An Archive

of Possibilities

An   Archive

of

CRITICAL GLOBAL HEALTH: Evidence, Efficacy, Ethnography
A series edited by Vincanne Adams and João Biehl

Possibilities

HEALING AND REPAIR
IN DEMOCRATIC
REPUBLIC OF CONGO

RACHEL
MARIE
NIEHUUS

Duke University Press
Durham and London   2024

© 2024 DUKE UNIVERSITY PRESS
All rights reserved
Printed in the United States of America on acid-free paper ∞
Project Editor: Livia Tenzer
Designed by Courtney Leigh Richardson
Typeset in Minion Pro and Helvetica Neue
by Westchester Publishing Services

Library of Congress Cataloging-in-Publication Data
Names: Niehuus, Rachel Marie, [date] author.
Title: An archive of possibilities : healing and repair in Democratic
Republic of Congo / Rachel Marie Niehuus.
Other titles: Critical global health.
Description: Durham : Duke University Press, 2024. | Series:
Critical global health: evidence, efficacy, ethnography | Includes
bibliographical references and index.
Identifiers: LCCN 2023029106 (print)
LCCN 2023029107 (ebook)
ISBN 9781478025757 (paperback)
ISBN 9781478021018 (hardcover)
ISBN 9781478027881 (ebook)
Subjects: LCSH: Healing—Congo (Democratic Republic)—
Psychological aspects. | Violence—Health aspects—Congo (Demo-
cratic Republic) | Racism against Black people. | Political violence—
Congo (Democratic Republic) | Feminism. | Afrofuturism. | Congo
(Democratic Republic)—Race relations.
Classification: LCC RZ401 .N544 2024 (print) | LCC RZ401 (ebook) |
DDC 615.8/528096751—dc23/eng/20230921
LC record available at https://lccn.loc.gov/2023029106
LC ebook record available at https://lccn.loc.gov/2023029107

Cover art: Thonton
Kabeya, *La vie est belle*,
2018–2022. Walnut
powder, woods, metallic
net, and transferred
newspaper ink on
sculpting canvas,
245 × 185 cm. Sanaa
Collection. Courtesy the
artist.

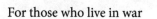

For those who live in war

CONTENTS

ACKNOWLEDGMENTS

Authorship seems to have two components. First, it implies responsibility and accountability for published work. In this respect, I am the sole author of this book. The analytical slippages, theoretical oversights, and factual errors are mine and mine alone. In addition to conferring responsibility, authorship also bestows social, academic, and financial status—this despite the fact that the anthropologist is, as Michael Taussig argues, a thief, a voyeur. Writing, as I do, as someone who uses the stories of others, specifically Black Others, for (white) personal gain, I would like to acknowledge here those to whom all credit is due.

My deepest gratitude goes to the men, women, and children in eastern Congo who shared their stories, homes, and lives with me over the past ten years. This project would not have been possible without the support and generosity of the "Kishabe" community. In particular, Furaha, Marie, Florence, and Bernadette were selfless hostesses, thoughtful discussants, and genuine friends. Claude and Jules provided endless conversation and amusement. The staff in the maternity ward were ultimately patient with my unending streams of questions. My interest and belief in otherwise presents arose as I observed the diligence and compassion with which they approach their work. Dr. Guellord was also a valued interlocutor, inspiring in his introspection and the tireless efforts he continues to make on behalf of his patients.

Outside Kishabe, too, many thanks are due. Lyn Lusi taught me to listen for quiet expressions of care and forgiveness. Mama Modestine, Mama Neema, Mama Noella, and Mama Domina took me into their homes, fed my curiosity, and encouraged my personal and intellectual growth. During my earlier stints of fieldwork, the leaders at HEAL Africa provided invaluable guidance and support, which ultimately enabled me to move my research to Kishabe. When M23 invaded Goma, logistical support from HEAL contributed crucially to my safety. Jean-Pierre, Ilot, Amani, Washikala, and

Dr. Luc intervened at several key moments, providing analytical direction in the research stage and innovative advice during the writing process. The four ethnographers with whom I conducted research on the Ebola epidemic in 2020 will, for their safety, remain anonymous here, but may they know that they are the reason that I have been able to see—and write—Congo in a new light.

My advisors at UCSF and Berkeley have been deeply engaged in the project since its embryonic stages. Vincanne Adams first introduced me to theoretical medical anthropology and has been a constant source of direction, motivation, and mentorship as my roles have shifted from anthropologist to surgeon to mother. Conversations with Liisa Malkki have pushed me toward a more thoughtful and compassionate approach to anthropology. I have yet to encounter a more careful scholar than Mariane Ferme. In addition to her theoretical rigor, I am especially appreciative of her incredible warmth and unabating support. This book would never have been written if not for the generosity, encouragement, and intellectual nourishment that Ian Whitmarsh continues to provide. His sustained meditation on the projects of empathy and justice in anthropology and in life is radical and profoundly inspiring.

Na'amah Razon, Carolyn Sufrin, Marlee Tichenor, and Dana Greenfield have provided companionship, laughter, and life advice since my earliest days in graduate school. Joshua Craze provided sage advice at a critical time that allowed this project to continue. My conversations with Sam Dubal, even after his passing, helped elucidate the structure that this book has taken. The years of WhatsApp conversations that I have shared with Clare Cameron about poetry, medicine, and life have nourished me deeply. Christoph Vogel has been an unwavering friend, a formidable colleague, and a source of joy for more than a decade. The many porch dinners shared with Freya Sargent and Michael Hicks buoyed my spirits and helped me move this project forward at a time when I, and it, felt profoundly stuck.

Josh Dugat, Maureen Shay, and the students in a writing class I taught at UCSF in the spring of 2020 read very early versions of the material that would become this book. So, too, did Joanna Cooper, Joelle Fraser, Michelle Lanzoni, and students in the classes at Creative Nonfiction that I took in 2020. Their thoughtful feedback and continued encouragement kept me writing when I felt most alone. Seminars at the UCB's Center for African Studies as well as Emory's Department of Women, Gender, and Sexuality Studies, together with thoughtful critiques from the four anonymous reviewers, Ian Whitmarsh, and Sheyda Aboii helped give the book its final push.

At UCSF, the research that underlies this book was funded by Graduate Division Fellowships and the Andrew V. White and Florence W. White Dissertation Fellowship. Through the Center for African Studies at the University of California, Berkeley, I received the Andrew and Mary Thompson Rocca Dissertation Scholarship and the Foreign Language and Area Studies Fellowship in Swahili. The research on Ebola was funded by the European Union and managed by NYU's Congo Research Group. At Emory, my two-year research sabbatical was funded by the Daniel Collier Elkin Research Fellowship in the Department of Surgery. The project would not have been possible without the (mostly blind and) unwavering support of Dr. Keith Delman in the Emory Department of Surgery.

I am most thankful for the family and friends who have stood steadfastly at my side since this project began. My father taught me the value of determination and of humor. My mother remains one of my role models for compassion. My brothers never cease to make me laugh. The relationships that I share with Mélanie, Julie, Milli, and Nadine are deeply intimate, inspirational, and generative. They push me to listen keenly, live fully, and love with reckless abandon. The six months that I spent with Nadine in 2019 and 2020 taught me more about joy and grace than most people learn in a lifetime.

Finally, I am forever grateful to the people who helped me build family. Though new to the scene, W, Z, and bb are the brightest lights in my life. Their presence in this world has ignited within me a fire to listen for new worlds being spoken into being. Walk through the world with care, my loves / And sing the things you see.

MAP 1. Democratic Republic of Congo. Map by author.

MAP 2. North Kivu Province. Map by author.

FIGURE I.1: *Belgian Colony*. This painting was photographed in a pharmacy in Mangina, North Kivu, in 2020. When asked what the painting meant to him, the owner of the pharmacy shrugged casually and said, "This is from the time of the Belgians. But today, it is the same. The whites [*wazungu*] still rule, and we, Congolese, run to escape the violence." Photograph by author.

Where the Scars Are So Thick

she taught them about shoulders. how upside down, they could still carry the world. she taught them about air and how one way to get it is to scream. she taught them about breathing and that the first way to do it is underwater. she taught them about the necessity of lubrication, the bright beauty of blood, the elasticity of membrane, the flexibility of a body holding on to itself, the grace of a first dive. and she would continue to teach them so many things. simply by being alive. —Alexis Pauline Gumbs, M Archive

The end of this world has already happened for some subjects, and it is the prerequisite for the possibility of imagining "living and breathing again" for others.
—Kathryn Yusoff, A Billion Black Anthropocenes or None

This book is set in eastern Congo, in and around Goma, the provincial capital of North Kivu. A city on the national border between Congo and Rwanda, Goma is home to some two million Congolese as well as the second largest population of humanitarian workers in the world. Nestled between Lake Kivu, one of the deepest lakes in the world, and Mount Nyiragongo, it's a border town that trembles sometimes in its embrace of a multiplicity of ethnicities, political ideologies, and languages.[1] Inside Goma's government buildings and hotel conference rooms, contracts are signed and business deals made that affect the stability of an entire region; and on Goma's streets, men, women, and children push, pull, and carry goods central to the global economy. Afrocentric haircuts and glasses pay homage to the 1960s, when Patrice Lumumba led Congolese politics. Abacosts—Mao-style tunics—and three-piece wax print ensembles hark back to a national uniform of the 1970s. Logoed T-shirts and hoodies—"My Grandson goes to NYU," a bedazzled "Queen of Sarcasm"—confirm the predominance of American Goodwill; slinky synthetic jumpsuits confirm open trade routes with China. Placards lining the road attest to the continued prosperity of the humanitarian-industrial complex; all the acronyms are present—UN, MSF, WFP, USAID, WHO. And a solar-powered traffic robot at Goma's center affirms the presence of a new generation. Designed by a female Congolese engineer to replace (potentially abusive) policemen, it is boxy, like a robot of 1950s science fiction. It has a breastplate that pivots as the traffic lights on its surface change from green to red and mechanical arms that raise to stop the traffic on one road and wave to vehicles on other routes to pass.[2] Like most of Goma's inhabitants, it speaks both French and Swahili as it instructs drivers to "leave the road to pedestrians."

At the intersection of a booming humanitarian complex and a visionary youth, Goma, and perhaps eastern Congo more generally, seems to be simultaneously solidly Congolese and also one of the most cosmopolitan places in the world. Where the darkly tinted private cars of mine, oil, and farming brass rumba with white Land Cruisers carrying humanitarian aid, and motorbike taxis and their oft-subversive passengers—students, artists, activists, and young businesswomen—weave their own paths across soccer fields and around traffic barriers, collisions are commonplace; and the diversity of lives that come together here create new possibilities in Congo and across the globe.

The repair of vesicovaginal fistulas in eastern Congo garnered international attention in the early 2000s. War had characterized life in eastern Congo for a decade; and then stories began to circulate about brutal sexual violence in which women's bodies were destroyed through penetration with guns, knives, and broken bottles. The violence created abnormal openings between women's urinary tracts and their vaginas or rectum, and a group of women now leaked urine and/or stool constantly. Human rights organizations described men in uniform raping en masse; subsequently, Congo was given the epithet "the worst place in the world to be a woman."[3] As a result of the international attention, centers were established in Goma and in Bukavu to take care of the women whose rape and subsequent fistulas had left them social outcasts, ostracized from their families and communities for their inability to control their excrement. Or so the stories initially went. Gradually, other narratives surfaced. A Swedish group documented that the overwhelming majority of fistula cases undergoing repair in eastern Congo were not due to sexual violence but actually the result of poor obstetric care.[4] Eschewing the imagined scenes of gang rape creating fistulas, the report presented retrospective data on the etiology of fistula for 604 women who had undergone fistula repair at the center in Bukavu. Their conclusions: where even public health clinics charged exorbitant fees, many women were left to give birth at home; even for those who attempted to pursue health care, the poor state of roads and security in rural areas resulted in prolonged transit times for women with obstetric emergencies; and there were large numbers of untrained or undertrained providers who performed cesarean sections without attention to the proximity of the uterus to the urinary system.

As critique of the rape-as-a-weapon-of-war narrative grew in Congo, stories about the use of rape narratives to access services appeared elsewhere.[5] An analyst of transnational humanitarian aid, Erica Caple James, illustrates the emergence of "trauma projects," which seek to care for those deemed to be "victims of human rights violations" in the Global South.[6] Where these trauma projects were the gatekeepers to much-needed food, economic, and medical aid, James describes the way that people were taught to perform trauma narratives that include shocking and egregious acts, including rape, in order to receive access to the services they needed. A similar phenomenon is described by Mats Utas in Liberia and Sierra Leone, where women and girls were taught to perform the role of the victim so as to establish themselves as "legitimate recipients" of humanitarian aid.[7] Gradually, in eastern Congo, researchers began to speak out against the creation of the category of the "traumatic fistula" and the "commercialization of rape."[8] And still, despite the research and advocacy efforts of those who sought to change the narrative around sexual violence, obstetric care, and vesicovaginal fistulas in eastern Congo, in 2018, Dr. Denis Mukwege, heralded founder of the fistula repair center in Bukavu, received the Nobel Peace Prize for his work with "raped" women.[9] From Goma, all of the hubbub around traumatic fistulas created fertile ground for thinking about who was responsible for the injury of certain Black lives, who was tasked with their repair, and how healing might be achieved amid continued injury.

Repair: to mend, to put back in order.

Healing: that which comes after repair, the process of making whole again.

When I first began research in Congo in 2010, I was interested in the way that chronic war marked bodies: the aberrant holes, the meager frames, the minds of those who had seen too much. I embedded myself in a private hospital in Goma that had become well known for its care of women with vesicovaginal fistulas and began studying. Early in my time in eastern Congo, I met Dr. Jerome. In Goma, Dr. Jerome was the gynecologist who performed the majority of the surgeries there. Because he traveled often into rural areas to teach other physicians how to perform fistula repairs, he was acutely aware of the way that poor surgical care, and poor primary care more generally, contributed to bodily injury. Our conversations, which have now spanned more than a decade, began with the structural factors that lead to fistulas in Congo. We spoke often about how structural adjustment programs in the 1980s had decimated the Congolese health system, and the ways in which the vertical programming in the humanitarian and development aid that followed continued to hollow out medical training so that many physicians performing cesarean sections in Congo were never taught how to perform a safe operation. We discussed rampant malnutrition in a country that had an abundance of fertile land, and we debated the lasting impact of pronatalist policies under colonial rule, which encouraged women to birth ten, twelve, or fourteen children.[10]

Seven years after I first traveled to eastern Congo, I finished medical school and began surgical training. As I advanced through residency and became more familiar with the process by which tissue heals, my discussions with Dr. Jerome shifted to include the technical aspects of repair. Because of his expertise in the field, Dr. Jerome often operated on the most difficult of cases: the women whose fistulas continued to recur despite multiple attempts at repair. While many surgeons in his position would choose to permanently divert the woman's urinary tract, because of scarring that had become too great to reconnect her urinary tract to its usual anatomy, Dr. Jerome insisted on performing multiple attempts at primary repair. "Permanent diversion is not an option here," he said. He reasoned: supplies that would allow patients to care for a diverted urinary system did not exist in the country. Even if they could be obtained, they would be prohibitively expensive. But, practical concerns aside, Dr. Jerome's approach also rested on a commitment to repair in a place where severe and recurrent injury was common. In response to my suggestion that, in cases of deep scarring, other surgeons might opt for diversion over repair, Jerome stated resolutely, "The surgeons you speak of have clearly never worked in a place like this. In Congo, the war has lasted for so long. Our wounds are deep, our scars are thick [*Nos plaies sont profondes, nos cicatrices épaisses*]. If we refused to operate on scarred tissue, these women would have to live with their bodies in ruin [*en ruine*]. Someone has to repair [*réparer*] these wounds."

Where structural and physical violence continued to injure years after the wars were declared over and peace treaties were signed, it was repair and healing—*kurekibisha, kupona*—not injury that dominated conversations. In the fistula ward in Goma, Dr. Jerome attempted a third try, a fourth try; the tissue graft, the muscle flap. His patients, many of whom had already undergone a handful of failed operations, declared that soon, they would once again be whole (*mzima*); they would no longer leak urine. Even when presented with overwhelming evidence to the contrary—persistent leakage after the nth attempt—they left open the possibility that this time would be different. "Hatujui," the women said, "labda ile itakamata." We never know: maybe this one will hold.

The belief in repair and healing extended beyond the fistula ward. "These kids will walk," the orthopedic surgeon said to me of the three children that sat at his feet in casts. They had been born with clubfoot, and he and a team of orthopedic doctors had been using a combination of surgeries and frequent recasting to correct their crooked limbs. Several months into the process, war had come to Goma, and the children and their parents had fled to their homes in rural areas. It had taken some time to find the children and convince them to return to the hospital. In the intervening time, ligaments had again shortened, and the children had gone from walking with crutches back to crawling and scooting on the ground. And still, Dr. Freddy remained confident in his assertion. "They might walk differently from you or I—there's no way to fully remove the scar tissue that has developed in the interim. But they will move through the world on two feet. Of that, I am certain."

Outside the hospital, too, people sought to mend what had been destroyed. As they went about their daily lives—farming, trading, fighting, laughing, and grieving amid the threat of war—people returned to that which had been torn apart, and worked to suture livelihoods, families, communities back together. Where the damage had been so extensive, rubble often blocked any simple path to return. And so attempts at repair and healing required imagination, ingenuity, invention, the forging of new paths. "Tunajikaza tu," people said. We just force ourselves. Whether in the hospital, the fields, or the home, people returned to their wounds, pieced together what was left, and worked to move beyond, toward satisfaction and flourishing. The wounds have been deep, the scars thick; and yet the work to make whole continues. Because, as the women in the fistula ward assert, "Labda ile itakamata." Maybe this one will hold.

A History of Scars

Eastern Congo has been marked by two and a half centuries of terrible violence. This violence created deep wounds. Some of these wounds have festered; others have become scars. The festering wounds stink, bleed, and hurt. The scars pull, throb, and constrain movement. Much time has passed; and still the wounds that colonial and postcolonial violence etched continue to be felt in the present day.

In Central Africa, unlike the Atlantic coast, the extracontinental trade of enslaved people was a brief, if brutal, force. Arab traders arrived in central Africa in the 1880s and quickly began leveraging the greed of local leaders to enslave people and extract raw materials to the Zanzibari coast. Within a decade of the Arabs' arrival, Belgian king Leopold II had declared Congo to be his personal property and had begun his own processes of extraction. While decrying the brutal practices of the Arab enslavers, Belgian imperialists under Leopold also operationalized violence for financial gain. Under the dual auspices of profit and civilization, Congolese were chained, their hands and feet amputated, their wombs violated. Blinded by greed and overcome by force, Congolese leaders participated in the graft.[11]

Surely, the precolonial period in central Africa was not without violence; no human society is. However, the arrival of lighter-skinned outsiders, and their institutionalization of antiblack violence, disrupted existing religious, political, and social structures in a way not previously seen. As brutal labor practices on rubber and coffee plantations dismembered individuals, they also crushed the life force of collective bodies. Complex systems devoted to maintaining balance were dismantled, and the regional balance of power that the precolonial kingdoms had maintained for centuries ruptured. And this structural wounding has had lasting effects: historian David Schoenbrun writes, "The particularly violent conquest of the Inner Congo Basin destroyed the premise of autonomy at the core of an Equatorial African political tradition."[12] Many transitions in power have taken place since the

Arab enslavers and their Belgian counterparts arrived in eastern Congo. And still, the destabilization of precolonial balances of power that occurred in the nineteenth century continues to reverberate through the region today.

In 1908, the Belgian state took over the governance of Congo and instituted indirect rule. As overt physical violence began to draw criticism in the metropole, demonstrations of power become more insidious. As part of their civilizing mission, Belgians enrolled Congolese children in primary and secondary school, where French language and European cultural assimilation were rewarded. After they completed school, these *évolués* were then recruited into the colonial system as nurses, priests, and local administrators, where they served as middle figures. Tasked with the local enforcement of colonial rule, these middle figures often reproduced the physical and psychic violence that they had witnessed. As Congolese *évolués* upheld, even enacted, colonial-era racial and class hierarchies, antiblackness overflowed the formal limits of the colonial structures and permeated the tribe, the clan, the home.[13]

In June 1960, Congo achieved independence from Belgium. Six months later, the country's first prime minister and a staunch freedom fighter, Patrice Lumumba, was assassinated in a covert Belgian-American operation undertaken to ensure that the newly independent state remained compliant with Western diplomatic suggestion.[14] For several years, the country was paralyzed by a deeply divided government and successive armed rebellions. Then, in 1965, Mobutu Sese Seko took power in a bloodless coup. The first decade of Mobutu's rule was characterized by relative prosperity: Mobutu's nationalization of foreign-owned companies filled state coffers, and as profit flowed in from copper mines and other exports, his government worked to expand public services to the entire population. But the divisions fostered during colonial rule were deep, and many Congolese (Zaireans) still opposed a centralized government.[15] Facing many threats to his leadership, Mobutu began doling out land, companies, or political positions.[16] By the 1980s, however, there was no more to give. Further, with the end of the Cold War, Western support of Mobutu's regime waned. Given empty state coffers, public services ground to a halt: schools started charging enrollment fees to pay teachers; hospitals began requiring patients to pay for medications prior to treating them. Violence became commonplace, as the national police and army began to extract their salaries from the population.[17]

In the east, the poverty and violence that followed Zairean (Congolese) state failure was exacerbated by land expropriation. Conflicts that had begun under colonial rule were stoked by Mobutu's warlord politics. By the 1990s, many people in the east found themselves landless and hungry. And just as local militia groups had begun gathering to protect their land or fight for its return, the Rwandan genocide began. In 1994, one million Rwandan refugees spilled into eastern Congo. Some ran from the genocide; others ran from the Rwandan Patriotic Front, which was killing perpetrators as it attempted to stop the genocide. Both victims and perpetrators coalesced together on the western shores of Lake Kivu, where they formed the world's largest refugee camps. The camps were crowded; there was cholera, there were guns, and there was fear. Hungry and in search of employment, many refugees climbed out of the lakeside camps into the surrounding hills, which exacerbated local land conflicts. At the same time, Congolese militias that had begun to assemble to defend their land descended into the camps, making alliances with the Hutu militias already present in the camps and profiting from the humanitarian aid that was being distributed. Fearing invasion, the new government in Kigali called upon Mobutu and the international humanitarian apparatus to clear the camps of armed groups. The presence of armed groups in the camps was condemned; and the armed groups grew even more powerful.[18]

In October 1996, citing self-defense, Rwandan-backed forces entered eastern Congo. This marked the start of the First Congo War. After chasing the armed groups from the camps, the troops spread out over the east of the country, began to integrate into the regional economy, and awaited reinforcement. Several months later, the resulting coalition of troops marched across the continent to the western capital of Kinshasa and toppled Mobutu's dictatorship. The leader of the invading troops, Laurent Kabila, a Congolese man who had grown up in exile after Lumumba's assassination, was declared president. For a year, there was a brief reprieve in fighting. Then, like all leaders before him had done, Kabila attempted to clear the country of foreign influence. Within weeks of being escorted out, Rwandan forces again entered the country. Between 1998 and 2002, nine African countries and twenty-five armed groups fought over control of Congolese soil in what became named the Second Congo War. Eventually, peace treaties were signed, and a transitional government took power in 2003. However, the continued presence of Rwandan and Ugandan influence in the region—and the militarization of all sectors of the economy more generally—has combined with persistent local land conflict to produce a growing list of armed groups and war that does not end.[19] Two decades after the formal end of fighting, people in eastern Congo still insist, "Tunaishi mu vita." We live in war.

As written, this history tells of the pattern of wounds that the West's encounter with Congo has left: amputated hands and syphilitic wombs during Belgian imperialism, the deeply internalized prejudice of Congolese *évolués* with Belgian colonialism, Lumumba's assassination and Mobutu's rise to power in the immediate postcolonial period, and, most recently, the persistent war that lingers in part because of the West's tacit support of the Rwandan government's cross-border meddling. While the historical specificities of Congo's scars are unique, I believe that the particular story of wounding in Congo can also tell a more general story about the intersection of antiblackness and violence at the present moment. "Ce monde n'appartient pas à nous. Les bons ne durent jamais," is a common refrain in Congo. This world does not belong to us. The good never lasts. It's a nonspecific statement, one that attests to the general and enduring experience of impermanence and erasure in Congo. The statement is muttered in a variety of geographic settings—after the pillage of a single household in rural North Kivu or when discussing the finances of the flow of Congo's natural resources into the global economy. It is also used across time—I have heard it used to describe present expropriation as well as the losses of the colonial and immediate postcolonial eras: traditional land tenure, political autonomy. Recently, I have heard the statement take on another meaning with the addition of two words: "Ce monde n'appartient pas à nous, les noirs. Les bons ne durent jamais." The world does not belong to us, Black folks. The good never lasts. In this usage, it gestures toward a shared experience of loss in Congo and in other Black worlds; and in so doing, it echoes the growing body of Black critical studies literature that attests that antiblack violence is a common experience of Black and brown folks across the globe.[20] Having described the particular ways in which violence and expropriation have functioned in Congo, I now turn to query how the particulars of war and its consequences—including the impulses to repair and healing it generates—are shared with others outside its borders.

War, Antiblackness, and Fugitivity

For decades now, scholars have debated the underlying causes of persistent war and early death in eastern Congo. Most would argue that the conditions of life in present-day Congo are largely shaped by locoregional forces: they might discuss laws that govern citizenship and land ownership in the east, or, more broadly, agrarian reform; or they might speak about the way that regional economic activity, traditional political and social structures, and the *longue durée* of identity formation in the frontier between neighboring countries affect grievances.[21] In their own ways, my interlocutors, too, spoke of these forces. Additionally, however, my interlocutors also attributed persistent war in Congo with a more general force: the valuelessness of (Black) Congolese life. To prove their marginality, people often repeated characterizations of them as "dirt" (*udongo*) or "insects" (*vidudu*). They also spoke of a racial hierarchy: when fighting stopped in 2012 in anticipation of a Western diplomat's visit, one of the hospital orderlies said, "Wacongomani tunakufa kila siku na wazungu hawajaii": Congolese die every day and white folks don't care. For my interlocutors, the persistence of war in eastern Congo was a product of geographical and historical specificities—and also war was a consequence of the general disposability of Congolese life.[22] War continued in Congo because no one valued Congolese life enough to stop it.

By attributing the war that characterized their everyday to their general disposability, my Congolese interlocutors rejected the characterization of Congo as exceptionally violent, as an enduring "heart of darkness."[23] Instead, they asserted that the fact that they were thought of as dirt or insects permitted them to become subject to recurring violence, thus creating a through line between their suffering and that of other marginalized folks around the globe. They also infused race into the discussion about violence in Congo—"Congolese die every day and white folks don't care"—and thus opened a conversation about how Black critical theory might be used to understand violence in Congo.

Sylvia Wynter argues that the category of the human cannot be thought without attention to race, for modern understandings of humanity came into existence amid dense global antiblackness.[24] Building on Wynter, Alexander Weheliye asserts, "If racialization is understood not as a biological or cultural descriptor but as a conglomerate of sociopolitical relations that discipline humanity into full humans, not-quite-humans, and nonhumans, then blackness designates a changing system of unequal power structures that apportion and delimit which humans can lay claim to full human status and which cannot."[25] For Wynter, Weheliye, and other Black critical theorists, because the enslavement of Black folks is so deeply written into modernity—into our understandings of value, freedom, democracy, progress—antiblackness is not limited to places where chattel slavery was practiced, but rather is a global force that continues to stratify who has the right to a good life and who does not.[26]

Of the western Congolese capital, Kinshasa, anthropologist Filip De Boeck writes, "Dying [was] no longer a departure from life, it [had] become that which gives life its significance, density, and directionality. Life in fact cannot be lived, nor spoken, nor even imagined, outside of the space of death."[27] In eastern Congo, as in Kinshasa, war, violence, and death are overbearing forces; and, as elsewhere in Black worlds, the omnipresence of death has occasioned the rise of particular ways of living with and in death. In this book, I am interested in the fugitive and monstrous ways that people in eastern Congo make life in the wake of war and death.[28] In Goma, a woman returns for her sixth attempt at a fistula repair; an orthopedic surgeon recasts a limb that has once again contracted. Outside of the hospital's walls too, amid the ever-present threat of more bloodshed, Congolese work to mend that which has been, and will continue to be, destroyed. Like characters of visionary fiction who forge lives in the aftermaths of apocalypse, Congolese are creating worlds they, and we, have never seen. This book traces the wild and dogged efforts of repair and healing in eastern DRC today and records the otherwise presents they create.

Apposing Skin, Repair, and Healing

In an essay that accompanies his exhibit titled *On Injury and Repair*, artist Kader Attia describes two kinds of repair: "Occidental" and "non-Occidental."[29] In Attia's formulation, Occidental repair is defined by the effacement of the trace of the wound and the restoration of a body to its pre-injury state. To illustrate Occidental repair, Attia offers the example of facial reconstruction surgery, which has as its goal the erasure, or concealment, of all scars. In contrast to Occidental repair, Attia suggests non-Occidental repair, which makes no attempt to hide the wound, but rather maintains it in the repair. According to Attia, the non-Occidental repair of the crack in the ancient African mask follows three steps: first, there is a recognition and preservation of the original wound, the identification of the losses and cracks; second, there is the integration—rather than the rejection, erasure—of these wounds; and finally, as the wounds are integrated, there is the creation of possibility for deep healing. Because non-Occidental repair opens space for healing, Attia declares it to be a superior process. He states, "To deny the wound [in Occidental repair] is to maintain the pain it generates. By repairing history's cracks with metal staples, with yarn or with patches from other, often contradictory cultures, I give voice to the victims; I allow trauma to speak to us and thus to pave the way for catharsis."[30]

As a surgeon, I have read Attia's work with interest. Traditional surgical teaching dictates that one must know how to repair something before one can cut; and so, I wondered if I was encountering a limited version of repair in my surgical textbooks. Before we picked up a scalpel, we learned about the four stages of wound healing. On an index card somewhere, I have written: hemostasis, inflammation, proliferation, and maturation. Within sixty seconds of injury, hemostasis has begun: blood vessels constrict, platelets aggregate, and a clot forms to plug the hole in the vessel wall. Shortly thereafter, inflammation begins. As white blood cells flock to the area, there is leaking and swelling, the removal of damaged cells and bacteria, and the prevention of infection. Then comes the proliferative stage, when type III collagen is laid onto the wound bed, granulation tissue builds up, and the wound contracts. Finally, during the maturation phase, the tissue is remodeled. Disorganized collagen that was laid down in the proliferative stage is realigned along lines of tension and cross-linked, which reduces scar thickness and increases the tensile strength of the scar.

This is how wound healing is supposed to progress; but after outlining normal wound healing, the textbooks all describe a litany of ways in which the linear process can be derailed. Usually, there is a single illustration of normal wound healing followed by multiple pages of pictures of infected, nonhealing, and hypertrophic wounds. Alongside the pictures, the textbooks list strategies for assisting the healing of chronic wounds. Depending on the size and location of the wounds, there are various options: sharp debridement, negative pressure, steroid injections, skin substitutes, hyperbaric oxygen. With experience, one learns which wounds require sharp debridement, which require special dressings, and which require a more complicated regimen. Learning how to get wounds to heal is an integral part of surgical training. After years of practice, I continue to study wounds closely, to learn the methods required to help even the most complex wounds eventually heal.

In all of my years studying the human body, I have never seen a wound heal without a trace; that is, I have never observed Occidental repair. Wounds always leave a scar, a reminder of the initial injury, a testament to a painful event that happened in the past. Neither have I observed Occidental repair in eastern Congo. Despite the recurrent violence they have endured at the hands of the West since imperialism, my interlocutors never speak of a return backward. They can't imagine a time before the Arab slavers—they know there was violence then too; and they state that it is not possible to recoup the lives lost under imperial or colonial rule. And still, their drive to repair is strong. Instead of some kind of return backward to some idealized past, however, theirs is an assertion of the possibility of presents and futures otherwise. Maybe this one will hold, the women in the fistula ward said. These children will walk, the surgeon asserted. The otherwise begins now, today, and extends forward. But the trajectory it takes is not the future of European modernity, in which Africa will forever be consigned to becoming, in which Africa can only draw near but never arrive.[31] Rather, the future of Congolese repair is a very proximate future—what will happen *kesho*, tomorrow. Tina Campt calls this "the future real conditional." Like the future of Black feminist writing, it is "a performance of a future that hasn't yet happened but must. It's an attachment to a belief in what should be true, which in turn realizes that aspiration. It's the power to imagine beyond current fact, to envision that which is not but must be. Put another way, it's a form of prefiguration that involves living the future now, as imperative rather than subjunctive, as a striving for the future that you want to see."[32]

Where chronic wounds fester and scars are so thick, healing is a complex task that stretches across multiple temporalities. In Congo, where present violence leaves many without records or recognition of their wounds—there are no museums that attest to violence; there have been no large-scale reconciliation efforts; and the only discussions about reparations keep getting pushed farther and farther into the future—repair begins in the here and now, the everyday encounters. As bodies, livelihoods, futures continue to be blown apart, repair assembles the pieces, stitches together two sides of the wound. Often, so much has been lost that new techniques are required to move forward, to live together again. As with physical wounds, the healing of the chronic, complex psychic wounds in eastern Congo requires attention, ingenuity, innovation. In addition, however, healing in Congo also requires a shared belief in the imperative, in "a performance of a future that hasn't happened yet but must." The description of this latter aspect of healing in Congo is the motor that drives this text.

The research for this book was conducted at a particularly turbulent time in Congo's history. Congo has not always been, nor will it always be, the way that it is depicted in these pages. Perhaps that is a limitation of this work. I believe that this is also its beauty. By telling this story now, while the fate of the Congolese nation and state is so nebulous, I have sought to create an archive of the future that is to come. At a time when, as Jean and John Comaroff state, "the global south is running ahead of the global north," I believe that Congo has much to teach us all about the possibilities of healing amid political and economic collapse.[33] As the climate continues to change and we all draw nearer to widespread energy scarcity, hunger, and conflict, Congo's lessons on repair and healing feel both radical and increasingly urgent.

Positionality and Method

I initially began research in eastern Congo as a graduate student interested in the bodily effects of violence. I followed the traditional path through anthropological graduate studies and defined a field site in a place foreign to me. I learned French and Swahili, so as to be able to communicate with my interlocutors, and secured a grant that would enable me to travel halfway around the world to conduct my research. The coloniality of the endeavor was evident to me at the time—and yet, it still seemed that postcolonial Africa was the site par excellence to examine the physical and psychic effects of enduring violence.

For the first several years that I worked in Congo, my white skin and American passport served to create distance between myself and my subject of study. While I studied violence during the day, I always retreated behind the safety of tall walls with armed guards at night. As I became more proficient in Swahili and began to feel more comfortable traveling outside of Goma, friends encouraged me to relocate to a rural area to advance my research. "You say you want to learn about how we live. Well, you'll never know how Congolese live in war every day if you stay behind those walls," one friend pushed. "Besides, Kishabe [a rural town south of Goma] has been safe for years. There's a hospital and a women's empowerment program there. You would learn a lot about what Congolese women live every day," she insisted. In July 2012, I moved to the small lakeside town that I will call Kishabe.[34]

Initially, I began ethnography in the hospital because it made sense—I was a medical student, and hospitals, as key sites of employment and humanitarian and development assistance in eastern Congo, were also central places of sociality. In a rural area like Kishabe, the hospital had a further advantage: because hospitals are largely considered neutral in war—"both sides of the conflict need medical care," people would say—the hospital provided safety to those affiliated with it. Those known to be doctors or nurses—these terms were broadly defined and often applied to me despite my nonclinical role at the hospital—were often waved through military barriers and spared violence in uncertain times.[35] In active conflict, the physical building of the hospital became a refuge for medical professionals, and also for the surrounding community more broadly. While I never used the hospital for this purpose, many in the region considered it to be an asylum within deep structural and physical violence.

In November 2012, the war that had been brewing in the area for some time engulfed my field site. Because of the connections that I had fostered in Goma for years, I was able to leave the country ahead of the war. And yet, the moment in which I, also, fled for my safety marked me deeply. While I was grateful and relieved that my privilege afforded me safe passage out of war, I also felt deep shame and guilt for having left behind the Congolese people that had become family to me. When the war stopped and I eventually returned, my attention shifted from studying the chronic wounds of war to noting the ways in which, for many Congolese, war was both a real, recurrent, life-threatening force and also a symbolic marker of the deep inequalities that allowed me, a white American woman, to leave the country when shells began falling and required them to remain in the violence.[36] Before I ran from war, I had recorded the phrases "vita inatuaribisha"—war ruins us—"vita inleta maisha buchungu"—war brings bitter life; however, it wasn't until I witnessed bombs fall on Goma that I began to understand the way war became a way for Congolese to make sense of their marginalization. "I was born in war; I grew up in war; and I live in war," a friend said when I called to see how her family had weathered the recent fighting. "To be Congolese is to know war." Eventually, I wrote a dissertation about the affective experience of living in wartime violence that has no end. I knew there was more to the story, but I couldn't yet articulate what the story of war in Congo had to offer to the rest of the world.

The week after I filed my dissertation, I returned to medical school. For two years, I spent my days in tertiary hospitals in Northern California. With time, medical terms took the place of Swahili and French in my brain, and Congo seemed to fade into the distance. When I moved to Atlanta to start my surgical residency, I thought that I would not be returning to Congo for some time, as my clinical training needed to take priority. I boxed up my books on war, Congo, and Africa and filled my bookshelves with medical texts. I screened calls that came in from WhatsApp—people always called in the middle of the day, and I was learning to operate. And still, despite my efforts to focus on clinical work, my mind often traveled back across the Atlantic. On busy nights at the trauma center at which I worked, I encountered twenty or thirty youths who had been violently injured. Sometimes, they were lucky—the bullet or blade had missed its intended target. As I stitched up their wounds and they spoke about their food insecurity, their inability to find a job or get out of the war they were born into, I was reminded of my Congolese interlocutors. Sometimes, they came in too ill to speak, and my hands worked quickly to find a pulse, to figure out where the blood had gone. In these moments, my mind returned to the maternity ward, where I had also worked frantically to keep breath in Black bodies. One year into the grueling training program, I wrote a note to myself: "I don't know why Congo matters here, but it does." Two years later, I decided to take a sabbatical from surgical residency. I had a hunch that learning about repair and healing in eastern Congo would change my clinical practice—and I needed time to figure out how.

****

This book is based on the ethnographic research that I have conducted in and about eastern Congo since 2010. For three months in 2010, I spent my days in the fistula ward of a private hospital in Goma. For two months in 2011, I traveled through North Kivu with a team charged with evaluating the far reaches of the hospital's women's empowerment program. Between July 2012 and June 2013, the Kishabe Referral Hospital—and the community that surrounded it—served as the site for continued ethnographic research on wounding in war. While I had undergone some medical training at the time, I entered the hospital as an anthropologist and remained in this capacity throughout my time there. In October 2013, a conference on violence occasioned a return trip to the region; between May and July 2014, a research consultancy on gendered violence in a refugee camp led to prolonged time spent amid displaced Congolese in Tanzania and South Kivu; and in May 2016, friendship motivated a return to Goma. In September 2019, I returned again to the region and spent six months immersed in conversations about structures of healing in the region.

In what now amounts to more than a decade of back-and-forth living between DRC and the United States, I have compiled the ledger on which this book is based: thousands of daily field notes, hundreds of interviews, and an entire cloud full of articles, photographs, and journal articles about the region. As much as was possible, I created and sustained daily encounters with interlocutors, who became friends: I followed some women from the fistula wards to their homes to their fields to the markets; I asked the people working in the guest house in Goma at which I stayed whether they would share their stories with me; every time I returned from a stint in the United States, I sought out people I had previously interviewed and learned about the directions that their lives had taken since I had last seen them.

And yet, regardless of the depth and longevity of my friendships, of the different contexts that I have explored and learned from, the material I collected remains fundamentally fragmented. As a privileged white American woman studying antiblackness, every encounter between myself and my interlocutors was punctuated by incommensurability. Silence often interrupted our conversations, especially when I asked people about their fear, their losses, or their desires for the future. Even when my friends and interlocutors were able to speak more openly about their daily lives, they often answered my questions about their experiences during active conflict with "huwezi jua ile"—you couldn't know that. I was and always would remain fundamentally an outsider to their experiences of hunger, poverty, and violence.[37]

And so, in place of the linear, cohesive sketches that often characterize ethnographic writing, I offer narratives of friends who only displayed aspects of their lives, relationships interrupted by flight or distance, and questions that remained unanswered irrespective of the extended time I spent researching. Where possible, I have avoided filling in the silences or flattening the incongruencies of these narratives.[38] For, fundamentally, I understand my ethnographic material, like the affect theorist's archive, to be composed of "lines of potential," of "trajectories that forces might take if they were to go unchecked."[39] The text that follows, then, gestures "not toward the clarity of answers but toward the texture of knowing."[40]

Where new ways of being were developing, and new forms of healing becoming, a sense of "perhaps" clung to so many encounters. Sometimes, these moments of possibility were identified and flagged by my interlocuters; and sometimes, people fell silent just before speaking aloud what could be, for fear of the performative power of a speech act. Regardless of how it was communicated, where violence and expropriation have dominated for centuries, the language of possibilities—possibilities of repair, possibilities of healing, possibilities of a present otherwise—was everywhere; it was also ever changing, with doors closing as soon as they had cracked open, and new cracks being encountered every day. And so, understanding Congo to be a society on the edge of transformation, as I do, I have sought to archive the possibilities that I have encountered there.[41] What follows is an archive that I have created about a place where I will forever be *mzungu*, a foreigner; and, a product of ethnographic contact, it is also an attestation of a particular moment in time in which a group of people believed that Congo could lead the world into a better future.[42]

The Chapters

Such is the theoretical and methodological framework of this book. What remains is an overview of the structure of the text. Overall, the book is organized into five chapters, each of which examines a different register of healing in eastern Congo. Between each chapter, there are also interludes, which contain more proximate encounters with the chaotic affect of insecurity in DRC. Like the threat of violence that intrudes into the everyday in Congo, these interludes interrupt the more cohesive narratives and offer more direct insight into the kinds of ethnographic contact that undergird this text. Surely, the particularities of this contact, the ways that I recognized and cataloged emergence, shape what I have chosen to archive. And so, as a means to explore ethnographic contact that produced this particular archive, the interludes stay close to my field notes, to my personal experiences of people and place in eastern Congo.

Chapter 1 queries Congolese relationships with soil, subsoil, and the natural world more generally. In Congo, as across Africa, the past 250 years have been characterized by the prying of autochthonous peoples from their land. First, there were the Arab slavers, who marched Congolese off their land in chains. During the imperial and colonial eras, land dispossession functioned as an important tactic of rule. In the postcolonial era, the wounds created during previous exploitative regimes have festered, and disputes over who has the right to which land fuels much of the current fighting in eastern Congo. As people seek to reconcile with this violent past, they return to the land—to the soil, the subsoil, and the ancestral power it contains. Through farming, mining, and conservation efforts, Congolese work to rebuild relationships with the natural world from which they have been severed. By returning to soil in a place where land has been so divisive, Congolese suggest that the ecological might serve as a register of repair, a form of public healing.

In chapter 2, I describe the way that insecurity functions as both a deep psychic wound and generates affect, which serves as a register for repair. The inhabitants of eastern Congo have always lived in a menacing environment, at the foot of an active volcano, on the shores of a methane-containing lake. When conflict erupted in 1993, the threat of physical violence compounded that posed by the region's topography. Where more than 132 armed groups are fighting to control a geographic area smaller than Texas, people in eastern Congo continue to live with the threats of violence and of repeated displacement. By narrating one particular period of insecurity, I query the affective experience of living in bad weather, as Christina Sharpe calls antiblack regimes, at the convergence of death, disaster, and possibility. Where violence looms, destruction is always a risk; but inhabiting affect offers healing, as victims and perpetrators work together to create anew.

Chapter 3 investigates the role of the body and the hospital in wounding and healing in eastern Congo. Where material possessions and food security are so fleeting, the body is both one's dearest and most vulnerable asset. Because the line between life and death is so thin in Congo, hospitals have risen in prominence, often serving as focal points through which social and economic activity are brokered. However, due to an absence of running water, electricity, and essential supplies within its walls, the hospital in eastern Congo often fails to provide physical healing. Rather, as it bears witness to the screams and the dreams of the population, it teaches endurance, witnesses pain, and stokes visions of presents otherwise, in which people and things can be counted on, in which life is less fragile.

The next two chapters examine the limits of repair and its unending possibilities, respectively. Over the past two and a half centuries of violence in eastern Congo, so much has been lost: progressive time, the promise of social reproduction, a sense of belonging in the global community, all in addition to the lives cut short. Drawing heavily on Achille Mbembe and Frantz Fanon, in the fourth chapter, I ask whether violence can be therapeutic in this context. Through an analysis of children who stop eating, youths who taunt death, and armed groups who commit massacre, I explore how killing, or making die, fits into a shared present in eastern Congo. I ask, are there ways in which violent refusal of the current order might beget an emphasis on tomorrow, on durable healing?

Chapter 5 then moves from the healing power of refusal to other radical propositions of what could be. By attuning to the poetic register, the chapter explores alternative ways of seeing and speaking Black survival. Through an analysis of visionary play, of performance and prophesy, and of the dreamworlds of interpersonal intimacy, this chapter interrogates the healing power of future worlding within antiblack regimes. For people of African descent, it is an audacious and emboldened notion to envisage a collective future. But a new discourse is emerging in Congo, which questions and affirms how Congolese will survive in the future, not if they will. The final chapter is devoted to this epistemology of Black/Congolese aliveness.

The conclusion that follows chapter 5 is brief. It begins with a meditation on the radical nature of cohabitating, of living with violence. Drawing on research conducted during the Ebola epidemic in eastern Congo, it examines the commitment to survive, to breathe, to aspire in Congo despite dense antiblackness, a world committed to Black death. It then offers a final glimpse of Congo, the return of M23 and continuation of violence, before concluding with a vision of what could be. When the world of Man is crumbling, as it must, the plural, multisited understanding of healing that is emerging from the undercommons, which is devoted to trying out other ways of living in a broken world, lights paths forward to otherwise futures for us all.

Fundamentally, this book is dedicated to archiving the possibilities Congolese espouse, both the devastating and the liberatory ones. So many refuse the politics of death that has been thrust upon them. So much Congolese culture—idioms, music, poetry, dress, and stories—asserts possibilities besides the "apocalyptic interlude" that characterizes the present.[43] By following visionary Congolese who are forging paths within pervasive death, by studying their efforts at repair amid profound wounding, we hear articulations of presents and futures otherwise. As war becomes the "sacrament of our times," it is my hope that the articulations of possibilities archived here might serve as guideposts for what could be.[44]

Dirt Work

And that it *is* the ground lays out that, and perhaps how, we might begin to live in relation to this requirement for our death. What kinds of possibilities for rupture might be opened up? What happens when we proceed as if we *know* this, antiblackness, to be the ground on which we stand, the ground from which we attempt to speak, for instance, an "I" or a "we" who know, an "I" or a "we" who care?
—Christina Sharpe, *In the Wake*

These are the abysses that await us and that will always lie in wait for us—not as accidents to avoid but as the ground [*fond*] itself, the ground without ground or groundless ground [*fond sans fond*] of the thing itself.
—Jacques Derrida, *Aporias*

On the road that leads west out of Goma, there is some asphalt left over from the early postcolonial period; much has been eroded, however, and the road is punctuated with meter-wide potholes and stretches of only gravel. Brightly painted rectangular buildings, each containing several small boutiques or

FIGURE 1.1. The road to Kishabe, 2013. One of the few national roads in the area. Like most roads in Congo, it boasted more foot traffic than vehicles, as people walked miles to work their fields, to bring their goods to market, and to visit family and friends. Photograph by author.

bars, line both sides of the road. Men in starched three-piece suits flirtatiously engage women wrapped in floor-length ensembles whose stiletto heels somehow move smoothly over the piles of lava rock, dirt, and refuse that rise up to meet them. Eventually, the crowds of Goma start to thin, and the fertile, green hills of the rural Masisi territory, the breadbasket of Congo, appear on the horizon.

Forty-five minutes into the drive, cars, trucks, and motorbikes stop at the semipermanent military barrier. The men surrounding the barrier wear the camouflage uniforms and red berets of the Congolese army. Sometimes they exact a small fee from those who pass; and still, they are often jovial as they examine identity cards and check vehicles with their automatic weapons on their backs.

Thirty minutes from the military barrier, one reaches Kishabe, a small farming town in the Masisi hills. Originally a colonial border post supported by lucrative Belgian coffee plantations, Kishabe is now a quiet map dot, known primarily for its hospital. The town center, composed of the nine-building hospital complex and the narrow strip of shops that sit in its shadow, is surrounded on three sides by vertical cassava, bean, and potato farms. Though these hills have always been inhabited, the last fifty years of land expropriation, unemployment, and war have pushed much of the population off their land and into a town center. Many Kishabe residents now live in rotting, brick colonial houses or newer dirt-and-plank houses that extend south and west from the town center. Single-track dirt pathways weave through town, around household gardens, connecting homes and the hospital with the town's other features: a secondary school, two primary schools, six churches, and the dozen or so households that sell palm wine or beer around town.

Life in Kishabe moves more slowly than it does in Goma: people walking on the main road stop often to chat with their neighbors; bicycles are more frequent than motorcycles; women selling their goods off bamboo tables and out of plastic bins finish their conversations before serving their next customer; a crowd gathers on the steps of the hospital to exchange news, buy fresh fish, and enjoy each other's company.

Marred by decades of war and neglect, Congolese soil is heavy with memories of loss. Sixty years after independence, many roads in eastern Congo have turned back to dirt, and hospitals and schools built during the colonial era sit in ruin. Where asphalt roads once existed, sticky red dirt evokes nostalgia for a past more modern than the present. In Kishabe, expressions of longings for a more modern past were common: "At least when the Belgians were here," people said, "we had roads, and hospitals, and schools. They were violent, but there was a standard of living." There *were* roads; there *was* employment other than farming; Congo *had* a future—all always composed in the past tense. With the continued destruction that violence has wrought, much of the promise of a more modern future has dried up. At a time when urbanity and mechanization have become such important symbols of forward progress, the pervasiveness of Congolese soil—the dust, the manual farming and mining practices, the land disputes—reminds people of all that they lack: security, modernity, a future that can be counted on. Thus, the common saying, "Tunakula na udongo yetu, lakini tunakufa na hii udongo pia." We eat by our soil, but we die by it also.

In the fertile Masisi hills outside Goma, people often hold clumps of soil when talking about their present vulnerability. Surely, working the fertile ground yields many a cabbage and potato. Theodore Trefon has argued that "Congo could feed a billion people—or the equivalent of the entire African continent."[1] And yet, where land conflicts continue to drive war, food insecurity is common. In 2012, when I was living in Kishabe, UNICEF reported a 9.9 percent rate of acute malnutrition in the area.[2] Today, across the country, the burden of food insecurity has become even more pervasive. In a report from the first quarter of 2020—prior to the COVID-19 pandemic—the World Food Program described significantly expanded operations in Congo from the year prior. Despite its vast swaths of fertile farmland, even though farming remains the most common occupation in eastern Congo, Congo was determined to have the world's largest food crisis in 2021.[3]

Much like Congo's fertile farmland, Congo's subsoil also holds great potential. Congo produces much of the world's cobalt ore; it is also a major contributor of copper, industrial diamonds, gold, silver, tantalum, tin, zinc, uranium, and timber to global markets. In many ways, the minerals beneath the soil's surface power the laptops, cell phones, and tablets of Western modernity; and yet three-quarters of Congo's population lives on less than $2 a day.[4] Trefon calls this "an environmental paradox." In Swahili, people say simply, "Udongo ya kongo ni tajiri, lakini waKongomani, tuko waskini." The Congo's soil is rich, but we, the Congolese, are poor. Whether because of or despite Congo's enormous environmental wealth, war, displacement, hunger, and deep poverty characterize the everyday for most living in eastern Congo.

In this chapter, I examine Congo's soil and subsoil as a lens through which to view the everyday conditions in which Congolese live. As I seek to characterize the experience of living in war, I am interested in elucidating "the ground on which [Congolese] stand, the ground from which [they] attempt to speak," to borrow from Christina Sharpe's words that begin this chapter. In eastern Congo, where life is defined by poverty, hunger, and violence, the ground is made of contradictory injunctions and impossible choices. People attempt to dig their way to a stable job, three meals a day, a year without running, but each step out of the depths lands them two steps back under. For, where antiblackness continues to dislodge all trajectories toward possibility, the ground—both the soil and subsoil, and the ground on which people stand—is, in Jacques Derrida's words, "ground without ground or groundless ground [*fond sans fond*]." Everywhere passage is denied, progress paralyzed. In their desperate hunt for escape, people turn toward that which has always fed them—the soil. The resulting dirt work is instructive for what it unearths about the experience of standing on groundless ground, of living in aporia that does not end.

Land, Identity, and Slippery Belonging

Geographer Kathryn Yusoff argues that changed relationships of land under global capitalism play a critical role in the establishment of a general regime of Black disposability, and thus aporia, as I explore in this chapter.[5] Yusoff posits that where people had lived for centuries in a reciprocal relationship with land, enslavers' cleavage of people from their land marked a new era in which the human and nonhuman worlds could be thought separately. For if Man now ruled over the nonhuman world, it followed that he also had dominion over anyone or anything he relegated to the nonhuman world. His association of Africans with the nonhuman world, then, inaugurated two related movements: first, it expropriated Africans from their land and enslaved them; and, second, it dismissed previous regimes of collective ownership and instead proclaimed large tracts of land in Africa and elsewhere to belong to Westerners. As the newfound owners of many people and much land, Westerners developed new forms of rule: in America, this took the form of chattel slavery; on the African continent, it began as imperialism and transitioned into colonial rule at the beginning of the twentieth century.[6]

In Congo, these new regimes of power—and the shifts they engendered to the ideas of the individual, property, value, and humanity more generally—transformed the landscape. Customary land was seized and turned to export-oriented, extractive industry. First, there was rubber and copper. Then, coffee, gold, cocoa, palm oil. The loot needed a way to leave the country, so Congolese labor was harnessed to build railways and roads. With time, both the small-scale societies and the elaborate kingdoms of precolonial Congo were replaced by Belgian-created and Congolese-led administrative units, each with a school, health center, and mission church.[7]

The domestication of the Congolese landscape exacted heavy human losses: millions lost their lives under Belgian imperialism alone—and this does not count those who were maimed but survived. But the losses under colonial rule were less tangible too: livelihoods, belonging, and possibilities for social reproduction disappeared with the reorganization of territory under Belgian rule.[8] In many ways, it is these losses—together with attempts made to recuperate them—that undergird violence in the east today. A report by a leading group of regional conflict experts begins,

> The Banyamulenge, a Tutsi community in the Eastern DRC, have despite their small size, been at the centre of many of the disparate conflicts in the eastern DRC for most of the past two decades. The initial 1996 invasion by a Rwandan-backed insurgent coalition that aimed to topple Mobutu Sese Seko became known as "the Banyamulenge rebellion," and the Second Congo War of 1998–2003 saw Banyamulenge take on top positions as rebel commanders and political leaders. During this period of nearly 20 years, the community has been stuck in a cycle of persecution and insurgency.[9]

Historian Gillian Mathys identifies four waves of migration of Banyamulenge—or more broadly, Kinyarwanda speakers—into present-day Congo.[10] Long before the colonial period, there were people who left present-day Rwanda in search of farmland and settled in Kivu. These were the first wave. Then, there were the Banyarwanda immigrants, whom the Belgian colonists brought to eastern Congo between 1927 and 1950 in an effort to increase agricultural production in Congo. Initially, the indigenous population profited from the Banyarwanda immigrants, who paid tribute to the indigenous chiefs for access to farmland. As the number of immigrants increased, however, tensions developed between the indigenous and immigrant populations. In 1937, in response to pressure from the new wave of immigrants, the colonial government bequeathed a block of land to the Banyarwanda immigrants. But the bequeathed land was not vacant, and the distribution of Congolese land to the Banyarwanda immigrants displaced some Congolese while also interrupting the traditional system of tribute that would keep Congolese profiting from the presence of the newcomers. Between 1959 and 1963, a third wave arrived, the "fifty-niners," who crossed into Congo to escape violence in neighboring Rwanda. Finally, the fourth wave fled Rwanda in the aftermath of the 1994 genocide.

Regardless of when they arrived or why they came, the status of the Banyarwanda—a general term for people with Rwandan origins—remains heavily debated. The 1964 Constitution granted citizenship exclusively to those who could claim ancestral ties prior to the establishment of the Belgian Congo in 1908, thereby denying citizenship to the tens of thousands of Banyarwanda in the first wave. In a 1971 decree, President Mobutu extended citizenship to anyone living in Congo at independence, thus awarding legal status to the first through third waves; however, ten years later, in an effort to regain support in the east, Mobutu passed another decree that denied citizenship to all Banyarwanda by limiting citizenship to people whose ancestors were present in the country in 1885.[11] Paradoxically, even as his decrees rendered their legal status in the country tenuous, Mobutu's patronage politics continued to reward Banyarwanda with large swaths of valuable land. Ninety percent of colonial plantations that were nationalized under Mobutu's rule were given to members of his inner circle, many of whom were Banyarwanda.[12] By giving valuable land that, according to customary tenure, belonged to "sons of the soil [autochtones]" to "visitors [wageni]," as Banyarwanda are pejoratively called, Mobutu rendered the relationship between land, belonging, and profit even more slippery. And so, although the current law, passed in 2004, reextends citizenship to those in the first through third waves by defining Congolese nationality by ancestral presence in Congo in 1960, the rightful presence of Banyarwanda in Congo remains a subject of great contention.[13]

In the murkiness generated by colonial and postcolonial identity politics, Africanists Jean and John Comaroff assert that history has come to assume a particular narrative structure, which is linear and legalized and used to point to past wrongs.[14] In eastern Congo, surely, the repetition of justice-oriented historical narratives is common: the Hunde speak of Banyarwanda stealing customary land; and, conversely, the Banyarwanda speak of [violent] Hunde efforts to displace them from land that was rightfully theirs. But, as anthropologist Stephen Jackson demonstrates, because someone can always be more indigenous than someone else, one's historical claim to land in eastern Congo "is adjectival, relational rather than absolute."[15] And thus, even as history guides narrative structure in Congo, questions—about who is (more) indigenous, about who has (more) rights to the land and the resources that the land contains, about why ancestral connections with the rich Congolese soil and subsoil do not open doors to global capital flows—abound.[16] In this context, where land tenure remains spectacularly unclear, conflict researchers Koen Vlassenroot and Chris Huggins argue that land has itself become a "resource," driving and sustaining conflict: customary leaders incite local youth to grab land, to take back what is rightfully theirs; politicians gift land as a reward for loyalty to new politico-military leaders; and armed groups occupy land as a means to finance their operations.[17] Each land transaction generates another potential point of conflict. In 2013, thirty discrete armed groups operated in eastern Congo. By 2017, this number had grown to 132.[18] The propagation of armed groups in rural areas has resulted in a dramatic trend toward urbanization of the population—there is protection in numbers.[19] As they attempt to distance themselves from conflict, many Congolese leave the land that is their birthright and seek livelihoods elsewhere.

Masonry and Movement: "Some Days, I Ask Myself Whether I Am Even Human"

When I asked him what he did for a living, Jean-Baptiste answered "movement." Born in 1980 to a mason and a businesswoman, Jean-Baptiste lived in a rural town outside Goma for the first decade and a half of his life. In early 1994, when Rwandan refugees fleeing the genocide began streaming into their town, Jean-Baptiste's family provided them food and shelter. However, several months later, when the spread of cholera in the ever-swelling refugee population resulted in the abandonment of corpses in the street, Jean-Baptiste's family moved away from the camp, to the commercial center of Sake.

For two years, Jean-Baptiste went to school in Sake, farming his parents' field on weekends or school holidays. Then, in 1996, Rwandan troops invaded eastern Congo. When they surrounded the camps and began killing camp inhabitants, Jean-Baptiste's family ran from the violence for several days. Upon his return to Sake, Jean-Baptiste found that many of his classmates had begun to, voluntarily and involuntarily, join the army. Because he had already lost so many members of his family—seven of his nine siblings had passed away from childhood illness—Jean-Baptiste avoided military service. In 1998, when war again erupted in Sake, Jean-Baptiste and his family ran again, this time back to the small town where he was born. For a year, he and his family waited for Sake to become calm again. Given the fierce fighting that was taking place in the interior, school was closed for a year.

When the intensity of the fighting decreased in Sake, his family returned to their home, and Jean-Baptiste went back to school. However, his school attendance was short lived, as his father had already started teaching him to be a mason's aid, and Jean-Baptiste wanted to continue his training. After dropping out of school, Jean-Baptiste worked for a short time as a mason's aid before he started an apprenticeship with one of his father's friends. At the age of twenty, he finished his training as a full-fledged mason and began working independently. His first job was building bridges and drainage ditches across North Kivu for a German NGO. At the time, fighting was still taking place over large swaths of North Kivu; however, Jean-Baptiste and his colleagues were, for the most part, able to work without significant disruption. A year into his contract, he met Solange, the woman who would become his wife, on one of his trips back home. It took him two more years of work before he could come up with the money necessary for the bride price, but he and Solange were eventually married in 2003.

After the wedding, Jean-Baptiste looked for other masonry jobs, to no avail. At first, he waited. Then Solange told him she was pregnant, and he began to worry about how he was going to provide for his growing family. Soon thereafter, he bought a bicycle and began transporting charcoal. For two years, he pushed the loaded bicycle up and down the Masisi hills, from the rural areas, where it was fabricated, to Goma, where it was sold. It was back-breaking work, but, with the war, the opportunities in masonry had all but dried up. Eventually, he saved up enough money hauling charcoal to change professions. One day, he sold all his charcoal and began transporting used shoes from Goma to rural markets on a weekly basis. Every Tuesday, he climbed aboard a large cargo truck with several sacks of shoes and spent the week making his rounds through the nearby markets. While he was away from the house for a week at a time, he was able to keep food on the table.

In late 2006, war came to Sake. Jean-Baptiste and his family were away visiting family, but the house was pillaged and much of the shoe inventory taken. Judging Sake to be too insecure to return, he moved his family to Goma and went back to the markets to sell shoes. At one point, the truck that he was riding on was stopped, and armed men took both his merchandise and his cash. The next day, he took some money from his savings and invested in another round of merchandise. For several more months, his used shoe business again thrived. Then, one day, war erupted at the market where he was selling. With bullets flying nearby, Jean-Baptiste left his merchandise and ran into the forest. When he eventually made it back to Goma, he was penniless.

For a few months, he sat and waited for the next opportunity. Then, he found a small job as a mason. While this project was short lived, it provided him the capital he needed to start moving again. Although Jean-Baptiste had never dealt in livestock before, he had heard that it was a more stable line of work than masonry during war. After all, even if people weren't building in the war, they would still need to eat. In 2009, Jean-Baptiste began buying goats in Goma, loading them on trucks in the evening and driving across the border at night, where he sold them in Uganda for a sizable profit. At first, business was good: he was able to sell all of the goats he brought within a day or two. However, when war worsened in the area where the market was located, many of the buyers fled. After a particularly unprofitable trip, Jean-Baptiste returned to Goma and again sat as he waited for the next opportunity.

After a few months, an acquaintance in his social network gave him a loan to buy a small motorcycle. Jean-Baptiste taught himself how to drive and was soon making good money as a moto-taxi driver in Goma. While profitable, driving entailed significant risk—accidents, nonpayment, theft by armed men at night—and his wife had just had her second child. Thus, as he drove, Jean-Baptiste kept his ear out for masonry jobs. On one such job, his boss was especially pleased with his work and asked him and his family to move to Kishabe to guard a piece of land she had there. It was then, when I took up residence on the land that Jean-Baptiste was guarding, that I first got to know Jean-Baptiste.

During the time we lived together in Kishabe, Jean-Baptiste's only job was as a guard and property manager of my landlord's house. He was paid relatively well, as was his wife. With the sum of money that they were able to save during that time, Jean-Baptiste and his wife bought a large field not far from town. This was the first long-term investment that they had been able to make in the ten years that they had been married. When I left Kishabe after a year of fieldwork, they were just beginning to plant beans, cassava, and eucalyptus trees in their newly acquired field, and they seemed optimistic about their future.

Four months later, when I returned to Kishabe for a short fieldwork visit, this optimism had faded. Jean-Baptiste and his wife both looked weary, and their five children had lost weight. Solange explained to me that the month after I had left, Jean-Baptiste's employer had stopped paying him. Instead of a monthly salary, she had given him a case of beer and instructed him to start an open-air bar on the land. Jean-Baptiste and his wife had done as she instructed; however, few people in Kishabe had money to spend on beer, and Jean-Baptiste and Solange were only able to eke out a meager profit.

As his family ate through their savings, Jean-Baptiste made several trips to Goma to try to find masonry work. However, it had been more than a year since he had spent time in Goma, and his connections were tenuous at best. He went several times to see his employer and plead again for work, but she was always unavailable. That was in November 2013.

In the intervening years, Jean-Baptiste's efforts to find steady employment have dwindled. As food became more scarce in the house, he and Solange began fighting. Despite being heavily pregnant with her sixth child, Solange was farming the field they owned together, and Jean-Baptiste wanted to sell it to put food on the table. Several months into the argument, Jean-Baptiste sold the land and then used the money to marry a second wife. Furious, disappointed, and hurt, Solange left and took the children with her. With only a first-grade education herself, Solange had little choice but to rent a plot of land on credit and begin planting anew. After several seasons, she saved up enough money to buy a plot of land; after several more, she was able to build a small house for herself and her children. When I visited her several years later, Solange was frustrated at Jean-Baptiste, who provided no support to feed or clothe the six children. And yet, she empathized with his position:

> If for one night, we didn't have to hear about war—pillage, displace-
> ment, bullets, rape; if for five years, we didn't have to run, imagine
> what this country would be like. There would be jobs and roads and
> movement. It is war that brings laziness. In war, you have to fight for
> life [piganisha maisha]. So we fight. We all fight. But at some point,
> after you have been pillaged or let down enough times, you just get
> discouraged. Even if your kids are dying of starvation, you stop going
> to the field or going to work. Because in war, life doesn't lead to what it
> should. Even if you plant, war will start before you harvest, and you'll
> never eat what you planted. When you invest in transporting beans or
> charcoal, war starts, and the soldiers steal it from you. You earn a little
> money, put it in the bank, and then M23 [an armed group] comes in
> and steals it from the bank. You see, war always returns us backward
> [inaturudisha nyuma], so far backward.

"Returned backward" is the phrase that Solange used most often to describe Jean-Baptiste's position. Whereas several years prior, Jean-Baptiste
was invested in keeping his informal activities going, after his split with
Solange, he rarely did more than circulate in the neighborhood. During
a recent visit, I asked Jean-Baptiste about his plans for the following year.

He replied matter-of-factly, "Without a salary, you can't have projects; you can't plan. You live day by day and just try to eat." Despite the many business opportunities he had pursued over the years, despite the expertise and skills that he had built up over three decades of movement, Jean-Baptiste had no savings and no job prospects. And, while before, he had fundamentally believed that movement would help put food on the table and pay his children's school fees, with repeated sabotage in war, he had lost both the economic means and the drive to embark on yet another venture. "Movement," writes anthropologist James Smith, is "the positive, socially collaborative, and temporarily incremental mobility of things and people."[20] Where so few had access to stable employment, the bricolage of informal activities and fleeting collaborations called "movement" helped people feed their families; however, for Jean-Baptiste and many others in Congo, war destroyed everything, even that which had the capacity to morph into something else when bullets got too close. Even if he kept moving, he feared his efforts would never produce enduring effects. "Where would I go from here?" he asked me on a day when he was feeling especially down. "These days, I am so poor. Some days, I ask myself whether I am even human."

Where land disputes have continued long after independence, so many have become disconnected, displaced from their ancestral land. This has stripped them of the means with which to survive; it has also deprived them of any durable sense of belonging. While many of the landless attempt to engage in the informal economy through movement, violence fractures their efforts and renders them bereft of the financial and social community that makes life livable. And so, many Congolese, Jean-Baptiste included, resembled Achille Mbembe and Janet Roitman's seemingly timeless characterization of "Figures of the Subject in Times of Crisis." Regardless of how hard he worked, he was caught in "the physical and mental violence that issues from the lack of coincidence between the everyday practice of life and the corpus of significations or meanings."[21] Even as he remained proximate to great wealth, even as he saw the possibility of a better life on the horizon, he was not able to "explain and interpret what happens, to act efficaciously and, in so doing, attempt to overcome the specter of nothingness." In Jean-Baptiste's case, his inability to act durably on the world has led him to question his place in the world, whether or not he even belongs to humanity.

On the one hand, Jean-Baptiste's statement, "These days, I am so poor. Some days, I ask myself whether I am even human," could be understood as an expression of fatigue, of desperation. But I think its meaning extends beyond the metaphorical register. Where war has obliterated formal economies,

Jean-Baptiste worked for years to create movement, to build capital and/or the social networks that generate capital. Despite decades of hustling, despite the hardship and violence he endured for future gain, he and his family continued to live in extreme poverty. And so, at some point, he came home, sat down, and did not leave again. As he watched his family get thinner, he wondered, "Is this it?" Will he, and by extension his family, remain forever marginal? Will he ever be able to save money, ever be able to feed his family? Will he ever be able to count on some kind of future? Surely, these questions unite him with other African postcolonial subjects trapped in late-stage capitalism—thus my invocation of Mbembe and Roitman above. But I wonder if his last statement, "Some days, I ask myself whether I am even human" drives deeper still, to questions about the intersection (and potential coincidence) of Blackness and humanity ("Man" in Sylvia Wynter's writing).[22] In an article titled "The Social Life of Social Death," Jared Sexton poses several questions that undergird the field of Black critical theory about the (im)possibility of Black humanity:

> what is the nature of a human being whose human being is put into question radically and by definition, a human being whose being human raises the question of being human at all? Or, rather, whose being is the generative force, historic occasion, and essential by-product of the question of human being in general? How might it be thought that there exists a being about which the question of its particular being is the condition of possibility and the condition of impossibility for any thought about being whatsoever? What can be said about such a being, and how, if at stake in the question is the very possibility of human being and perhaps even possibility as such?[23]

For Black critical theorists, Blackness within antiblack regimes is an aporia—an impasse, a double bind. This aporia has been given different names: for Sexton, it is "social life in social death"; for Saidiya Hartman, the "position of the unthought"; for Sharpe, "the wake"; for Hortense Spillers, the "impossible monstrosity."[24] For all of these theorists, staying in the aporia is impossible—how to make a life when you are condemned to death? So, too, is exit: after all, *aporia* broken down is *a-*, without, and *-poros*, passage. Within dense antiblackness, there is no possibility of Black life freed of the requirement for Black death. And still, people search incessantly for a door, a route that leads them out of the double bind. Of those who endured the Middle Passage, Mbembe writes, "the work of producing symbols and rituals, languages, memory, and meaning—and therefore the substance necessary to sustain life—never stopped. Nor did the interminable labor of caring for and repairing that which had been broken."[25]

Jean-Baptiste's life, like that of many Congolese, is characterized by deep wounding. He has lost much in war, and despite his recurrent attempts to make a route out of poverty, he remains desperately poor, unable to feed his children. And though these wounds seem extensive, and, in many ways, Jean-Baptiste seems to succumb to these wounds—he stops moving, at least for now—I do not believe that his positionality is fixed. With repeated injury, tissues contract and scars become more dense. With every insult, a few degrees of range of motion are lost; there is less and less room for movement. And still, healing is possible: steroid injections can remodel keloid, contracture releases might restore mobility to frozen joints. While his wounds leave him wondering if he is still human, they have not permanently arrested time or annihilated future time, as Emery Kalema argues scars in Congo are want to do.[26] Rather, as Derrida argues, the aporia demands interruption, even if "the interruption always resembles the mark of a borderly edge, the mark of a threshold not to be trespassed."[27] Said another way, the aporia is both the abyss and the impossible possibility of passage through the abyss. In this section, I have suggested the contours of the aporia, of the contradictory injunctions, that is life in Congo today. In the remainder of this chapter, I query what "going through" the abyss, toward healing, toward a different present, might feel like in Congo.

"To Be Congolese Is to Have Soil on Your Hands"

During the time that I lived and worked in Kishabe, Jean-Baptiste was one of my closest interlocutors. Through time spent at the hospital, I also became dear friends with Anne-Marie, a nurse-midwife who worked in Kishabe's maternity ward. Anne-Marie had a house in Goma, where her husband and five children lived, worked, and attended school. She also had a house, a job, and fields in Kishabe. While she often claimed to live in Goma, the majority of her time was actually spent in Kishabe, where she split her time between the maternity ward and her bean and cassava fields. Anne-Marie was among the small minority of Congolese who had secured formal employment. And yet, given the meager and inconsistent salary that she received from the hospital, she insisted that her family would not be able to survive if she did not farm. "I farm to keep the shelves in Goma stocked and to keep hunger at bay," she said. Often, she went straight from a busy overnight shift to her fields. When I remarked on how hard she worked, she always responded with "Sisi waKongomani, tunaishi kama ndege; tunakula na neema ya Mungu." As Congolese, we live like birds; we eat by the grace of God.

Anne-Marie and I lived but a few houses apart, and we shared many meals together. One Saturday morning, I was leaving Kishabe for Goma for the weekend, and Anne-Marie flagged me down. She asked for a ride to Goma but needed some time to gather food for the children. Several hours later, she loaded fifty kilograms of beans and about as much cassava into the back of the car. As she opened the passenger door, she explained that her husband had called to say that the pantry was completely empty in Goma. "Hunger [*njala*]," Anne-Marie said, rubbing her abdomen in the common way that people do when the pangs have set in. "Njala ni vita ya kila siku." Hunger is an everyday battle.

When we arrived at her house in Goma, I helped Anne-Marie unload the car and got back in the car to leave. While we spent a lot of time together in Kishabe, Anne-Marie's time in Goma was limited, and I never wanted to take away from time with her children. On this day, however, Anne-Marie invited me in. Her home was cozy even with the kids at school. As in many houses in Congo, laminated posters decorated the wall. While these posters served a functional purpose—covering spaces between the boards of the house to keep rain and mosquitos out—their too-bright images also seemed to be a reminder to all who entered that a good life was possible, if always elsewhere: an Asian couple lounging in a park with plush grass feeding each other fruit, a blonde child holding hands with his thin, blonde, well-dressed mother and father.

For a few minutes, there was some rustling in another room, and then Anne-Marie joined me in the living room. She carried with her a small bundle, which she extended toward me. I took the bundle from Anne-Marie, who then used both hands to unwrap it slowly, deliberately. As she pulled back the wax fabric one corner at a time, she revealed an opaque, black stone. In a hushed voice, as if out of reverence for the stone, Anne-Marie asked me whether I knew of anyone who would buy it from her. She said that she was looking for a "white [*mzungu*]" middleman who would give her a fair cut for moving the stone between the mines in the rural areas surrounding Kishabe and Goma, where it could enter the global market. She stated that she was worried about being cheated by a buyer, of not receiving what she actually deserved. "At least some people have gotten rich off of stones," she said, with reference to the large houses on the lake shore that were owned by whites and successful Congolese businessmen.

Congo has long been known for its subsoil. In the 1920s and 1930s, the Belgian government, like many colonial powers on the continent, invested heavily in the mining industry. Extensive infrastructure was developed to extract copper, tin, and iron from the ground and export these heavy metals for largely extracontinental construction projects—roads, railroads, schools, hospitals. Because they offered formal employment and the possibility of a middle-class life, mining inspired dreams of modernity, of progress. Potentially, if they resettled in mining towns, the colonized would finally achieve the stable, prosperous lives that they saw their colonizers living: their kids could go to school; they could afford health care. While, for a few years, there might have been profit in the mines, when global copper prices plummeted in the mid-1970s, opportunity seemed to dry up. Within a decade, even bilateral aid couldn't keep the mines open. Where mines did continue to function, miners' salaries dropped below subsistence levels—and still the miners returned to the shafts, for the dream, the possibility of a better life seemed so much more promising than a return to subsistence agriculture.[28]

With the dawn of the digital age in the 1990s, Congo's subsoil was infused with new visions of reverie. In contrast to the infrastructurally laden extraction economies of copper, tin, and iron, rhizomatic networks of artisan miners developed to extract coltan, a key mineral used in the production of digital devices. After a decade of war had destroyed livestock, land, children, and other markers of progressive time, coltan seemed to offer a possibility of building anew. With dreams of entering the global market from which they had been long excluded, farmers put down their hoes and entered the forests where coltan had been found. In the heavy, voluminous material, people again saw a glimpse of an invitation into modernity.[29]

Given how lucrative and vast the tech industry has become, coltan should provide the possibility for a better life, one that connects the forests in Congo to Cupertino; and yet, most coltan diggers continue to live in extreme poverty, unable to feed their families. Like most lucrative sectors of the Congolese economy, coltan mining is largely militarized, and those at the top of the hierarchy retain most of the profit. In the end, coltan, like copper before it, has only provided a new life to a select few. Like many who entered the coltan trade for the promise of riches, Anne-Marie admired the "big men with the big houses and big cars" around Goma. However, as the mother of three boys, she also had other plans: "Once I sell this stone, I can buy some land so that my sons can marry," she daydreamed aloud. She paused and then added, "Kuwa mkongomani ni kuwa na udongo mkononi." To be Congolese is to have soil on your hands.

I never heard what happened to this particular stone. I do know, however, that Anne-Marie has remained poor. During the fall of 2012, armed men pillaged her beans and corn just before harvest. Anne-Marie stood in her razed fields for some time mourning for the empty shelves to come. By the time she had returned home, however, she was in better spirits and had already begun to prepare seeds for the spring's planting. A year later, the owner of the land that Anne-Marie had previously farmed demanded a higher rent, and, when she could not pay it, banned her from planting there again. For a season, hunger again gripped Anne-Marie's household, and her children did not go to school. Eventually, though, she was able to secure farming rights to a different plot of land in Kishabe and, once again, Anne-Marie started over.

Eight years have passed since I first met Anne-Marie. Despite the many interruptions and recurring challenges, she continues to return to the soil, both as a farmer and as a middle person in the coltan trade. When I last visited her, her face was gaunt and her eyes were tired. She talked, as she has always done, about what it might feel like to stand in front of an overflowing pantry like the ones she has seen on television, or to drive to work in a luxe car on an asphalt road and to arrive at work on time and dust free. This time, she added a new vision: "I'm going to visit America," she proclaimed confidently. "I'm fifty-two. I've made it past the life expectancy of this country. Farming has been hard on my body, and I can barely breathe sometimes. But I am not dying, and I am still trading [minerals]. Mark my words," she said with a grin before she hugged me goodbye. "I will knock on your door and sit at your table with you someday soon, even if today I am hungry."

Whereas Jean-Baptiste turned to movement when his initial plans of masonry did not produce a secure salary, Anne-Marie continued to return to the soil. The soil sometimes left her hungry and did not deliver a better life. And still, Annie-Marie returned. For, it seemed, the soil provided something nothing else could—a refusal of the placelessness of continued displacement. Proximity to soil in Congo offered her the chance to sink her fingers in the dirt, to engage in the work that her parents taught her, the work that fed her grandparents and their parents. And, with the products she pulled from the dirt, Anne-Marie dreamed of an exit from a life of poverty, where full pantries and dust-free roads abounded. In this way, dirt work seemed to create a through line for Anne-Marie from the centuries-old tradition of land tenure, through the recurrent displacement, to a present otherwise. Where temporariness and radical uncertainty characterized the everyday, returning to the dirt, that which had fed her ancestors and engendered belonging, was an insistence of the possibility of exit from aporia, war. "To be Congolese is to have soil on your hands," Marie insisted. In a country so destroyed by land conflict, dirt work itself was a register of healing.

****

I have found examining dirt work in Congo to be instructive, for it was in listening to Anne-Marie's and Jean-Baptiste's stories that I first began to think about the abyss, the impossibility that is the Congolese everyday. Neither Anne-Marie nor Jean-Baptiste seemed to think that their lives were harder than those around them. When they talked about suffering, they both tended to use the first person plural: "Sisi waKongomani, tunaishi kama ndege; tunakula na neema ya Mungu." We Congolese, we live like birds; we eat by the grace of God. The ordinariness of their stories is precisely what makes them valuable when thinking about aporia. There are not just a few people in Congo—the brutally raped or the desperately poor—confined to the abyss; rather, Anne-Marie and Jean-Baptiste insist that they are joined by eighty million other countrymen and women in the impossibility. "We Congolese," they say.

If these two people teach about the shared experience of aporia, I argue that they also offer important lessons about the shared, or public, component of healing and repair amid deep wounding. Historian Steven Feierman posits that in precolonial central Africa, healers worked at two levels: that of individual misfortune, treating a woman's infertility, the illnesses of children in a household, the suffering and pain of an elderly man; and that of group survival and well-being, acting on epidemics, famines, warfare, cattle disease. Where much of the writing on African healing has focused on the first level— for Western conceptions of the individual permeate everywhere—Feierman emphasizes how people understood the collective health to be reflective of political and social functioning. He writes, "The criteria on which people could evaluate their public leaders and assess the public conditions of their survival were grounded in a practical knowledge of childbirth or of the environment, of animal diseases, and of epidemics."[30] When the collective was well, the healers remained aligned with the groups' leadership; when the survival of the collective was imperiled—such as sleeping sickness epidemics in the 1880s and 1890s and the dramatic rise of syphilis in the 1990s[31]—healers led the collective in therapeutic forms of social healing. Feierman discusses the drumming ritual called *ngoma*; but there were also rituals involving spirit mediums and other forms of public healing in precolonial central Africa.[32]

Fast-forward to present-day Congo. Many of the public health rituals of precolonial times no longer exist. Much was lost under colonial rule.[33] But much has been transformed as well. Anthropologist Luca Jourdan describes healing rituals undertaken by the Mai Mai armed group as one form of public healing in eastern Congo today.[34] Here, I am curious about whether dirt work might also be a form of public healing. Could dirt work function like *ngoma*, which, in Schoenbrun's description of it, incorporates the afflicted into larger communities of people, thus enabling them to make sense of their marginalization and creating the possibility for them to imagine, demand, create something different?[35]

It is said that the relatives of the enslaved who were forced into the hulls of the ships that crossed the Atlantic braided seeds in the hair of the enslaved before they departed.[36] I try to imagine how this happened. The descriptions from this time speak of African people chained together in heavy iron shackles, led by white men. The drawings of the slave holds depict bodies on top of each other, without room to sit up or relieve oneself, let alone braid. The braiding must have been done after people had already been shackled but before they were loaded on the boats—which means that the braiding was done after it was clear that people's loved ones would be taken forcibly away from them and that they likely would never return to their homeland. And yet the families of the enslaved believed so strongly in the fact that their loved ones would continue to exist, that there was an alternative present, that they braided seeds in their hair to prepare them for whatever they would face.

When Anne-Marie returns to her fields, when she returns to the soil or to the sale of the subsoil, I believe she is doing something like braiding seeds. Surely, her action is, in part, functional—where there are few other opportunities, she is doing what she can to quell the gnawing hunger of her household. And yet I believe that Anne-Marie, like so many Congolese, returns to the soil, which has never truly sated her family, which is often the site of armed plunder, in a sort of demonstration of her belief in the potential that soil in Congo holds. Where the soil itself has been the scene of so much destruction—the site of enslavement, the basis of colonial power, the root of war—where the expropriation of ancestral land during colonial and postcolonial rule contributes to a general state of phenomenological alienation, might a return to it for nourishment, in the form of farming and mineral trade, be read as a profound gesture toward an otherwise?[37]

Dirt provokes ambivalence in Congo—both the site of the original wound in Congo and the possibility for a different future.[38] Because violence often tracks with mineral and agricultural wealth, Congolese assert, "Tunakula na udongo yetu, lakini tunakufa na hii udongo pia." We eat by our soil, but we die by it also. Motivated by an ambivalence toward the soil, some people use whatever means are available to them to flee the land, anything to get away from the violence and the pain of dispossession, of landlessness. Others stay, returning to the very land that has been the site of the crime, and digging their fingers into its soil. Like those of Black Americans who return to the soil after centuries of being forced to work it, Congolese relationships with the soil are not simple.[39] And yet I believe that those who doggedly return, in spite of the fact that the land has yet to provide for them, do so because they believe that a different present is possible—one in which the soil is freed from its ties to the global economy and can once again feed and nourish Congolese people.

The Patience of the Trees

For years, discourses of soil have dominated history and the assertions of presents otherwise in eastern Congo. Given that land conflict features prominently in discussions about the roots of the current violence, conflict mediation and resolution efforts have focused on recasting and rebuilding relationships with Congolese soil and subsoil.[40] Experts propose reforming land tenure, decreasing the impact of displacement on long-term inhabitants, and improving the structural factors that lead to hunger, poverty, and movement—and thus, to violence.[41]

While discourses about land loom large in Congo, new discourses are emerging too. As talk of climate change and environmental sustainability have become more mainstream globally, discussions about repairing relationships with the land from which they were dispossessed have expanded from a focus on self-governance of Congo's agricultural and mineral wealth to include other natural resources including biodiversity, air quality, and solar power.

Founded in 1925 by the Belgians, Virunga National Park, located just north and west of Goma, sits at the center of some of these discussions. Covering nearly three thousand square miles, Virunga is the most biodiverse area on the continent and home to many endangered and endemic plant and animal species. With vast timber and water resources, it is a "natural lung" and "an economic driving force."[42] For the four million people who live within walking distance of it, and for those who enforce its boundaries, it is also a site of significant contention. Like other protected land in the Global South, Virunga is the object of many debates about rightful land ownership in conservation areas created during colonialism, the ethics of prioritizing the protection of animal and plant life over indigenous food security, and the influence of increasingly militarized conservation efforts on regional conflict dynamics.[43] And, for some, it is the tinder that sparks conversation about a time in the past when Congolese enjoyed a rich, multifaceted relationship with the natural world and what forms richer connections with the land, which extend beyond the soil and subsoil, might take.

In 2015, a small, local NGO called LEAP was founded in Goma.[44] While most of its operations revolve around the economic empowerment of single mothers, due to a demand from its members, LEAP has also begun activities focused on environmental sustainability. Initially, these activities were limited to educational efforts among its members about the imbrication of health, clean water, proper disposal of trash, and organically grown food. However, even in the absence of dedicated funding to do so, the environmental arm of the organization has grown to include the founding of several conservation clubs in primary schools as well as the testing and distribution of charcoal-alternative cooking stoves in Goma. In 2020, I sat at a meeting with the LEAP founder and two UNICEF staff members who were looking to launch a small initiative to support conservation work in the east. When the UNICEF staff members asked LEAP's founder what had motivated the organization to start environmental work, she replied,

> We need to teach Congolese children that the [Virunga] park belongs to them too. It's not just a place where the whites [*les blancs*] go to see the gorillas or climb the volcano. Or a place to make charcoal. That is *our* park, those are *our* trees. They say the earth is warming, so we need those trees to clean our air. If we cut down all of our trees, how are we going to breathe? Our ancestors knew the value of trees: they talked to them; they preserved them. With the wars and the poverty, we have lost this respect. But the park is ours; it is our job, as Congolese, to protect it.

Assertions about the necessity of environmental protection are one way that people are remaking relationality with the land in eastern Congo. Social entrepreneurship in the form of solar energy is another. Initially, as elsewhere, solar energy in eastern Congo was only a possibility for the rich: panels were fragile and expensive; batteries were bulky and had to be replaced often; only those with connections to international capital could afford to buy or maintain the systems that were available. In 2011, a British start-up called Bboxx began offering affordable, small-scale solar energy systems in Goma. Since then, many other solar products have become available in the region. In both rural and urban areas, many households, small businesses, even health centers rely on small solar lanterns for light in the evening, and neighbors often share a solar panel to charge their phones and other devices. Discussion about the potential for solar energy has risen to the national level as well. In January 2020, at a press release that covered the launch of a partnership between the government and Bboxx, the Congolese president discussed the role of the solar sector in contributing to employment, electrification, and offsetting the four million tons of carbon dioxide emissions that the country produces annually.[45]

While Bboxx has, since its arrival in the country, largely dominated the market for small-scale solar systems in eastern Congo, in the last decade, several Congolese-owned solar companies have emerged in its shadow. For several years now, I have followed the growth of Congolese solar companies with interest. Because a friend costarted and co-operates one of the larger Congolese companies, I have watched the sector evolve at close range. On a rainy night in early 2020, my friend and I got together for a beer. After exchanging personal news, Remi talked to me about the business. In the last year or so, the company had developed two new products to meet the particular demands of rural, poor Congolese life. In addition, they had designed new financing models, which took into account the dramatic ebbs and flows that war created in people's monthly income. We spoke at length about his own company. Then Remi told me about the business models of a new Congolese start-up on the market, which had plans to install solar panels along the major roads in the region. Soon, Remi predicted, this line of solar panels would provide very remote villages with light; and this electrification would have far-reaching effects. Remi argued, "With solar, we can rid ourselves of reliance on government and international corporations that have been extracting from us for so many years. This is but one step in taking back our country."

Alternative Modes of Being Human

Where land conflicts continue despite—or because of—Congo's significant ecological wealth, the majority of Congolese remain poor, hungry, and insecure. When faced with the paradox that land poses in Congo—offering the promise of belonging and middle-class life, but delivering instead war—some flee the land and take up movement. Others sink their fingers into the soil: through farming and mining, they return to their deep wounds and work to create something different. Still others move beyond the land, toward the trees and the sun. Through advocacy efforts and social entrepreneurship, they seek to heal the ruptures created by enslavement and extraction and restore a multifaceted relationship with the earth.

As they return to the dirt (and the natural world more generally), Congolese experiment with whether relationality with the other-than-human world might offer passage through the aporia that is their everyday.[46] These trials take different forms: innovative uses of solar technology are emerging, which provide new routes out of poverty; novel ways to do and teach conservation are being developed, which center equity and local governance; and a return to dirt work continues to create new through lines, which connect centuries-old land practices with alternative presents. In a place where land has been so divisive, these suggestions that the ecological might serve as a register of repair, a form of public healing, are radical; they are also visionary. Mbembe argues, "If to survive the ecological crisis means to work out new ways to live with the earth, then alternative modes of being human are required."[47] As environmental collapse worsens in Congo as elsewhere across the globe, Congolese are working out new ways to live with each other and with the warming earth. If, as Mbembe argues, our collective survival depends on these alternative ways of being, we would be wise to see the healing potential in Congolese dirt work.

FIGURE 1.2. The hospital in Kishabe, 2013. Scrubs were washed by hand, then dried in the hospital courtyard, as dust from the farmlands above percolated through the open-air complex. Photograph by author.

EIGHT WEEKS PRIOR

In Goma, break-ins by "bandits" have been rising. It is spectacularly unclear who these bandits are, which is precisely why the term is used.

SEVEN WEEKS PRIOR

On the way to Goma, I pick up some folks walking on the road with heavy bundles. They are going to Mugunga, the biggest refugee camp in the world. They say that they have lived there for years. Home is too dangerous.

The roads are clear.

SIX WEEKS PRIOR

Every day this week, the nearby UN force has been detonating old artillery. The blasts shake the ground. They broadcast ahead of time over the radio that they will be doing this, but given the threats of impending war, it nonetheless remains unsettling.

FOUR WEEKS PRIOR

There are many more soldiers in Goma. The word on the street is that the invading troops are donning plain clothes and then hiring moto-taxi drivers from Goma to transport them into the city. When night falls, these invaders-in-disguise are then entering houses in Goma, not because they need to steal necessarily, but because they are trying to create a narrative about the inability of the Congolese army to keep the population safe. This will then make it easier for the invading troops to win over the population when they actually come to town. Regardless of whether this is true or not, there is now a moto-taxi curfew at 1800, which the government soldiers are enforcing.

The roads are still clear.

FIGURE 2.1. *DRC: The Most Coveted Woman.* Because it is so visible, performed without any fear of reprisal, the graft and plunder that take place in Congo are a common subject of political satire. Here, a painting being sold on the street in Kinshasa, in 2012. See also the work of famous Congolese cartoonist Thembo Kash. Photograph by author.

A Sea of Insecurity

It is in listening to that cacophony of troubled stories that we might encounter our best hopes for precarious survival. —Anna Lowenhaupt Tsing, *The Mushroom at the End of the World*

Finding things out, getting at the meaning of things, turns out to mean and to demand an investigation of instability, a courting of tumult, of riot, of derangement, of the constitutive disorder of the polis, its black market, border, and bottom, the field of minor internal conflict, of the minor occasion or event through which the essence of an interminable struggle takes form. It means settling down in the uninhabitable, where one is constrained to reinitialize what has been dismissed as the pathontological in the discourse of the militant onto-pathologist. —Fred Moten, "The Case of Blackness"

Lake Kivu features prominently in the daily lives of many of Goma's inhabitants. People bathe in the lake, swim in the lake, wash cars beside the lake, and take their sundowners overlooking the lake. In a city where few have access to running water, many drink from the lake, young girls filling yellow jerricans at its shore and delivering them home before they go to school. During the day, speed boats crisscross its glassy surface, bringing people and cargo to meetings, markets, and home. At dusk, fishermen in wooden canoes lure small fish from the water into their nets with song. And yet, even as they wash with its waters and celebrate its bounty, many fear its cool, black depths.

In the 1950s, long before the recent wars, some 60 billion cubic meters of methane and 300 billion cubic meters of carbon dioxide were discovered in the depths of Lake Kivu. To volcanologists, this was a terrifying discovery. For any lake with methane under its surface carries the threat of a limnic eruption, a phenomenon in which the layers of the water are disturbed, and the lake "overturns," releasing the gases formerly in the lake's depths into the air. Heavier than air, these gases, both methane and carbon dioxide, creep along the ground and asphyxiate all that is around: people, livestock, vegetation. Previously, limnic eruptions were textbook phenomena—theoretical and historical possibilities. However, in 1986, Lake Nyos, a small lake in Cameroon known to have methane in its depths, overturned. Within minutes, 1,746 people and an estimated 3,500 livestock were killed. According to news reports, there were only six survivors of this limnic eruption. They told of a white cloud that blanketed the town overnight, silently killing most, and leaving a lucky few with weakness, nausea, and burns on their skin.[1]

Lake Kivu is the continent's eighth largest lake, and the world's largest known methane-containing lake, containing one thousand times the methane of Lake Nyos. While it has not erupted in recent history, there is some geologic evidence that past eruptions have occurred in thousand-year cycles. In general, limnic eruptions are thought to be triggered by tectonic activity, which perturb the surface of the lake enough to allow the lighter gas below to escape—or potentially, from a sudden and massive temperature change of the water at the lake's surface, such as that which happens when lava flows into a methane-containing lake. Sitting, as it does, on the East African Rift, as well as at the foot of an active volcano, either an earthquake or a volcanic eruption could have contributed to past eruptions of Lake Kivu, and both threats continue to loom large in the region. In 2002, when Mount Nyiragongo erupted and covered one-fifth of Goma in lava, scientists watched Lake Kivu with concern. Would the molten lava flowing into the lake be enough to destabilize the lake? There would be no time for an evacuation once a limnic eruption started. With two to three million people living on the shores of Lake Kivu, this would be a natural disaster of unimaginable proportions.[2]

The lake didn't turn over in 2002. Nor did it erupt in 2014, when an algae bloom caused its black waters to turn an eerie turquoise blue, and scientists warned again about the danger the lake posed to Goma's inhabitants. Even as Rwanda has begun to extract methane from its side of the lake for electricity, a potentially risky activity, the lake has largely remained stable. Vents in the region occasionally belch lethal doses of methane, and everyone in town has a story of someone who swam into a cloud of methane and was lucky to have made it out.

Between April 7 and July 15, 1994, a million people were killed in what later became known as the Rwandan genocide. Men and women were hacked to death by their neighbors; fetuses were eviscerated while their mothers were still alive; children were clubbed to death. With neither the space nor the time to bury them, bodies were dumped en masse into the lake.

To escape the violence, and then the war that ended the genocide, two million Rwandans, perpetrators and their victims, fled into neighboring Congo. Some refugees traveled into the hills surrounding Lake Kivu; one million formed the world's largest refugee camp on the lake's shore. For two years, international humanitarian organizations worked to provide for the basic needs of those who could not return to their homes in Rwanda. And then, in 1996, the tensions that had plagued the camp from the beginning boiled over. The killing started in the camp and then continued along the lake's shore. As war began in Congo, the lake again turned red with blood.[3]

Over the years, other bodies have joined those at the bottom of the lake: a young man in a school uniform robbed, killed, and dumped offshore; a prominent member of the community who was targeted, tracked, and then silently disappeared because of conflicting political beliefs, affixed with a backpack of stones that might have taken him to the depths if it had been heavy enough; and all of the children who jumped or fell in without knowing how to swim. These losses are mourned, but burials cannot be conducted without a body—and, with depths of nearly five hundred meters, the lake returns few of the bodies that it receives. Instead, bodies gradually decompose in their watery mass grave, and the levels of methane continue to rise at the bottom of the lake.

Running That Does Not End

It was 2013, and I was sitting with a group of youths in Kishabe. I often spent afternoons at a center built for women's empowerment activities in the town, and youths often gathered at the center whenever training or teaching was taking place. On this day, there had been no training, but several youths had stopped in after seeing me enter and sit alone in the pavilion. It was the middle of the day; I had asked them why they weren't in school. In discussing the hardships in their households that kept them from school, several mentioned the recent violence in the region. Houses and fields had been plundered; there was nothing more to sell to scrape together the necessary school fees. In a moment of silence that followed, I asked how many of them remembered running from war in their lifetimes. The question elicited laughter as all eight of them, ages eight to sixteen, raised their hand. One young woman remarked, "Kuwa mKongomani ni kujua kukimbia." To be Congolese is to know running. "Ndiyo," several in the group muttered in affirmation. Yes. A young man added, "Even if it's not war, there is the volcano, there is the lake. Tutakimbia kwa milile au Congo." We will be running forever here.

According to a 2007 study, 83 percent of people living in eastern Congo have experienced the destruction of goods; 46 percent have been beaten by armed groups; one in three have been abducted for at least a week; one in two have seen the violent death of a household member; and four out of five have been displaced, have run.[4]

People in eastern Congo have run for a very long time now.

The regime of running, if we might call it that, began with the arrival of the Arab slavers. Surely, people had run long before this—but there was staying too. Societies farmed; kingdoms matured.[5]

In the mid-1800s, people ran from the slavers—the chains and the hunger.[6]

Then, in the 1890s, when Belgian imperialists arrived to chase the slavers, people ran again. There were screams, amputated limbs, wombs rendered sterile from all the pounding—a regime of "red rubber."[7]

On June 30, 1960, Congolese won their independence. Five days later, the running began again with the army's looting, which was intended to chase the Belgian colonists out of town, but resulted in significant collateral damage.

In 1964, the people of eastern Congo ran when the Simba Rebellion clashed with national troops.

In 1965, the people of eastern Congo ran again when Belgian and American troops entered Congo to crush the Simba Rebellion.[8]

After the tumultuous 1960s, there was a period of relative abundance in Congo in the 1970s. Soon, however, copper prices fell, structural adjustment policies consumed the state whole, and people began to run again.

In 1993, people in eastern Congo ran from the fighting in the Masisi hills. These were local conflicts, but they nonetheless caused displacement.

In 1996, large-scale war began, and all over the country, people ran.

In 1998, there was another war, so much violence. As nine countries battled for control of Congolese territory and resources, people ran, and ran, and ran.[9]

There was a transitional government in 2003, and elections.

And then, in 2006, the army splintered again, and the people in Goma ran from war.

The intermittent but repeated attacks on those in North and South Kivu continued through 2009.[10]

And then, in 2012, people ran again as another major armed rebellion fractured the fragile peace.

To be Congolese is to know running, the youths had said. We will be running forever here.

In chapter 1, I explored the general sense of aporia that serves as the backdrop for life in eastern Congo—as well as the dirt work that is aimed at passage to a present otherwise.[11] In this chapter, I add the staccato sounds of bullets and running, knock-knock-open-up to the idea of aporia. I am interested in affective chaos, what it feels like to live in a place in which even youth have a bodily understanding of the threats that are posed by their environment—the lake, the volcano—and by the recurrent violence. I query the particular wounds generated by the displacement, the insecurity; I also examine the novel spaces for repair that open. Where war and disaster are always looming for all sides involved, I argue that inhabiting affect—mutual affective attunement—has the capacity to paper over ruptures created by violence and open up new spaces for healing.

The material for this chapter is based on research conducted during a particular period of insecurity that took place in the Kishabe community when I was living there for my fieldwork. While it is but one episode in a longer durée of violence, I believe that this story provides a lens through which to examine the relationship between wounding and healing amid recurrent conflict. People in eastern Congo live with a constant awareness of how insecure their lives are, at the foot of an active volcano, on the shores of a methane-containing lake, in intimate proximity with armed groups. I believe that, even as it pushes them to run, this awareness also opens the possibility for return to the landscape and to the very groups that threaten their daily existence with hopes of mending the pain and working together to create a present otherwise.

When Soldiers Become Bandits and Bandits Become Neighbors

In April 2012, three hundred Congolese soldiers defected from the national army and formed Le Mouvement de 23 Mars (or M23 for short). The most recent iteration of the Rwandan-backed rebel groups operating in eastern Congo, M23 was quickly chased into the forest by the Congolese army.[12] At the time, there were forty other armed groups meting out significantly more violence in other parts of eastern Congo. Thus, initially, M23 was largely forgotten. Over the next two months, with the financial and logistical support of Rwanda, M23 trained and equipped a fierce fighting force.[13] Then, in mid-June, having amassed 1,500 soldiers, they reemerged and installed themselves just north of Goma. Within six months, they had become the strongest rebel force since the civil wars had officially ended a decade prior.

When I began working in Congo in 2010, I had never intended to research war. A major peace treaty had been signed the year before; things seemed to be stabilizing. Certainly, there was still urban violence, but as a white woman living in a wealthy part of Goma, I could keep my distance from the insecurity. Even in July 2012, when I returned to Congo for a year of dissertation fieldwork, I did so under the auspices of relative safety. Certainly, M23 existed at the time, and they had already threatened to take Goma. But with the UN guarding Goma, these seemed like empty threats. After all, much more established armed groups had threatened to take Goma in the past, and none had succeeded.

M23 didn't come to Goma in July. They didn't invade in August. Or September or October. In Goma and in Kishabe, traders continued their routes, farmers planted their fields, and I continued my research. In November 2012, however, M23 left its base and marched south. For twenty-four hours, M23 engaged in a fierce fight with the Congolese army for control of Goma and its surroundings. Inhabitants of Goma sheltered from heavy artillery, stray bullets, and marauding troops. On November 20, M23 took control of Goma and its surrounding areas, thus gaining international attention. For twelve days, M23 controlled the town.[14]

When troops arrived in Kishabe, I had already left. On the day that M23 had started their march south, the American ambassador had called to tell the head of the hospital in Goma that the bombs "were real this time." The head of the hospital dispatched an ambulance to bring me back to the safety of the city. Eventually, when M23 got close to Goma, I would climb aboard a boat with my landlord in leopard-print tights, and we would cross over to the country that had started this iteration of war but whose territory would always remain untouched.

From the other side of Lake Kivu, I learned about what unfolded in the place I had come to call home. On the first night, the family with whom I lived in Kishabe—Solange, Jean-Baptiste, and their four children—hid from the retreating Congolese army in the grass by the lake. The town was looted—shops, houses, and bodies violated as soldiers entered homes in waves. Vinny, a nurse at the hospital, recounted, "You would hear a knock at the door, and then someone would order [in a gruff voice] 'open up.' When you opened the door, they would just come in and take whatever you had." The first group took Vinny's motorcycle and some money. The second, suitcases of his family's clothes and large sacks of food. When the third group came, they found the house almost empty, so they hit Vinny with their guns and took clothes that hadn't yet been washed.[15]

With heavy artillery echoing in the background, the violence at times took on an absurd dimension. Julien, a custodian at the hospital, laughed as he recounted the crazed state of the retreating soldiers:

> The soldiers had run for a long time, and they were hungry, so they tried to catch some chickens [to eat]. When the chickens beat the soldiers, the soldiers just started shooting. So many gunshots rang out in Kishabe, and we all hid under our beds. But there weren't any people getting killed. It was only chickens. All the chickens of Kishabe were finished that day. Head one place, chicken, another. And the chickens were so blown up after that the soldiers didn't even eat them! They just left them and walked away. Head one place, chicken, another. Even though they had killed all of our chickens, they were still hungry. Later that evening, they began firing at the fish. BAM BAM BAM, the shots rang out in Kishabe.

After drinking and eating all of the town's provisions, the soldiers eventually lay down for the night. At dawn, before the soldiers woke up from their stupor, Jean-Baptiste and his family joined thousands of other Congolese in flight. Jean-Baptiste pushed his motorcycle, which was loaded with food, charcoal, and clothes. Solange, visibly pregnant, carried two children and held the hands of her two others. "We had to leave," Solange remembered. "The army was looking for porters to carry the things they had stolen. If they had taken Jean-Baptiste, he wouldn't have returned." As the sun rose, whole towns and their livestock filled the road. Solange said, "We joined a sea of people who were also fleeing. The road was so crowded that you could lose the person next to you." The sea walked en masse to a town twenty-five kilometers away, and then made camps in the surrounding forest. The soldiers, who had beaten them there, got drunk again on stolen beer, and then stumbled into the forest where men, women, and children had tried to hide. There was screaming and gunshots. Solange and her family stayed, for it was too dark to flee again.[16]

Eventually, as a result of the violence committed by both M23 and the retreating Congolese army, international pressure mounted on Congo and Rwanda to broker a peace. At the beginning of December 2012, M23 retreated into the forest north of the town, looting homes and state offices in Goma as they left. Several days later, the Congolese police and the national army returned to Goma. Superficially, life seemed to return to normal; however, so much had been lost, so much destroyed in the war. And M23 continued to threaten Goma and its surroundings for the better part of the following year.

Days after M23 left Goma, several hundred government troops entered Kishabe with orders to set up residence there. Much of the Kishabe community had fled during the brunt of the fighting and had just returned from Minova and its surrounding forests. Given the violence that the national army had perpetrated in Kishabe and in Minova, the Congolese army's subsequent return to Kishabe created significant anxiousness. Vinny remembered, "They wore the same uniforms as the troops that had invaded my house with their weapons drawn. No one knew if they were the same soldiers, and no one knew what their orders were."

It was a given that the residents of Kishabe would host the soldiers. When Mobutu Sese Seko had governed the country, he had instated a clear hierarchy, wherein the army held significant power over the population. Near the end of his rule, when no money remained in state coffers to pay the national troops, Mobutu had given the military explicit permission to extract their salaries from the population. Theft from and abuse of civilians by the military became commonplace.[17] While Mobutu has been gone for decades, Mobutu's edict, "The civilian is the cornfield of the military," colloquially referred to as "Article 15" (of the Constitution), still often governs civilian-military interactions, especially during times of active war.[18] Vinny recounted, "They did ask our permission. But are you going to refuse a man with a gun?"

And yet, even though the possibility always existed for predation and violence, civilian-soldier interactions were not merely governed by fear. For some years now, Congolese soldiers and their families have been some of the region's poorest and most vulnerable inhabitants. Despite reforms in military payment, soldiers often still struggle to feed their families.[19] As a result, the population feels a certain obligation to provide for the national troops, especially as they are, in theory anyway, fighting for Congolese soil. Within days of pillaging houses in Kishabe and committing atrocities in Minova, government soldiers entered homes in Kishabe again, this time to sleep.

For several weeks, soldiers and civilians cohabitated. Following Mobutu-era etiquette, Kishabe residents served their armed guests. While men in uniform had decimated their fields and flocks and pillaged many household goods only a few weeks prior, young women spent their days foraging, cooking, and cleaning for the soldiers. At night, men served the soldiers beer.

In the hospital, too, Kishabe residents cared for soldiers. To enable the hospital to better treat those affected by war, a Belgian NGO had donated some funds for an emergency project that targeted war victims. Even though the soldiers weren't acutely wounded in war, clinicians in Kishabe used the funds to treat soldiers and their families free of charge. Surely, they were fearful of the soldiers, who milled around the grounds with arms slung lazily over their backs. Anne-Marie, who was working in the maternity ward when the government troops retreated to Minova, explained, "When the army came through Kishabe [on their way to Minova], a soldier came into the hospital, pointed his gun at a nurse, and demanded reimbursement for the money he paid for his wife's cesarean the month before. Now, we give free health care to anyone in uniform. Otherwise, we are too fearful to work."

Fear presided over interactions between soldiers and staff in the hospital; but the fact that the NGO expected the hospital staff to differentiate between war victims and people who had not been affected by the war generated empathy, too. Anne-Marie protested, "But also, the money is supposed to go to war victims. Here in Kishabe, everyone is a victim. Especially the soldiers. Look at them. They don't have any other clothes than the ones that they are wearing. And because they are always moving, they don't have their own fields or animals. So they steal ours. Yes, soldiering is just an official name for banditry. But what choice do they have when they are not paid?"[20]

Both inside and outside the hospital, people spoke anxiously about sharing spaces with soldiers. There had been so much violence, and there was potential for so much more. In speaking about the soldiers that they housed, Kishabe residents often used the words *soldier* and *bandit* interchangeably. With M23 threatening to return to Goma, the population was acutely aware of just how unpredictable their arrangement with the soldiers was. At any point, war could come again to Kishabe, and the soldiers could turn again on the very people that currently housed, fed, and cared for them, and once again become bandits.

But embedded in the population's pronouncement of their own fear of the soldiers were acknowledgments of the soldiers' vulnerability. At the hospital as well as in the community, Kishabe residents claimed that soldiers were themselves suffering. Adding to Anne-Marie's assertion of the soldiers' victimhood, Julien said, "Soldiers are the poorest people in Congo. They live like street children, with nowhere to sleep."[21] One day, when I voiced my own anxiousness about soldiers' presence in the hospital, Julien remarked, "They are our army. What choice do we have but to care for them?" Although the soldiers wore the same uniforms as those who had pillaged the town two weeks prior, even as soldiers' presence in their homes rendered the lives of Kishabe residents precarious, people in Kishabe pitied the soldiers—and felt obligated to provide for them.

Within a few weeks of arriving in Kishabe, soldiers began building a camp in the middle of town. Gradually, they moved out of people's homes into temporary shelters constructed from reeds, banana fronds, tarps stolen from the refugee camp, and wax cloth. The town of Kishabe seemed to take a collective breath of relief, as residents settled back into their own homes and their prewar routines. A ceasefire had been called between M23 and the government, and people began talking about celebrating Christmas. Still, in the absence of a signed peace treaty, the potential for renewed conflict loomed, and people continued to take precautions to manage the risks associated with living intimately with soldiers. Françoise, whose house bordered the camp, remembered:

> We told our children not to play near the camp. They wanted to play at the soccer field on the other side of the camp, but we told them they had to play at the school instead. For people like me who lived near the camp, it was hard too because I didn't want to be cooking outside, always being seen by the soldiers. So I started cooking on the side of the house away from the camp. When walking to their fields, everyone took the long way. It's true—we had already lived with these soldiers, and we had lived with many others before them, but in war, people can turn.

Vinny, who had lived with soldiers in his house for a few weeks, added, "In the event that war starts up again, it won't matter that you were just eating together, out of the same plate. They will steal your plate. Because they are soldiers, and in war, soldiers become bandits."

For a few weeks, people in Kishabe watched the soldiers' movements for signs of impending war from a distance. However, with time, the boundaries between the camp and the community blurred, and the population developed a different kind of intimacy with the soldiers.

****

When the camp was first constructed, shelters were organized in rows on uninhabited land in the center of town, and soldiers lived three or four men to a shelter. Two months later, soldiers' wives and children gradually began to arrive at the camp—a sign that they would be staying for some time. As living arrangements changed, more shelters were built to accommodate the camp's growing population. Before long, the camp had developed finger-like extensions around and between the population's more permanent dirt-and-plank houses. As the camp grew, children began taking shortcuts through the camp. Then, businesswomen in Kishabe began approaching the camp with goods to sell. The circulation of soldiers and their wives around town further extended the reach of the camp. Dressed in some combination of T-shirts and camouflage, Kalashnikovs slung casually over their shoulders, soldiers strolled along the main road, visited friends in the hospital, and drank palm wine in the storefronts that formed Kishabe's center. On Saturdays, the town's children joined the soldiers for their morning drills. On paydays, the soldiers drank, laughed, and danced together with their civilian neighbors.

Two months into the town's occupation, the soldiers' cash stores ran out, and they began to ask their civilian neighbors for food and other essential goods on credit. Selling on credit is common practice in rural Congo, where farming is people's sole source of income. But these were soldiers, and it was still wartime. Although they readily accepted credit from the population, merchants worried about establishing debt relationships to men in uniforms. For it was common knowledge that in peacetime, the military was paid inconsistently. And during wartime, soldiers could be deployed to the front lines at a moment's notice, leaving unpaid any outstanding debts they had in Kishabe. Thus, taking soldiers' debt was a risky affair; it was also a potentially lucrative one. Months after she began lending to soldiers, the owner of a chapati shop explained the calculation she made:

> When you lend to soldiers, you bet against war. You never want to lend too much, because we live in Congo, and every day is war . . . but who else in Kishabe has access to $100 cash every month? Besides, they have guns. In the end, we pity them [*kusikia uhruma*]. They have a lot of needs: they have a wife and children to feed. Sure, it can also be profitable for us. But even when it's not, you can't say no to a hungry

soldier. He must steal from the population to live [*Inabidi anyanyase raia kumbi aishe*].

Care and obligation once again emerged amid the fear.

While the Kishabe community gradually grew more comfortable with the soldiers—their camouflage and their guns, their occupation of space, their buying and selling routines—people were always clear that living intimately with soldiers carried significant risk. Socially and economically, the soldiers and community were intertwined, even mutually dependent. And yet there was always the possibility that war would intensify and raw violence would again enter Kishabe. On multiple occasions after its withdrawal from Goma, M23 engaged the Congolese army within twenty miles of Kishabe. When conflict would begin, all of the combat-ready men in town would pack up and leave for the front lines. At once, anxiousness would peak in the town. As the soldiers were leaving, Kishabe residents shut their doors and windows, fearing that the men would take advantage of the chaos of war and pillage their homes. Once the soldiers had left, people gathered in storefronts to discuss the future of Kishabe without the soldiers. Some had sold entire harvests or inventories to men in uniform and worried for their financial future. Others worried that in the absence of the army, local militias, who often fought against the national army, would descend on Kishabe and exact revenge for all of the care the town had given to the army. Grandmothers went to church, knelt, and prayed for the soldiers' safety: "Mungu, ulinde watoto wetu," they said with hands raised to the sky. Lord, protect our children. Within the span of a few months, the soldiers had become integral, if mercurial, members of the community—even children to some.

A Militarized Society

The slippage that developed between *bandit*, *soldier*, and *children* in the Kishabe community was remarkable—how rapidly the context changed and, with it, the community's appellation of the soldiers; and the fact that the Congolese troops who took up residence in Kishabe had the potential to be several things at once to the surrounding population was unique neither to Kishabe or the army nor to the M23 war. Since the 1990s, civilian-military relationships, and especially informal war economies, have generated significant academic interest.[22] In Congo, as elsewhere across the continent where the lines between civilian and soldier have become so blurred, the conception of war—as distinct from peace, as separate from the everyday, as an entity that has a beginning and an end, which is fought on a defined battlefield—has become so slippery.[23]

In Chad, anthropologist Marielle Debos documents the ways that, for many years after the formal end of war, "living by the gun" had become an accepted occupation.[24] In Congo, living by the gun is not an occupation limited to former combatants; rather, many civilians actively participate in collaborations with and networks of armed men to feed their families.[25] And because armed groups in eastern DRC are constantly undergoing transformation—recruiting, demobilizing, splintering and reforming, joining alliances with other groups only to quickly fall out with each other—the specificities of the civilian-military networks, who is collaborating with whom to what ends, are constantly shifting.[26] During my tenure in Kishabe, the community collaborated with the Congolese army; however, prior to the M23 conflict, they were known to be supportive of various local militias in the region, which sometimes were at odds with the Congolese army and sometimes collaborated with it.[27]

As demonstrated in Kishabe, where war had become so boundless, it was not just that civilians had become increasingly involved as active participants in war economies, but also that the population collaborated with armed men in all economic exchange, from chapati selling to farming to beer buying. For years, advocacy efforts have focused on the need to demilitarize certain sectors of the Congolese economy: "No guns in my mobile" was a campaign that focused on the demilitarization of coltan mining.[28] While on a much smaller scale, the gold, coffee, timber, and charcoal sectors in Congo have also received the attention of activists.[29] The fact that civilian-soldier partnerships touch all sectors of the Congolese economy leads geographer Ann Laudati to argue that in eastern DRC, war is not the continuation of politics by other means, as Clausewitz famously claimed. Rather, where populations and armed groups live in such intimate proximity, "Wartime activities, then, are a continuation of economics by other means."[30]

As anthropologists Roitman and Debos illustrate in Chad, the imbrication of civilian and military, the knitting together of profit, statecraft, and violence that has taken place across the African continent, redraws the boundaries between politics and economics; it also creates new subject positions, alternative ways of inhabiting the world.[31] Writing on Congo, Jourdan describes the "Mobutuist habitus" that arose in the wake of the peace treaties that ended the Second Congo War.[32] Where the pact between citizens and their state has long been broken and the state monopoly on violence has given way to control by individuals, Jourdan argues that violence has become thoroughly embedded in everyday ways of life, for civilians who have never touched a gun as for those who have. Even where active war is geographically or temporally distant, violence is used—and legitimized—as a means to achieve social mobility and accede to modernity. Conflict researcher Judith Verweijen documents the way that in Goma, years after the last formal battle for the city, interpersonal conflicts and workplace disputes are settled through recourse to violence, and threats of violence are often used to ascend to positions of social and economic power.[33] Where AK-47s are plentiful and hit jobs are priced by how many bullets they will require, Verweijen shows how the slippage between soldier and bandit expands to encompass another category: that of the civilian.

****

Kivu Security Tracker holds a three-day conference in Goma. A project initially devised by a group of expatriate conflict researchers with significant experience in the region, the project has become a source of pride for the Congolese researchers who contribute to it. With the ever-changing conflict landscape in eastern Congo, being in the know about which groups are operating in which area, which groups are working together with the population versus exploiting their civilian neighbors, and which groups are protecting versus carrying out war crimes is a socially valuable expertise. Being able to predict violence, and/or to make sense of it after the fact, is a skill that allows people to keep themselves and their families safe. For some, developing an expertise in conflict is also economically valuable. In the case of Kivu Security Tracker—and similar positions have been created elsewhere in the humanitarian and corporate worlds, "security officers" who conduct reconnaissance in an area ahead of travel into "red zones"—the field of conflict research, whether academic or operational, offers the possibility of formal employment in a country where little such work exists. Finally, as some of the researchers at this particular conference point out, "It helps us keep track of the crimes. We have to know what is happening in order to demand justice on the behalf of the victims."

Over the course of the conference, there are talks on methodology. Several researchers explain their use of feigned intimacy with one's informants: *faire semblant d'être proche*, pretending to be close. "Some of the military men actually think that I am on their side," one boasts. This elicits laughter, and another chimes in to remind the boastful one that the ruse goes both ways: the colonels are also pretending with us, he says, and this affects the truth of the information they give.

There is a discussion about how to distinguish truth amid a sea of rumors and fake news.[34] Someone suggests that an original time-stamped picture of a body should be enough to report a case. Another person chimes in to describe the way that WhatsApp now imports all photos that one receives in one's photo roll by default. The speaker continues, this means that multiple people could have a time-stamped picture of a body in their photo roll. "Which one is truly the original then?" he asks. One woman offers, perhaps there is something in the time stamp that would allow us to distinguish between the original image and a copied one? She adds, "Because, there is the body, and there is blood, maybe even dismemberment, and so you tally the case—but then you find out that it is actually an image from another massacre at another time. I remember someone in South Kivu showing me a photo of a row of hands, and then finding out later that it was from Ituri several years prior."

One of the leads of the group offers triangulation as one possible strategy for distinguishing the original from its double.[35] Ask many unrelated sources; see if they offer the same details, he suggests. The room becomes silent. Everyone seems to agree that triangulation is a good strategy—but there is a sense that the deception is too deep, and triangulation alone won't get to the bottom of things.[36]

Near the end of the conference, there is a discussion about safety. It emerges as a given that everyone in the room uses hats and disguises, different SIM cards to communicate with different people. And all of the researchers seem to have developed a handful of identities—researcher, activist, student, NGO worker—along with the skills to strategically deploy different identities in different situations. One says, "You have to read the situation and decide which role is the safest, and also which will get you closer to the truth." Later, when someone is talking about the ways in which the armed men disguise themselves—"sometimes they change uniforms upon going to the mines, and then wear different uniforms around town," he says—I think about how everyone in the sea of conflict is capitalizing on the same strategies of multiplicity and deceit. I wonder, where everyone is putting up smoke screens, engaging in public secrets, how different these conflict researchers are from the soldiers-bandits-children they study.[37]

Several times during the conference, someone says, "On est dans un vrai confusion." We are in true confusion. As I hear these words repeated, I think of how this sentiment seems to expand far beyond the walls of the hotel. Where violence has become so deeply embedded into habitus, all truths feel relative, all people at once potential allies and potential enemies.

At a hotel in Goma, a group of twenty researchers works to turn the confusion into discrete map dots of "violent incidents," thereby quantifying the violence, and maybe denying it its power. But, I wonder, is it even possible to count something that has a volume? How does one put numbers to the crushing weight of a wave or the breathlessness of the almost-drowned?

"War is still here"

Sometime after the artillery fell on Goma and soldiers entered homes in Kishabe, once the situation seemed to have reached a new equilibrium, I returned to eastern Congo. For a few weeks, I stayed in Goma and made day trips out to Kishabe. When it felt safe, I moved back to Kishabe and restarted work at the hospital. Slowly, I grew accustomed to the new landscape—the military barrier, the soldiers on the road, the soldiers near my house. Surely, my days looked different than they had before: I no longer circulated at night; I texted people in the know often to get security updates; I used an extra lock on the door. For weeks, Jean-Baptiste accompanied me the four hundred meters from the house to the hospital every morning. In the afternoons, when I returned home, he told me about his day spent watching the road. With time (and much coaching by Jean-Baptiste), I, too, learned how to read the road, and the people traveling on it, for early signs of danger. Some nights, I lay awake for hours listening to the soldiers' movements for clues about where they were going and when they might come back. Many mornings, I awoke to find that Jean-Baptiste and Solange had done the same.[38]

Initially, Jean-Baptiste, Solange, and I had distanced ourselves from the soldiers. Living, as we did, on the land of a well-known woman in Goma, we had the privilege of being able to ask the military to stay off our/her yard—and they had done so. At some point, though, the distance between our routines and those of the soldiers began to lessen. Every day before sunset, a couple of soldiers in leadership stopped by to update us on the progress of the peace talks between M23 and the Congolese government in Kampala. On the days when the phone reception in Kishabe was poorest, these same soldiers asked permission to make calls from within our gates, where the signal was better. Eventually, we shared produce from our garden and even meals with these men. Like others in Kishabe, we never trusted them fully—"the war is still here, and soldiers can't be trusted in war," cautioned Jean-Baptiste—but we lived harmoniously with the soldiers who had become our neighbors.

Four months after I had returned to Kishabe, Jean-Baptiste fell quite sick and needed to be hospitalized. I came home from work early to help Solange cook for him, and together, we brought heaping bowls of food to the hospital. With the last rays of daylight streaming through the windows, the three of us sat together on his bed, eating and exchanging the day's news. As night set in, Jean-Baptiste stood and encouraged us to leave. The town had been quiet in the preceding weeks; and yet Jean-Baptiste and Solange's children were at home alone, and no one was guarding the parcel. "Vita ingali." War is still here, Jean-Baptiste said. As we said our goodbyes, I joked with Jean-Baptiste that I would be by in the morning for our usual morning run. Since the war, Jean-Baptiste had been joining me on my prework runs into the hills. Of late, it seemed like he had begun looking forward to the run even more than I. Jean-Baptiste laughed weakly before adding, in a more serious tone, "Muindo [Jean-Baptiste's cousin] will join you tomorrow."

I initially brushed off the offer. "The roads are safe these days—and I'll stick to the main roads," I objected. "No need to trouble anyone else." But Jean-Baptiste was resolute. "You cannot go alone," he said. "The soldiers haven't been paid yet. They're hungry." Both thin and less than five feet six, neither Jean-Baptiste nor Muindo provided much physical protection. Still, Jean-Baptiste was insistent: *vita ingali*. It wasn't safe to go alone.

Muindo and I ran together the following morning. In the afternoon, with food stocks in the house running low and Jean-Baptiste still in the hospital, I drove the five miles to the nearby market after work. After picking up a few staples, I stopped in to visit a friend who had recently been discharged from the hospital. We caught up for a bit, and then, seeing the sun begin to dip behind the hills, I bade farewell and got back on the road to Kishabe. With my attention drawn to the horizon—indigo was just emerging—I almost missed the four men in uniform who were sitting in the shadows at Murangaa, a corner notorious for road banditry. As I watched their silhouettes in the rearview mirror, I was reminded of Jean-Baptiste's warning the night before: "The soldiers haven't been paid yet. They're hungry. War is still here," he had said. At dinner that evening, Jean-Baptiste announced, "A house near the hospital was pillaged last night. No one was hurt. No one was home. But this is the first house to be pillaged since November. We were living well with them. Now you see that things turn quickly here. Hewa haiku nzuri hizi siku. Vita ingali." It is bad weather these days. War is still here.

The soldiers were paid the next day. In the evening, they celebrated. Together with a few civilian friends, they laughed and danced late into the night. The anxiousness that had characterized the previous two days quickly dissipated, and the bean harvest began, as planned.

****

Three weeks later, Jean-Baptiste had fully recovered and was back at home. We ate dinner together at my house, as we usually did, and then Jean-Baptiste and Solange and the kids bade me goodnight and walked across the lawn to their house. Within a few minutes of leaving my house, Solange was back. There was something I needed to see on the lake, she said. I put on shoes, and the two of us walked down to join Jean-Baptiste, who was standing quietly at the lakeshore. The moon was full and rising; the lake lapped softly at the shore. "Look," Solange instructed as she pointed toward several small islands of land, tufts of grass and dirt that floated on the surface a hundred meters from shore. Surely, these islands weren't usually in the middle of the lake. "Was there a storm today while I was at work?" I asked. I couldn't remember hearing rain or wind, but I couldn't think of how else these tufts of land would have ended up in the center of the lake.

Solange shook her head. "It's not how they got here," she said. "It's what they mean." Solange paused. My face remained blank. "There is land where there should be water," she said with some urgency. Another pause. "This is the lake telling us that war is coming," she concluded in a whisper.

For a few days, Jean-Baptiste and I didn't go on our morning run. With the lake predicting war, neither of us felt safe striking out into the hills at daybreak. But, after some time, when things remained quiet despite the lake's warning, Jean-Baptiste asked again when we would next go. On our first morning back, we stuck to the main road, winding up and down around the lake at dawn. On the way home, as we rounded a blind curve, we came upon a trio of men standing silent and still in the road. We greeted them and then followed their gaze across the lake. The sun was rising over the water, but it wasn't the sight that had caught their attention, but sound. In the distance, the booms of detonating artillery shells reverberated off the water. As the islands had predicted, war had begun again.

For three days, the Congolese army had a standoff with M23 on the outskirts of Goma. As they had many times before, the soldiers in Kishabe left for the front lines. In Brussels, negotiations began between the UN, the United States, Congo, and Rwanda. In Kishabe, people went home early from work and prepared to run again. To everyone's surprise, the fighting stopped as suddenly as it had started. The soldiers returned, but things did not feel settled. One morning, Solange knocked on the door as I was getting dressed for work. With a worried look on her face, she reported, "They've killed somebody at Murangaa."

The night prior, around 8 p.m., a group of armed men had gathered at Murangaa and began extorting money from those who passed. At first, they had stopped a few groups of people walking home from the fields. Small bills were given up, and the people were allowed to continue. Then they had stopped a moto-taxi driver coming from Sake. While they were exacting money from him, a second moto-taxi had attempted to drive past without stopping. "It was the end of the day," Solange said, "and he probably had a lot of money that he didn't want to give them." The men at Murangaa shot the fleeing motorcyclist in the back. "He was from around here," Solange said with regret in her voice. "Just two kilometers away. He was only thirty, and he had two wives and six children."

Solange and I stood in silence for a few minutes together. Then I asked whether anyone knew who did it. "Was it the soldiers or just bandits?" I pressed. No armed men were officially stationed at Murangaa. Thus, either the soldiers from Kishabe had gone to Murangaa to steal; or men with guns had come down from the hills in search of profit. Given that we were still living intimately with the soldiers in Kishabe, it felt important to know if they had been involved.

"Hatuwezi kujua," Solange replied. We can't know. "They put masks on when they steal. And it was dark." From the tone of her voice, I could tell that Solange worried that the soldiers were to blame. I could also tell that she did not expect to ever really know who had pulled the trigger.

That evening, with the events of the night before on my mind, I went to a friend's for a beer. We were sitting outside, watching the traffic on the road, when a group of twenty or so moto-taxis pulled up. Several of their radios were turned up; everyone was honking and yelling; a couple drivers carried cases of beer. From their demeanor, I knew that they were en route to the funeral of the driver who was killed the night before. From my perch a bit removed from the group, I watched in silence as they greeted those around me. "Come, Rachel," one called jovially up to me. "We're going to eat and dance until the morning." I declined. The deceased motorcyclist's house was quite close to Murangaa, and it was too close to sunset to travel in that direction.

The following morning, on our run, we passed the deceased man's home. Congolese hip-hop played loudly inside. Outside, three men stood moving their bodies to the rhythm. Tables and chairs were strewn across the yard, and these men were somewhat scattered, as if they had been dancing in the same place all night. Eyes closed, hands to the sky in prayer, they slowly rotated their hips. Dawn was just starting to break, and their silhouettes began to emerge from the shadows. One wore army fatigues, the other two jeans. A gun stood in the doorway. A soldier had come to mourn the loss of the young moto-taxi driver, and the family of the deceased man welcomed him, mourned serenely beside him. In the sea of insecurity, soldiers had become neighbors, even family. They could protect or they could kill. And yet, where people live in war and the running never ends, the only thing that is certain is that *huwezi kujua*. One could never know.

****

In November 2012, Kishabe was plundered by retreating Congolese troops. Two weeks later, the same soldiers returned to the town under orders to protect it. For seven months, the town's residents lived in intimate proximity with the soldiers. The presence of the soldiers added to the everyday forces of hunger, illness, and poverty that already hung heavily over the town and created a loud and gnawing sense of anxiousness and insecurity. Everything, from whether people would eat that day to whether they would flee into the hills the next, felt uncertain. People slept in the hospital, put new locks on doors, prepared again and again to flee. Watching the road together became a town pastime, and every conversation included some reference to safety.

While anxiousness and fear were prominent during this time period, so too was opportunity. New economic partnerships were created; new alliances were made. This, I believe, is what Sharpe meant when she spoke of weather as "death, disaster, *and* possibility."[39] The weight of the present is crushing for those living in the global regime of antiblackness—and this crushing weight is precisely what opens up the potential for new intimacies, new economic networks, and new pleasures. And so, back to Sharpe: "To be in the wake [of antiblackness] is also to recognize the ways that we are constituted through and by continued vulnerability to overwhelming force though not *only* known to ourselves and to each other *by* that force."[40] The men who danced outside their deceased friend's house at dawn danced not in spite of their abjection, their anguish, but amid it, because of it. Their serenity was neither reducible to, nor extricable from, the tragedy that surrounded them.

****

When I returned to Goma and Kishabe in 2020, few people spoke about the war of M23 or the military occupations that followed. The army had largely moved out of the area, the burned-out tanks had long been removed, and direct Rwandan intervention in the region seemed to be a thing of the distant past. And yet the lake and the volcano continued to threaten the region; banditry continued in Goma and Murangaa; and, outside of Goma, intermittent fighting continued.

Whether posed by soldiers, bandits, the lake, or the volcano, insecurity continues to threaten daily life in Congo. This is traumatic, devastating, life limiting. It is also generative.[41] Across eastern Congo, people continue to run from insecurity; however, they also return—to the lakeshore, the soldiers that have become neighbors. Often, the goal of their return is not to stay—to remain next to a lake that threatens destruction, to linger in exploitative relationships and militarized economies—but rather to make new relationships that allow them to move beyond the current vulnerability, to the potentiality that lies in the paths that lead outward from it. Through shared affect, Congolese continually remake relationships with insecurity— soldiers who could be bandits or neighbors, a lake that could offer life or rapidly seize it. As Harney and Moten write, the power of affect lies in its ability to fill the space between:

> This form of feeling was not collective, not given to decision, not adhering or reattaching to settlement, nation, state, territory or historical story; nor was it repossessed by the group, which could not now feel as one, reunified in time and space. No, when Black Shadow sings "are you feelin' the feelin'?" he is asking about something else. He is asking about a way of feeling through others, a feel for feeling others feeling you. This is modernity's insurgent feel, its inherited caress, its skin talk, tongue touch, breath speech, hand laugh. This is the feel that no individual can stand, and no state abide. . . . The capacity to feel through others, for others to feel through you, for you to feel them feeling you, this feel of the shipped is not regulated, at least not successfully, by a state, a religion, a people, an empire, a piece of land, a totem.[42]

Instead of trying to resolve the tension between victim and perpetrator, soldier and bandit, life and death, Congolese allow affect to be the healing force that re-pairs that which has been blown apart over centuries of violence. At times, when violence is proximate, affective solidarity can be loud, chaotic. For a while, distance might be sought; people might eat alone. But, if Kishabe's story is an exemplar, the pause doesn't last long—it can't, for survival in war rests on interdependence. And so, Congolese return to forging intimacy with armed groups, thereby healing old wounds and stitching past worlds back together. In the sea of insecurity that governs Congo, these sutures bridge the ruptures that separate people in war and create new paths through which all people, regardless of their political affiliations, might work together to build different presents.

FIGURE 2.2. Soldier's hut, 2013. The walls are reeds and grasses; the roof is a UNHCR tarp. The rectangular jug inside the entrance contains water carried by hand from the nearby lake. "We are so poor, we live like swine," soldiers say. In the background, a civilian's home for comparison. Photograph by author.

Many of my field notes begin with me running. How many times Jean-Baptiste and I ascended and then descended the hills that rose above the lake.

I never really asked Jean-Baptiste to run with me—he just came along that first time, and every time thereafter. Within a few months, we had found a rhythm together, and I had begun to find the synchronized rise and fall of our feet and our breath meditative. I now looked forward to this daily hour with Jean-Baptiste, to silently traversing the farms that fed us together, to wordlessly sharing the experience of the smell of eucalyptus and dew with another human being.

For a while, it was just us in the hills. We would start in the dark, with our vision limited to two or three meters ahead of us, and arrive at the summits before the sun came up. Occasionally, when we were returning home, we would see a farmer. We would greet them warmly—for we were all neighbors, and it was calm. But, more often than not, we finished the run without our vocal cords ever having made a sound.

And then a new armed group moved into the region, and strange soldiers covered the hills. We didn't run for several weeks—the new faces and uniforms provoked fear. Even the word *kukimbia*, to run, made us think of the day when the bombs came, the day we had run separately. And then, one day enough time had passed from the tanks and the gunshots, and I called Jean-Baptiste's name in the dark, and his gangly figure emerged already dressed in running clothes, and our bodies were again side by side, our feet again pounding the dirt road beneath us, the rise and fall of our paired breath bearing witness to survival, to life.

***

"Let's go . . . this way," Jean-Baptiste says between breaths. Because he grew up close to Kishabe, he usually leads us up one of two routes into the hills above the town. Today, he proposes a third alternative.

I turn to follow him, and we take a few strides in silence. I see that we are on a small footpath and that we are heading high above the lake. "What's up here . . . at the top?" I ask.

Jean-Baptiste smiles and says a name that I recognize as a village. I had heard this name mentioned in the hospital and was curious about where it was located. As we make our way slowly uphill, talking becomes an effort. I think about the vista we will have at the top, the whole valley at sunrise, and silently enjoy this small delight.

We climb and wind, climb and wind. As we make what seems to be the last turn before we reach the top, a row of huts built just off the path comes into view. With war coming closer, I have spent the past few months learning to read fear in people's stride and in their breath. I now know that the banana-leaf shelters ahead are a reason to slow, and I can sense Jean-Baptiste's fear. I look to the man next to me and realize that I'm already a step ahead of him—he has made sense of the shelters' silhouettes before me, and his eyes are now searching for clues that might tell him how long the soldiers have been here: How weathered are the leaves that constitute the hut? Are they fresh? Or perhaps they are long dry, and the holes that they leave have been reinforced with a tarp? This would mean that they have been here at least some months. New soldiers can never be trusted, but those who have made homes here are likely trustworthy, even neighborly.

Jean-Baptiste's analysis of the huts is silent. Even when I have asked him before to explain how he knows whether the soldiers are good, whether the road is good, whether war is close, he struggles to put words to his process. "Ninajua tu," he usually says with a laugh. I just know. Now, he exhales, and, in the lightness of his breath, I sense that it is safe to continue past the huts. Our pace quickens, and we are once again running step for step. But our stride has become deliberate and will stay this way until we return home.

The vista must have been beautiful—eastern Congo is stunning, and especially the hills at sunrise—but it's not what I remember about this run. Instead, Jean-Baptiste's measured breaths of fear, the way his eyes searched for answers in the construction of the hut are etched into my memory. He is always relaxed, easygoing; but how rapidly his body had tensed at the sight of the huts. Every nerve was alive, every muscle at the ready, for his body knew something that mine never would: the other meaning of *to run* in Congo, running from war.

***

For a decade now, I have been wrestling with what to do with myself in this story. For years, I could only write about experiences like these, which, taken together taught me how to read the road during war, to know when it was safe to stay in an area, and when to leave. My own fear seemed to elicit a certain verbosity and foreclose the possibility of writing about Congolese lives. Surely, in any ethnographic research, part of the task of writing is deciding how much of the story is told in the first person. When the researcher is white and the subjects are people of color, as is the case here, this task is both more charged and more critical. There was a time when I tried desperately to write myself out of this book so as to give primacy to Congolese voices; but my experiences of fear kept returning to me, in dreams, but also in interviews and policy meetings in which I presented my research. Even when I wasn't talking about war directly, the understanding that I had of fear—my fear and that of my interlocuters—seemed to frame everything. In Kishabe, I had learned to read roads and hills and crops and population movement for signs of past and future violence. I had also learned to hear clamor in silence—all that wasn't said, for fear or, in other circumstances, out of hope that it might come true. And so, whether I was studying war or health-seeking practices during the Ebola epidemic, my understanding of fear in Congo shaped my understanding of what counted as data, and thus also, what data I counted.

With extended time away from Congo—so long away that the anxiousness that I used to have around a full tank of gas, for you never knew when you would have to leave town and just keep driving, has long dissipated—I have learned something else about fear, which is actually about commensurability, "remaining in the face of one another's unshared vulnerability" in Angela Garcia's words.[1] From the beginning, my fear was never mine alone. Rather, fear was something I experienced with people—feeling my interlocuters' bodies tense before mine in the early days, and then, later, once I had learned to read the roads and recognize signs of impending danger, feeling my breathing stop at the same moment as Jean-Baptiste's, as Solange's, as Anne-Marie's. Surely, my experience of fear was always mediated by my privilege, my ability to leave the country at any time; and yet, because my interlocuters and I often shared a common vulnerability, the soldier at dawn, fear became a commensurable experience. Once I understood fear to be commensurable, it became communicable in a multitude of ways— verbally, nonverbally; directly and indirectly; with laughter, and in silence. Communication about fear then opened up other topics of conversation. Eventually, I began to see that, in addition to war, another topic often occupied my interlocuters' minds: possibility. *Labda*, people said frequently. Perhaps. Perhaps the soldiers would get paid today; perhaps the artillery was far way, in the park. Gradually, as I had with fear, I came to hear *perhaps* in silences, too—in the way that people held my eye contact too long, or looked away nervously before completing their thought. As I had with fear, I sometimes asked questions of people's understandings of possibility, discussed their visions of what could be. And sometimes, I allowed the possibility to remain just below the surface, a feeling that was mutually recognized but never voiced—for it was in these moments of remaining in the face of unshared vulnerability that I began to wonder if a belief in a Congolese otherwise could itself be a commensurable experience.

The Body, the Flesh, and the Hospital

How to care for the injured body,
the kind of body that can't hold
the content it is living?
And where is the safest place when that place
must be someplace other than in the body?
—Claudia Rankine, *Citizen*

In the absence of kin, family, gender, belonging, language, personhood, property, and official records, among other factors, what remains is the flesh, the living, speaking, thinking, feeling, and imagining flesh: the ether that holds together the world of Man while at the same time forming the conditions of possibility for this world's demise.
—Alexander Weheliye, *Habeas Viscus*

"Mwili, njoo yote," Solange said. The body, it is everything. I had just gotten home from work and taken a look at a red and inflamed lymph node that had appeared several days earlier under the chin of Solange's youngest child.

FIGURE 3.1. The Kishabe Hospital, 2013. To the left in the photo is the pharmacy cabinet of the maternity ward; to the right is the unit's hand-washing station. The medication was often purchased through partnerships with various international humanitarian organizations. Because the water was carried in by hand, it was a precious commodity. Photograph by author.

I had very minimal clinical training at the time, having only finished half of medical school; but Solange was intent on managing the abscess with compresses, and so I checked it every day to make sure it wasn't getting worse. Overall, Jo Jo was doing well, and as Solange and I sat watching him play with the other children, Solange expressed relief at having avoided the $5 consultation fee at the hospital. "Bandits might take your clothes and your crops. But, God willing, you can buy more clothes and you can find food. The body, though. The body is everything." *Mwili, njoo yote.*

This chapter investigates the role of the body in healing in eastern Congo. As Solange states, where material possessions and food security are so fleeting, the body represents that which one always has if (and when) everything else disappears. It is also the last, most intimate frontier of vulnerability. Where so few have access to safe food, water, or preventative care, sickness and injury are common, even expected; this even though healthy bodies capable of manual labor are necessary for survival. In eastern Congo, where healthy life expectancy has been estimated to be forty-four years, the body serves as undeniable proof of the poor standard of living that people share.[1] Both reflecting shared experience and demanding witness, the body opens up conversations about the possibility of a present otherwise, in which people and things can be counted on, in which life is less fragile.[2]

One note on terminology: in this chapter, I use "the body" to refer to the individual physical body; however, as the field of medical anthropology established long ago, many other bodies exist—the social body, the body politic, the body and the flesh.[3] Whereas, in Western epistemologies, these bodies—and the healing practices they require—are sometimes separable, in the Congolese context, the physical body has little meaning outside of its social context.[4] Thus, in a collection devoted to establishing the social basis of health and healing on the continent, historian/anthropologists Steven Feierman and John Janzen write, "Healing ideas and practices are not a separate domain. They are an integral part of politics, kinship relations, religion, trade, farming and sexual life."[5] Certainly, the specific ways in which some bodies fall ill in eastern Congo, and the forms of repair and healing that their affliction makes possible, tells more about the social condition of living in war than it does about the success (or lack thereof) of biomedicine.[6] As a physician, I have often found it difficult to observe physical pain, loss, and death in Congo and know that, elsewhere, other outcomes are possible. And, through my ethnographic work, I have learned that the act of inhabiting affliction is what allows the physical body to function as a register for repair, a site through which greater social healing might be demanded and presents otherwise imagined. In this chapter, I seek to portray both the devastation and the possibility that accompany illness and the demands for bodily healing.

The Hospital: A Site of Healing or of Harm?

The first Belgian excursions in Congo were oriented toward morality—stopping the Arab slave trade—territorial control, and profit. With the field of public health still nascent in the metropole, the imperialists devoted little attention to improving the health of the Congolese.[7] Instead, hands were severed in forced labor campaigns, and the porters who died of hunger, exhaustion, and infectious disease were simply replaced.[8]

By the early 1900s, photographs of imperial wounding had begun circulating in Europe. As news of the atrocities committed in Congo spread, another iteration of Western intervention was proposed: perhaps the natives could be civilized; perhaps they could be saved from their Godless ways.[9] In 1908, King Leopold's personal grip on the country loosened as the Belgian parliament assumed control of the country. Shortly thereafter, in the words of historian Nancy Rose Hunt, "medicalization became a form of colony building."[10]

By 1910, mining companies had begun rewarding employees who had more children with food support, bonuses, and tax breaks. These pronatalist measures accompanied vaccination efforts and institutionalization of the traveling mission doctor and marked the beginning of hygienic rule. Over the next decades, the footprint of the colonial state grew, and Belgian authorities built an extensive network of health centers and maternities. As they sought to transform health from a traditional practice to a modern one, they used coercive and forceful practices to wrest authority from Congolese healers and move healing into the newly constructed centers.[11] Throughout this process, birth work came to occupy a unique place in the Belgian colonial state. Given the population decline that followed the brutal imperial period, state health officials, religious authorities, and company leaders advanced a pronatalist agenda. In an effort to shorten birth intervals and achieve a higher birth rate, traditional forms of birth spacing were outlawed and monogamy, breastfeeding schedules, and early weaning were institutionalized. By 1958, the Belgian Congo boasted the most extensive medical infrastructure in post–World War II Africa. By medicalizing birth, the Belgians successfully reversed population decline, thereby producing a large and robust labor force. They also expanded the reach of the church and the state, with maternities serving as an important opportunity for evangelization and for bureaucratic inscription.[12]

And so, the Belgian colonial state, together with its Congolese middle figures, built world-class maternities and laboratories; but the intent had never been to create an autonomous health system. When Congo obtained independence in 1960, not a single Congolese physician had been trained.[13] In the political upheaval that followed independence, many Belgian nationals—including much of the health care force—left the country. For nearly a decade, health care in Congo was piecemeal, provided by a combination of Belgian missionaries, Congolese nurses, and other international humanitarians.[14] In the early 1970s, the nation's health finally drew the attention of then-president Mobutu. Taking seriously the idea that nationalized primary care would strengthen the people, and thus the country, Mobutu worked to develop a nationalized, decentralized health care system.[15] For a short time, the national government expanded to provide clean water, sanitation, treatment of most common ailments, maternal and infant health, family planning, and essential medicines to all Congolese free of charge; however, the state collapse that began in the early 1980s spared nothing. As he attempted to cut expenditures from the state's quickly emptying coffers, Mobutu first minimized public investment in the national health care system.[16] Several years later, he tightened the budget further, introducing user fees to help keep the doors open. But his hold on power was quickly unraveling, and local health care administrators soon began seizing these user fees for their own enrichment.[17] Within a decade, the robust nationalized health care system had been transformed into the weak and often predatory market-based system that exists today.[18]

The Kishabe Hospital, eastern Congo's first hospital, was built in 1963. For the first twenty years of its operation, it was overseen by Belgian physicians and supported by a combination of Belgian donations and state money.[19] With funding from a Belgian nonprofit, a nursing school was later established nearby, and the hospital became a regional training site for both nurses and physicians. During this time, people traveled hundreds of miles to Kishabe to receive what was widely considered to be the best health care in eastern Congo. In addition to providing health care, the hospital also offered formal employment, the first of its kind, to residents of Kishabe. Men and women who had grown up picking coffee on Belgian plantations were educated and employed as nurses in the hospital; others took up custodial duties; and still others operated small stores in the market that arose to support the hospital's needs. Over time, the hospital became the focal point in the small farming town.

In 1976, a Belgian cooperative named CENAB began supporting the operation of the hospital as part of a project aimed at rehabilitating health care in the eastern Congo.[20] Still, by the early 1980s, the nine-building complex had begun to show evidence of "the Zairean sickness," *le mal Zaïrois*, that plagued the rest of the country.[21] When state collapse became more imminent in the 1990s, the state's role in health care became limited to "a legal framework for non-state actors," and international NGOs entered en masse.[22] At various points in the 1990s and again in 2007 and 2008, during periods of brutal fighting in and around Kishabe, Médecins sans Frontières (MSF) labeled Kishabe an emergency zone and took over full operational support of the hospital. Before and since then, operations at the hospital have been supported by a bricolage of different national and international entities: Ministry of Health, CENAB, UNICEF, Save the Children, World Food Program, and HEAL Africa. Despite receiving a relatively high level of support, the Kishabe hospital often lacked the personnel and supplies it needed to help those who passed through its doors. As a result, the hospital harmed as much as it healed.

The ô in *Hôpital* has fallen off the sign out front of the building; the paint is peeling, the cement cracking. Many windows are broken, and the roof leaks in places. Water is all over the floor, but never from the spigots. Some of the bed frames date to the hospital's construction; others, broken, litter the courtyard. The lab has a light switch but no light bulb. In order to take an X-ray, families first have to buy gasoline to start the generator. Episiotomies are done with a kerosene lamp. Babies are born on the hospital's single metal obstetric table, on which sits a thin, torn piece of foam covered by a piece of vinyl. In the dry season, when the air is thick, the smell of pus clings to this vinyl, even after a dousing with bleach. In spite of the infusion of hundreds of thousands of dollars of humanitarian and development aid, the hospital appears weary with decline.

****

In the Kishabe hospital, as in any biomedical space, cleanliness was everywhere attempted: surgical (fabric) towels and drapes were carefully washed by hand, dried in the sun, and then autoclaved; disinfectant was liberally applied to the floors in the operating room and the wards; patients were meticulously washed and shaven before surgeries; surgeons scrubbed their hands until the skin cracked and then doused them with alcohol. Despite all this effort, however, dirt entered the hospital. Patients walked in barefoot, with mud caked on their feet. Fine granules of sand clung to the clothes of visitors who had traveled many miles to see sick family members. The afternoon breeze brought the black earth from the vertical farmland surrounding the hospital through the open windows. And in a context in which supplies, water, electricity, and time were always in short supply, dirt worked its way into bodies.

Upon entering the maternity ward, I heard the restrained cries of a woman on the obstetric table. Instead of the deep, sustained sounds of childbirth, the cries that emanated through the tarp that separated the nursing station from the obstetric table were staccato and irregular. Lydie, a nurse-midwife, stood on a stepstool, neck craned over Pascaline, a woman who had recently delivered via cesarean, examining Pascaline's belly at close range. What should have been a neat line of stitches appeared red, swollen, and disfigured. Infection had set in. Lydie stood back up and began squeezing both sides of the incision toward each other, as if trying to pop an abdomen-sized pimple. The depth of the infection required significant force, and Lydie's jaw was set for the effort. Pascaline writhed in pain and then let out a visceral howl. Lydie sternly chastised her for moving; Pascaline inhaled sharply and lay still. As Lydie pressed even more of her body weight into the wound, Pascaline held her breath. Finally, a yellow line of pus erupted from the site. Lydie relaxed momentarily. To Pascaline, she said, "See, I told you it was dirty [*mchafu*]. I have to keep going now; we have to get all of this out of there. It will never heal if it stays dirty."

For several agonizing minutes, Lydie moved along the full length of the eight-inch incision, pressing deeply around the sutures to break up any pockets of infection. Pascaline breathed rapidly and unsteadily. Several times, she moaned, then hummed in pain. With her arm covering her face, she turned her head left, right, then left again as if refusing both the procedure and the pain. Several lines of blood-tinged pus ran down her belly and met the table beneath her. When the wound stopped producing discharge, Lydie relaxed the pressure. With great relief, Pascaline exhaled.

A combination of the infection and the squeezing had torn the skin around several of the sutures. Where once a line of black stitches had held two pieces of flesh together, there was now a half dollar-sized hole. Lydie used disinfectant-soaked gauze to clean the hole before beginning to pack it. As she pushed piece after piece of gauze into the dark hole, Pascaline let out a quiet cry. At some point, the wound stopped accepting gauze, and Lydie applied a clean bandage over the incision. Then, she gestured for Pascaline to get up. Pascaline slowly curled to a stand. She took a breath, then, grimacing in pain, started to get dressed. As Pascaline walked out the door, Lydie said sternly, "Come back tomorrow, and every day for a while." With the wound infected and now open, it would have to be cleaned and packed on a daily basis until the pus gave way to new, pink flesh.

For the next thirty-seven days, Pascaline joined the long line of women who returned daily for the cleaning of their infected incisions. Sometimes she was turned away for lack of time or clean bandages. However, on most days, she endured a painful, prolonged dressing change—the pieces of gauze had to be fished out piece by piece—before returning to the common room, where she waited for the infection to pass so she and her baby could return home. As the days became weeks and the weeks, a month, Pascaline's figure returned and her baby grew a head of hair. Still, her incision remained open and oozing. Finally, to expedite her recovery, a physician decided to sew the open area of her incision back up.

The secondary sutures were placed on the obstetric table in the maternity ward. Dr. Alex began the procedure by injecting the area to be sewn with local anesthetic. Pascaline flinched but remained silent. Dr. Alex waited a few moments for the anesthetic to take effect, then began sewing. As he placed the first stitch, Pascaline wailed and grabbed for his gloved hands. Wary that Pascaline might introduce further infection into the wound, Dr. Alex called for nurses to restrain Pascaline. "I put lidocaine in," he said, confidently. "It will work soon." Then, with three people holding Pascaline down, he continued to sew up the hole in Pascaline's abdomen. At first, Pascaline struggled; then she wailed; then she fought again. One nurse barked orders at her: "Stop moving! Be patient!" Another offered more gently, "Close your heart. Stop crying and be strong." Dr. Alex sewed resolutely, stopping only to slap Pascaline's leg and repeat the nurses' orders. For several minutes, the torture scene continued: Pascaline, restrained by three nurses, wept; Dr. Alex berated her for being emotional and continued to stitch. Finally, he tied the last knot. As he put his instruments away, Pascaline continued to cry. Dr. Alex shook his head and looked at Pascaline in disgust. On his way out of the room, he chided the nurses: "I'm not coming back in here again, if this is how your patients behave." When the door closed behind him, the nurses turned to scold Pascaline. "We should make you pay a fine," they said. "A woman is she who silently toils for her family's benefit [*mwanamke ni kufunga kamba kichwani*]. You must learn to close your heart. Suffering is a valuable lesson [*mateso njoo masomo*]." Pascaline got dressed and, with tears still streaming down her face, walked out of the room.

In the Kishabe maternity ward, pain was considered an expected part of any intervention. As a result, nurses never asked about it, and patients seldom mentioned it. Instead, whether it was labor pain or the pain of wound care, it was most often endured quietly and individually. On rare occasions, women who had just returned from the operating room were given Tylenol to take the edge off; stronger pain medications were reserved for exceptional cases—traumatic injury, orthopedic manipulation. Sometimes, as Pascaline's story demonstrates, no pain medication was offered at all. But this is not to say that pain wasn't acknowledged. In fact, quite the opposite. After wound care or during the later stages of labor, nurses steadied patients as they got down from the table, helped them get dressed, and walked them back to their beds. When the pain was too great for a woman to move or to speak, nurses waited silently, patiently until it passed. When younger women cried out in pain, as Pascaline had, the nurses first encouraged them: "Be patient, stay strong, close your heart [*funga roho*]," they said. If women continued to cry out, nurses (and doctors) sometimes slapped their legs or their arms. Though occasionally done out of anger, this was most often done in an effort to discipline, to teach. As one nurse said to Pascaline, "Suffering is a valuable lesson." In response to my questions about hitting during labor, another nurse said, "If a woman learns to bear suffering quietly now, when war comes and she is in labor, she will be able to birth a child on the side of the road and get up and run again. We are teaching them how to survive."[23]

Since the colonial era, the hospital in Congo has intervened on more than the physical body. Of colonial medicine in northeast Congo, Nancy Rose Hunt writes, "Lowering maternal mortality was never the express purpose of colonial midwifery at Yakusu. Evangelization, 'getting the girls,' and producing a 'trained staff of female nurses' were the missionaries' goals."[24] Where many (still) lacked a formal education, the hospital in present-day Kishabe also performed an educational role. When women presented without birth supplies—a plastic sheet on which to birth, a bucket that would serve as a chamber pot, a piece of fabric to swaddle the newborn—nurses instructed them on "proper" birth supplies and "proper" birth etiquette. When women left the hospital after delivery, the nurses reminded them about "proper" ways to wash (away from the family so no one would be bothered by the smell) and "proper" ways to avoid falling pregnant too soon (abstinence). Much of this talk felt disciplinary, occurring as it did down a power gradient, characterized by a sense of right and wrong, and sometimes accompanied by a slap or a harsh word. Because childbirth made women the most frequent users of health care in Congo, it was always highly gendered. And, if one looked to nurses' physical efforts—Lydie's determined squeezing of Pascaline's wound, the pushing and pulling midwives engaged in to deliver a stuck baby—a profound sense of duty, a deep dedication to one's brethren came into view.

Over the thirty-seven days that Pascaline underwent wound care, the whole team of nurses took part in the very fleshy work of pressing down, digging in, and bandaging the festering wound.[25] As they cared for Pascaline's wound, these nurses also taught her about pain. For, both nurses and patients claimed, if a woman could learn to bear physical pain in the hospital, she would more gracefully be able to carry the other (physical and emotional) burdens of life. Where daily life often involved hunger, heavy work, and violence, fostering fortitude—training women to endure severe pain silently—equipped them for life in war. And so, as they chided and pushed and slapped, thus blurring the line between harming and healing, the nurses in Kishabe did what they could to deliver mothers and babies to safety while also ensuring that their patients had the tools they needed to survive in the longer term.[26]

"Ninakufa": Dying and Transformation

Since its construction, the hospital has been composed of four wards: internal medicine, surgery, pediatrics (which also housed the malnutrition ward), and maternity. Because the maternity service was the busiest in the Kishabe hospital, I spent the majority of my time there. Although its census often reached seventy-five—a handful of gynecological cases, thirty or so recently delivered women, and about the same number of women with high-risk pregnancies who had come down from rural areas in their final weeks to give birth—only two nurse-midwives were on staff at any one time.[27] As a result, the ward was often bustling. Patients waited to be admitted, discharged, examined, and served their medicine; beds filled up too quickly and emptied too slowly; blank charts piled up. On especially surcharged days, the nurse-midwives half-joked that their assignment to the maternity service was punishment.

In addition to being busy, the service was unpredictable. The only sure thing about days in maternity was sign-off from the night crew at 7:30 a.m. After that, the day's activities depended on whoever walked in the door. Some days were occupied with routine tasks such as medical rounds,

dressing changes, paperwork, and prenatal visits for the high-risk pregnancies; other days included deliveries, miscarriages, hysterectomies, and
obstetric emergencies. Since Kishabe's was a referral hospital, most of its
patients had passed through one of the smaller health centers in the hills
first. Often, they had complications with deliveries and needed a higher level
of care; however, with no state-run transport system, many had to walk or
arrange other transportation between the health center and the hospital. By
the time they arrived in Kishabe, many were gravely ill, and about half required emergency surgery.

The common room in the maternity ward was one of the most active places
in the hospital: patients' family members, who did most of the care work and
nursing, laughed together as they doted on their charges; mothers murmured to their newborns as they nursed; and babies became ruddy-faced
in their protests against being bathed, changed, or dressed.[28] At the far end
of the long, rectangular block, women with long faces and feverish babies
knocked impatiently on the delivery room door. From behind the door, a
nurse-midwife barked that she couldn't see the sick babies yet—and so the
line of women holding their newborns grew. Across the aisle, women who
walked with the hunch of a new incision did their own knocking. As the din
grew louder, a nursing student came out to disperse the waiting women. "The
bandages haven't been sterilized yet," he shouted. "No bandage changes until
after noon." But for every woman who went back to her bed, another one
stood up.

In the next room, a delivery was always in progress. A slap, a stern voice,
and then the sounds of a delivery penetrated the tarp that surrounded the
obstetric table. From within the womb to a world of tarps, plastic sheets,
and metal instruments. But she wouldn't stay there for long—now that the
baby had proven herself strong, she would be wrapped in onion layers of
soft blankets and danced around the room in joyful celebration. At least this
one, at least on this day.

On Monday of my second week in the Kishabe hospital, I walked into
the maternity ward as shift change was starting. The off-going midwife began:
there had been a "a catastrophic case." Her first baby had been a term stillbirth.
(Where few women have access to prenatal care, this was a too-frequent oc-
currence.) Then, during the seventh month of this second pregnancy, she
started hemorrhaging suddenly. Her family brought her to Kishabe, and the
doctor tried to stop the bleeding. The fetus lost a heartbeat, and the woman
continued to bleed. Where there was little capacity for blood transfusion,

the on-call doctor performed a hysterectomy to stop the bleeding and save the mother's life. She is alive for now, the off-going midwife reported. "But watch her closely."

After several clucks from the incoming team, one of the incoming midwives recounted the story of another tragic case from the weekend. A woman had given birth at the health center in a town five miles away. After delivery, she began hemorrhaging. They gave oxytocin and did uterine massage, per the protocol for postpartum hemorrhage. When she kept bleeding despite these interventions, they began the process of transferring her to a higher level of care. According to the nurse telling the story, the nurses at the transferring health center had taken several hours to prepare her paperwork. On their end, the family had taken a few hours to come up with the money necessary to pay the first health center and rent the bus that they would use for the transfer. More than twelve hours after giving birth, the woman finally arrived at the emergency room in Kishabe. The Kishabe staff had worked quickly to mobilize an operating team and an operating room. But the woman's blood pressure was already too low, and the single IV she had in her arm too small. She had died shortly after rolling into the operating suite.

For a minute, the room was quiet as all present digested the two stories. Eventually, the nurse-midwives continued sign-out: there were three women laboring, dressing changes to do, and two other women on the ward who had undergone cesarean sections overnight and still had low blood pressure. As the incoming team began preparing for the day, the off-going team finished their charting and left. The bustle began, and still a sense of the fragility hung in the room.

After report, I rounded with the team and attended several (live) births. Every time I walked out of the nurses station into the common maternity room, I was cognizant of the fact that the woman from overnight, who had lost her baby and her uterus at once, was the only woman in the room without a child. At some point, after her blood pressure had come up and she was able to sit, I went over to extend my sympathies. "I'm so sorry," I said. She looked at me with tear-brimmed eyes and took a moment to compose herself. Then she bit her lip and murmured, "I am healed [*nimepona*]." It was the response I expected—the one that traditionally followed sympathies in eastern Congo—but what could healing possibly mean in this context after such a tragedy?

One week after the first that I recorded, there was another neonatal death in Kishabe. Four days later, I recorded another. In the same week, I watched three neonatal resuscitations.

****

The next two neonatal deaths took a month to tally.

There was a baby who got ampicillin. The mom had said, "My baby is warm and she is not eating." The neonate was two days old. "Bring me a spoon and some water," the midwives said to the mom. And then they picked out a tablet of ampicillin from the bottle, cut it into fourths, and crushed it on the dirty table. They used a paper to lift the powder from the table to the spoon and then put some water on the spoon and held the mixture to the lips of the lethargic, febrile child. The next day, the baby was a bundle on the floor, waiting for her parents to pay her hospital bill so that she could go to her own funeral.

At some point, I began counting bundles on the floor. Many days there are none. One day there were three.[29]

It was shift change. The loud humming of the oxygen condenser threatened to drown out the handoff between the night nurse and the women coming on duty. There had been a cesarean, a baby boy who had come out screaming. But he had deteriorated in the past few hours and now needed oxygen.

Justine's report had been brief, to the point, and she was out the door before we said goodbye. I got up to visit a woman who had lost her child the day before. As I walked toward the maternity ward, I passed by the crib in which the struggling newborn was lying. The baby's brightly colored swaddle had fallen over his face, and I brushed it away, eager to see a new little ruddy face. Instead, as my hand pushed back the *kikwembe*, I saw blue lips. The oxygen condenser had shut off at some point without anyone noticing. "Anne-Marie, Anne-Marie!" I screamed. "ANNE-MARIE!"

As I clawed frantically through the layers of blankets, Anne-Marie came running from the other side of the room. Somehow her hands reached past mine. She grabbed the baby by the ankles and pulled him out of the crib and upside down in one motion. As she slapped his back, I rummaged on a shelf below for an oxygen mask. And then the baby was back in the crib and Anne-Marie had started CPR. While her hands worked, her eyes searched the shelves for a vial. When she found what she was looking for, she stepped away, grabbed a syringe, and drew from a half-full vial. While Anne-Marie was away, I squeezed the oxygen bag in small, quick bursts, then took the child in my arms for another round of CPR. As I alternated back to the baby's head, Anne-Marie skillfully injected epinephrine into his umbilical vein. Then she went back to chest compressions. As we worked, Anne-Marie looked nervously at the clock and pleaded urgently, "Come on, come on, little one."

Fifteen minutes elapsed. Anne-Marie's hands stopped. We both knew that if the baby didn't make it now, he wouldn't. We gazed down expectantly at the baby in the crib. Slowly, the baby's face contorted, and he let out a weak cry. Anne-Marie and I looked at each other with tears of relief. This one would make it. Several hours later, his screams would become loud and rigorous, and, having become a disruption in the delivery room, he would be given back to his mother to hold. Meanwhile, the three other bundles on the floor would disappear and would never be spoken of again.

****

At some point, I discovered that the hospital did not keep records of infant deaths, those bundles on the floor. Stillbirths were captured—in the birth register, there was a column for the status of the infant, and when the fetus was already dead, this column contained an M for *mort-né*. But the birth register was usually filled out immediately after delivery, and there was not a separate register that listed infants as patients. This combination of facts meant that babies who were born alive but died shortly afterward—the majority of the bundles on the floor—were never tallied. I tried to think of how many bundles I had seen, how many cold bodies I had personally wrapped. When I couldn't come up with a number, I started keeping track. Between February and June 2013, my field notes are punctuated by numbers: 0 bundles, 0 bundles, 1 bundle. On the days that I did not go to the hospital, I wondered how many bundles I missed. As I thought about this tide of bundles that no attempt at counting would stop, I wrote:

> How many times will I watch them reach for bicarbonate? Today, there was no gas for the generator and the power had gone off, or perhaps it had just been too long since someone had checked on the fragile new being. At some point, the baby had stopped breathing, and now he was blue and cold. The covers are pulled back from his face and chest, two fingers pump his chest, too fast, but maybe this is what it meant to jump start. It's always an emergency when then they reach for the bicarbonate. But how many emergencies can a body take?

In my quest to tally the deaths, I descended to medical records, an office at the bottom of the hill. I made Excel sheets from the hospital's monthly reports that were submitted to the state. From observing how the midwives filled in registers, I knew the numbers would only be partial. Still, it seemed important to quantify the loss. For the period April to June 2013, I recorded: Births: 60, 71, 52; Cesareans: 44, 32, 32; Stillbirths coming from health center: 5, 7, 3; Stillbirths during labor: 0, 0, 0; Neonatal death: 1, 2, 0;

Maternal death: 1, 0, 0. Looking back over the last two years, this three-month period—in which there were eighteen neonatal deaths, one maternal death, and three hundred deliveries—seemed typical. I put the numbers into a calculator. Officially, nearly 6 percent of all births in Kishabe ended in death of the baby. And this was not counting the six other bundles I had tallied during this time.[30]

When I discussed my math with the midwives, they were adamant that they were not to blame for this number, which, if generalized across the country, would mean that Congolese neonates were ten times more likely to die than infants born in the United States. We work so hard to save them, the nurses maintained. But the running and hunger, the inability of the Congolese state to care for and protect its citizens, put limits on what they could do in the hospital, they insisted. Besides, this was not a new phenomenon, or specific to Kishabe. "In Congo, we have died like animals for years and no one has cared," they argued.

It is true that elevated infant (and maternal) mortality rates have a longer history in Congo. In the precolonial period, before the Belgians built maternities, childbirth was often likened to war: "childbirth is dying," the saying went; "giving birth takes women to the mouth of the grave."[31] Under imperial rule, dying became more generalized. Some were worked to death; others saw violent ends. At some point, the loss of able-bodied laborers combined with high rates of infertility to engender a Belgian panic over population decline. Would there be enough hands to pick rubber, to sift for gold? Fifty years later, the pronatalism instituted during this time lingers. Despite evidence that increased parity increases both neonatal and maternal mortality, the hospital's family planning offerings were characterized by supply chain ruptures; and even when Depo-Provera was available, midwives would not inject it without a husband's signature. And so, where many women presented with their sixth, seventh, eighth pregnancy, often after long labors elsewhere, where prenatal care was a rarity and life-saving blood products were more than an hour away, despite midwives' efforts otherwise, giving birth still took women to the mouth of the grave, and in Kishabe, laboring women still said, "Ninakufa": I am dying.

But the medical aspects of maternal and infant mortality are only part of the story. Anthropologist Filip De Boeck writes, "Without children, there are no gifts. Without gifts, there are no kin, no allies or social body."[32] Everywhere, children are figures of social reproduction. However, where so many households and communities have been fractured by war, children's ability to build new kinship, new connection, affords them a unique position in the social fabric. In a regime of nothingness, children offer a potential exit—toward relationality, recognition, a future that can be counted on. When I asked the midwives what they liked about their jobs, they stated, "Our children are our tomorrow"; "Our children allow us to dream [*kulota*]."[33] And yet, the oxygen rarely worked, the bandages were rarely clean, and bundles continued to accumulate on the floor. How to reconcile these two facts?

****

In "Variations on the Beautiful in the Congolese World of Sounds," Achille Mbembe traces the well-being of the Congolese people through different eras of Congolese music popular at different times.[34] First, he examines the choral music popularized during Belgian rule. He writes, "One of the most important contributions to Congolese music made by Christianity proved to be aesthetic indoctrination—an imposition of view as to what constitutes beauty, rules concerning correct harmonic progression, voice leading, types of vibrato and timbral characteristics."[35] Surely, Mbembe posits, other music existed during colonial rule—and many other subjects, too—but what was recorded were the voices that fell in line, adhered to the standards set in the metropole.

After choral music came the rumba, that buoyant genre popularized in the celebrations that marked Congolese independence. Mbembe asserts, "In many respects, [postindependence] music epitomized joy, festivity and happiness, elegance and serenity. It enabled the Congolese to sing what cannot be spoken about in any other kind of speech."[36] But soon after independence came the crushing weight of rock-bottom copper prices, crippling structural adjustment policies, and the heavy hand of a nervous dictator. By the 1990s, joblessness, hunger, and state violence were widespread. It was in this context, Mbembe posits, that contemporary Congolese music emerged. He writes: "Screaming, howling, throughout the last quarter of the 20th century and into the new millennium, part noise-sound, part musical scream, Congolese music has endeavored to account for the terror, the cruelty and the dark abyss—for the ugly and the abject—that is its country."[37] Where Congolese music has always been characterized by jubilation, ecstasy, the integration of the scream into music has allowed for a certain truth telling about the terrible, violent realities in which most people live. As it has freed dancers from the usual deception and ostentation that characterized the Congolese musical world, Mbembe argues, the scream has opened public space for people to inhabit the pain and loss that characterize their lives and bear witness to others doing the same.

Mbembe writes about Congolese music; but I have heard the scream that he describes, which reflects not only physical pain but also the "the terror, the cruelty and the dark abyss—for the ugly and the abject—that is its country," echoing through the walls of the Kishabe hospital. There was pride in grieving silently, and so many women did; but some mothers whose babies had become bundles on the floor screamed in the middle of the night, or in the showers, or when they got dressed to return home. And after she told me, "I am healed," once I had walked away, the woman who lost her child and her uterus on the same day uttered a gutteral "God, oh God" before falling silent again. In the realm of music, Mbembe suggests that, where crushing poverty and violence continued to threaten erasure, the socialization of suffering—the witness of the scream—is itself a form of healing.[38] Where life outside the hospital is so very hard—the hunger, the violence, the running, the fear—and the hospital cannot stem the tide of injury and death, I wonder if, more than saving individual lives, the central function of the Kishabe hospital might be the recognition of suffering and rendering it social? If one were to look only at the numbers, the Excel sheet of infant deaths that I made, it would be easy to chastise the nurse-midwives, to wonder why women returned—and many funding organizations did this. But if one listened to the nurse-midwives—"In Congo, we have died like animals for years and no one has cared," they said—if one sat with their frustration, recorded their exhaustion, witnessed their efforts, a different conclusion might be reached. It was not that the midwives were callous, or that the mothers they delivered did not notice the losses. Surely, the deaths of tomorrow were acutely felt—and shared—by all in the Kishabe maternity ward. But where oxygen was always scarce and clean bandages numbered, perhaps the witnessing of loss, of grief, of the screams that could not be hidden from all who slept in that large common room was itself a healing intervention.

Mtunzo and the Hospital's Promise of Care

At the foot of the hospital's steps, a handful of people operated small, wooden boutiques that provided the goods necessary for a prolonged stay: batteries for radios, quarter-sized bags of powdered soap, Fanta, and fried dough. A dozen women gathered in the open area in front of the boutiques to sell tomatoes, onions, and ten-cent denominations of powdered milk, sugar, and dried fish to patients well enough to walk to the market from their beds. At any one time, several young men waited with their moto-taxis at the foot of the steps for the next discharged patient who would become their next client; anyone without work gathered under the shade of the hospital's eucalyptus trees to relay news and exchange gossip.

The town didn't stop at the hospital entrance; rather, the hospital itself was deeply imbricated in the town's social and economic activity. At all hours of the day, a seemingly constant flow of people circulated through the wards: female friends and family delivered food and soap for the sick; fathers and husbands arrived to pay the bills of their charges; and counselors and pastors visited the sick and accompanied those who had been discharged home. In addition, women sold fish from baskets they carried on their head through the wards; children peddled kerosene from old water bottles on the walkways that connected the wards; and merchants hawked clothes, wax fabric, and plastic goods on the hospital steps. When night came and stillness fell over the town, the activity continued in the hospital: well after dusk, family and friends shared food with those who were hospitalized; after the food had been put away, mothers, wives, and daughters washed the sick and tucked them in before rolling out straw mats on the concrete between the hospital beds and taking their own reprieve.

Regardless of whether they entered as a patient or a visitor, a vendor or an employee, everyone in Kishabe spent time in the hospital. Above, I have explored the role of the hospital in relation to its patients, the way that it taught about physical pain and witnessed loss. But the hospital exerted a magnetic pull on the entire surrounding community, not just on the afflicted. And so, as I work to untangle the knot of the hospital that drew people into its gates despite the screams, the losses, in this section, I examine a more metaphysical kind of care, of healing. Though less corporeal, less intimate, it is a kind of care that continues to be brokered by the body and its vulnerability in war.

At less than five feet tall, Antoine was a slight man. The faded, threadbare blue coveralls that he wore swallowed his body, and his too-large white rubber boots reached almost to his knees, making him appear even smaller than he was. Born in Kishabe, he had grown up farming. For years after his father died, Antoine had continued cultivating the large plantation of banana trees that his father had overseen. In 2007, after he had married and become a father, pests came through the area and killed the banana trees. Finding himself unemployed and with many mouths to feed, Antoine began looking for work. It was 2006; war was everywhere, and MSF was running the hospital.

The high salaries that MSF offered lured him to the hospital in the first place, when, as he recounted, "the hospital was still clean." The work was physically demanding—he prepared the operating room prior to surgery and attended to the equipment and surgical supplies during the operation. And due to the frequency of surgical emergencies—so many gunshot wounds and obstetric complications—Antoine often found himself working seven days a week. But the regular salary of $100 a month that MSF paid enabled Antoine to feed his family. And with time, he was able to buy a plot of land and begin the construction of his house. "Farming kept us full," he remembered, "but with the hospital work, I could finally build."

In the 1960s, employment in the hospital had been prestigious, one of the few opportunities for upward mobility available to rural Kishabe residents. Nurses owned land. Some even drove cars.[39] During Mobutu's rule, the hospital, like all public institutions, had been hollowed out, and salaries became intermittent. In many ways, MSF's tenure at the hospital turned back the hands of time, to a time of prosperity and construction. However, when conflict died down and MSF left (at least for some time), working conditions at the hospital again deteriorated. Antoine remained one of the few people in Kishabe who was formally employed. And yet, because the hospital paid so little, his family often only ate once a day, and his children did not go to school. "We have such a bad life," Antoine said. "At least before, we could live, we could survive. Now, we have nothing." Instead of delivering on Antoine's expectations for a better life, the hospital rendered him hungry, frustrated, and in debt.

Antoine and I met on the hospital stairs in my early days in Kishabe, where I had descended to take a breather from the maternity ward and he sought cell phone service. At first, we crossed paths sporadically. With time, however, our paired descents to the stairs became more intentional. Antoine had a knack for animated dramatizations of precarity: like a jester, he pointed out the holes in the clothes of people who walked into the hospital and then put his own threadbare clothes on display as comic relief. With wild gesticulations, he told of the bills that he had that he couldn't pay—and, as if he were the host of a game show, asked those waiting at the accountant's door what they had sold to pay the hospital bill of their family members. By making light of the poverty, illness, and loss people were bearing, he transformed the mood at the foot of the stairs.

But Antoine had a quieter side, too, when he was deeply concerned about his family, how they were all going to get through. On one such occasion, I asked him why he continued to work at the hospital if it didn't pay. Why not return to the land? At least then, you could feed your family, I suggested. "At least, through the hospital, my family gets *mtunzo*," Antoine replied, repeating a refrain I had heard from others like Antoine who struggled to feed their families with the salaries they made from the hospital. In Swahili, *mtunzo* refers to physical care, health care, and/or the cost of this care; it also describes a more metaphysical, social concept, taking care of the sick and the vulnerable more generally. Antoine did not clarify what kind of *mtunzo* the hospital provided, but I believe that this slippage is precisely the point. If Antoine or his family were to fall sick, the hospital would pay their bill. In this way, it provided health care. And, through his daily work in the hospital, his ethical mopping and sterilizing, Antoine imagined that one day, the hospital would deliver a better life for him and his family. He wasn't sure how this was going to happen—perhaps MSF would come back and provide him with the means with which to finish his house—but even if not MSF, another organization would intervene and reward him for his long suffering, for his years of uncompensated toil. One day, Antoine insisted, the care that he provided to the hospital and its patients would be recognized, his own suffering seen, and a dignified salary paid. In this way, Antoine imagined the hospital as the doorway to a more metaphysical form of care, of healing.

Black critical theorist Hortense Spillers writes about the division of Black flesh from the body that has taken place in antiblack regimes. She writes, "before the 'body,' there is the 'flesh,' that zero degree of social conceptualization that does not escape concealment under the brush of discourse or the reflexes of iconography."[40] In Spillers's writing, flesh is captive, seared, whipped, deprived; whereas the body is liberated, self-possessed, recognized by legal personhood. Centuries have passed since the emancipation of enslaved people in America; however, the racializing assemblages that initially cleaved Black flesh from the body continue to organize life across the globe. Moreover, capitalist modernity is built on this division.[41] And so, Antoine has a sense that another present is possible but lives a very fleshy everyday. Because of his proximity to the hospital, however, Antoine's story does not end at the flesh. Rather, where he has seen the hospital provide for others in the Kishabe community—a stairway to a life beyond the hospital's walls—Antoine dreams that, through the connections with humanitarian organizations and NGOs he makes in the hospital, he might finish his house, provide three meals a day for his family, clothe his children. Through his ethical work at the hospital, he might one day live as a social subject in a regime of the flesh. For Antoine and many others who pass through the hospital's gates, this possibility, that the hospital might enable a suturing back together of Black flesh to body, a repair of the centuries-old wound, motivates return.

Too often, the Kishabe hospital failed to keep alive those who sought care at its doors. Decades of neglect, scarcity, and violence in Kishabe had taken their toll, and deprived of the human or material resources necessary to curb the precarity of life in war, the hospital could not stem the death and debility that passed through its doors. In 2007, members of an American NGO attempted to quantify the human cost of war in eastern Congo. They reported that between 1998 and 2007, war caused 5.4 million "excess deaths" in Congo.[42] Of these 5.4 million, the great majority were not direct results of conflict, but rather the consequence of nonviolent, treatable, and easily preventable illnesses such as pneumonia, malaria, diarrhea, malnutrition, and obstetric complications.[43] Despite the efforts of Antoine, Anne-Marie, Lydie, and others, these excess deaths continued in Kishabe long after Coghlan et al.'s report. And still, the Kishabe community rotated around the hospital. In this chapter, I have sought to reconcile these conflicting facts—that as bundles piled up on the floor, more people streamed through the hospital's gates.

In the epigraph that opens this chapter, Alexander Weheliye writes that "what remains is the flesh" in dense antiblackness, "the living, speaking, thinking, feeling, and imagining flesh: the ether that holds together the world of Man while at the same time forming the conditions of possibility for this world's demise." Today, the hospital in Kishabe continues to hold together the world of Man, where Blackness is relegated to a fleshy existence. But the people in Kishabe insist that their bodies, and the structures that care for them, have other futures too. While the hospital cannot save the lives of many that grace its doors, while the hospital sometimes even hurts its patients, people continue to come to the hospital because it performs a key function for the population in Kishabe: where so many people die unnoticed, the hospital allows Congolese the possibility to inhabit affliction, bears witness to their suffering, and teaches its patients to survive in war. Where suffering is everyday life and people have run from war more times than they can count, Congolese argue, the witnessing, the teaching to bear are themselves forms of healing. And so, the body is both the most proximate site of vulnerability and that which continues to motivate an outpouring of care, inspiring visions of presents otherwise, in which people and things can be counted on, in which life is less fragile.

FIGURE 3.2. A store in Kishabe, emptied by retreating troops, November 2012. An untrained eye might not recognize pillage in eastern Congo. For the most part, there were no broken locks, no doors swinging open, no empty beer crates lying around. There was no evidence of struggle, nothing that would attest to thieves leaving in a hurry. Only if you had visited before would you know that an event had taken place. Windows were shuttered, doors closed, shelves cleared. Where once there had been music, neighborhood chatter, children playing between houses, the silence was deafening. Photograph by author.

It had been two months since war had come to Kishabe, and things had seemed calm recently. The morning staff meeting had just ended, and Rachel, one of the nurse-midwives, was preparing to start rounds when Anne-Marie entered in a flurry and put the register on the table with an uncharacteristic brusqueness. "I need to go home early," Anne-Marie stated flatly. Her face was drawn, and her eyes were glazed with worry.

Her family had left several missed calls today, Anne-Marie explained. She hadn't been to Goma in two weeks. The security in Goma was bad. Last time it was like this, she didn't worry because she had already prepared for the kids: she had made a huge pot of *sombe* (cassava leaves); she had left beans for them; she had brought charcoal; they knew to get under the mattresses if they heard gunshots. So even though they were separated when M23 invaded Goma, she knew they would be okay. But when she left the house two weeks ago, there was only one cup of rice in the house. Otherwise, it was completely empty. "They must be beeping me because war is coming and they are hungry," Anne-Marie reasoned.

"I'm driving to Goma," I offered. "I can take you this afternoon."

As Anne-Marie and I discussed timing, Rachel interrupted. "I don't have any charcoal either. When war is coming, you need charcoal, oil, flour, and beans. I don't have any charcoal," she repeated in a panic.

Distracted from our logistical discussion by the fear in Rachel's voice, Anne-Marie turned back to discuss wartime necessities with Rachel. "No," she corrected Rachel, "you need salt more than you need oil. You can eat food with no oil, but you can't eat food without salt."

Rachel sat silently for a moment and then started to make a verbal list of the staples that one needed during wartime. "Of all the things, you need sugar, soap, salt, oil, coal, flour, and beans," she said, counting each item on her fingers. She continued, "If you have to run, you need sugar because the kids get tired, and if you have sugar, you can get some water and put some sugar in it and they will have energy. If you don't have sugar, how are the kids going to have energy to keep running?" After a pregnant pause, she returned to the subject that had launched the discussion: "But war is coming, and I really don't have any charcoal," she said.

APRIL

Four months had passed since the big troop movements of November. Now that the soldiers lived in the center of town, people circulated around Kishabe as if the war was long over. But on a random day in April, the town woke up to a deserted army camp. The government soldiers had packed up and left Kishabe without warning. Suddenly, all eyes turned northward, to where M23 had been stationed for months. Speculation about impending war dominated conversation. Everyone worried that war was coming again. Was M23 coming back? Would there be another retreat? If so, would Kishabe be spared? Again, people bought charcoal and sugar.

MAY

The peace talks had stalled, and now the war days seemed more frequent. Again, the banks were closed, commercial flights canceled, and students sent home from school. Again, people stayed at home waiting, wondering. Maybe this would be the day that M23 would return, people said out loud. Mothers cooked beans. Fathers cashed in on debts they were owed to buy supplies, just in case. There had been some days like this last month, and the month before, too, and nothing had come of the talk then. Now, there were shells falling within earshot. One always had to be ready to run.

JUNE

I had come to Goma to see a friend. With things feeling as tense as they did, I had decided against driving near sunset and had instead stayed the night in Goma. It was now sunrise, and I was starting to prepare to return to Kishabe. As I was starting to pack the car, my phone rang. I saw from the number that it was Solange—the woman with whom I lived in Kishabe. I answered quickly, for Solange never called me unless there was a problem. Skipping the usual pleasantries, she asked simply whether I had already left.

"No, I'm just packing," I responded. As I waited for Solange to say more, I thought about why Solange might be calling. Did she need me to pick up something at the grocery? Or perhaps someone had gotten hurt there and they needed the car? "Solange, is everything okay?" I asked when the silence had stretched out too long for comfort.

She paused before responding, "The bombs are like drums here. Everyone is in the street."

It had been six months since the war of M23. Some days had been calm, but so many others had felt like this, full of war talk, fear, worry, and sadness. The intensity of the threat ebbed and flowed, but it always returned. On this day, there would be changes of travel plans, more charcoal buying, more preparation. Once again, an entire population listened to artillery in the distance and wondered whether they would, yet again, run to save their lives.

FIGURE 4.1. Mugunga Refugee Camp, 2013. Nineteen years after one million people poured over the border from Rwanda, the camp remained. Tents stretched for miles across the volcanic rock. Where doors were but a flap of fabric, there was little security, and theft and sexual violence were commonplace. And yet the size of the camp and the humanitarian presence within it largely protected inhabitants from the dangers of living with armed groups. Photograph by author.

When Life Demands Release

Rape, what is that? It is connected to all that—stealing, killing, it is all in that. . . . You feel you have to do something bad, you mix it all: sabotage, women, stealing, rip the clothes off, killing. . . . It is suffering which makes us rape. Suffering. If I wake up in the morning and I am fine, I have something to eat, my wife loves me, will I then do things like that? No. But now, today we are hungry, yesterday I was hungry, tomorrow I will be hungry.
—Congolese soldier

not all of those Black people were afrofuturists, but to focus on afrofuturists in the Black social-justice tradition, I would note that:

africans leaping off of slaver ships were afrofuturists.
slave-era parents teaching their babies a foreign alphabet in the candlelit dirt were afro-futurists.
black women dissociating themselves through to tomorrow while being raped into mother-hood were afrofuturists.
those who raised the children of violence, and those who chose not to, all were predicting the future and articulating their choices.
slaves who ran to freedom, and slaves who ran to their deaths, were afrofuturists.

it is the emphasis on a tomorrow that centers the dignity of that seed, particularly in the face of extinction, that marks, for me, the afrofuturist.

—adrienne maree brown, *Emergent Strategy*

In her chapter "Health and Healing" for *The Oxford Handbook of Modern African History*, Nancy Rose Hunt devotes a long section to what she calls "the harming register" of African therapeutic practice. Hunt explains that, whereas healing practices in Western medicine are often imbued with positive valence—the paths by which individuals achieve better health—therapeutic practices in Africa have long been understood to contain both the potential to heal and the potential to harm. Here, Hunt builds upon John Janzen and Wyatt MacGaffey's foundational writing about the deep ambivalence surrounding medicinal charms and power objects in the lower Congo. In Janzen and MacGaffey's writing, *nkisi* derive their power, their therapeutic potency from their dual potential to radically heal or thoroughly harm.[1] Hunt suggests that this duality might be a shared pillar of African healing. Rather than leading people unidirectionally toward health—a widely held, if incomplete, characterization of Western medicine—African therapeutic practices often involve a certain liminality, a period of suspension during which the outcome of the practice remains markedly unknowable. Things could go either way, toward individual and communal wellness, or toward worsened dysfunction, imbalance, and even death.

In previous chapters, I have described new healing practices emerging from centuries of violence in DRC—dirt work, inhabiting, the transformative power of pain. In doing so, I have taken it as a given that healing from deep violence requires a turn away from the violence. In this chapter, I challenge this supposition. Over the past three decades in eastern Congo, so many have killed and been killed. Often, the violence of today tells of earlier terrors: hands and feet are cut off, vaginas pounded to sterility today as they were during imperial rule.[2] Sometimes, the violence becomes increasingly perverse: men are ordered to rape their mothers at gunpoint; older brothers, their younger sisters. In these cases, the devastation continues to reverberate long after the violence has ended. A woman who has endured such a rape strangles the baby that results from it, asking herself, "He was the child of who? My brother? My father? My mother? My grandmother? Me?"[3] In this chapter, I am interested in querying how these moments of profound devastation, made darker still by their repetitiveness, create particular drives toward healing. Certainly, this violence is world ending for many; and, where violence has become so chronic, so perverse, I wonder if it might itself be, for some, an attempt to refuse the painful present, a gesture toward other possibilities, when/where there is enough to eat, a way to make money, the possibility of political and social recognition. I ask: if, as the writing on African healing teaches us, therapeutic practices can always go either way—toward healing or toward harm—is it possible that violence might be the underside, the harming register, of a turn toward repair?

I begin the chapter with a return to the Kishabe hospital, to the malnutrition ward, where I examine *bwaki*, a form of severe malnutrition in Congo. Through a close look at experience of one young child in the Kishabe malnutrition ward, I query the relationship between death and healing in war. From the Kishabe hospital, I move to Rutshuru, a town sixty miles north of Goma, where I describe the way that M23's violent occupation of the town produced specific turns toward violence.[4] In this story, death has healing potential; so, too, does liberatory violence. From Rutshuru, I travel farther north, and forward in time, to the Grand Nord and the violence that characterizes the region. As I narrate the gruesome forms of violence utilized in the continuing conflict, I am interested in whether the killing of innocent civilians might also be motivated by a desire for healing.

My understanding of violence owes much to a lineage of writing on revolutionary violence.[5] During the civil rights movement, Malcolm X demanded freedom for Black people everywhere "by any means necessary."[6] When the African continent was fighting for independence from colonial regimes, Frantz Fanon became a leading theorist of the use of violence to attain political change.[7] In recent years, Achille Mbembe has gained much repute for his thinking about the intertwined relationship between dying, killing, and contemporary power, which he calls "necropolitics." Where colonial and postcolonial regimes have taken so much from their subjects—for decades, depriving those under their rule of food, land, security, bodily autonomy, sovereignty—Mbembe argues that many belong to the world of the slave. Always relegated to the shadows, they are neither dead nor alive, human nor animal. They struggle daily to achieve other-than-nothingness; and still, they too often become victims of state-sponsored violence, who never gain access to a voice in the courts, or a seat at the negotiating table. Until, Mbembe proposes, the rise of the Palestinian suicide bomber. He writes, "In this instance, my death goes hand in hand with the Other's death. Homicide and suicide are accomplished in the same act. Resistance and self-destruction are largely synonymous."[8] By killing—or brutally raping, or terrorizing—he who has forever been trapped in the state of becoming finally accedes to the status of subject. In this nocturnal world, Mbembe argues, "War has become both remedy and poison—our pharmakon."[9] In this chapter, I am interested in exploring the ways in which a close view of violence in Congo might further our understanding of what forms war-as-pharmakon might take.

Bwaki: Another Version of Necropolitics?

When I first starting visiting Muisha, a constant, low-pitch lament emanated from his mouth, like the drone of a helicopter, except more human. His father, an artisanal miner, had come back from several months in the mines to find all of the children thin. Muisha, one of the oldest children, was the worst off. By the time his father brought him to the Kishabe malnutrition ward, the swelling around Muisha's eyes had rendered him functionally blind, and the skin on his arms and legs was cracked and bleeding where it had broken under the swelling. After he was weighed in a hanging scale, for he couldn't stand, a feeding tube was placed in Muisha's nose, and dual diagnoses of chronic malnutrition with wasting and severe acute malnutrition were recorded. The admission logbook listed his age as nine years and his weight as fifteen kilograms (thirty-three pounds).

A few days into treatment, the fortified formula that nurses pushed through his feeding tube six times a day began to make a difference. Gradually, hollow eyes emerged from his face, and Muisha's constant drone abated. One day, his mouth formed a word, and he spat it through an emotionless face. "Uende," he said to his father. Go. Elated to finally hear his son's voice, his father laughed. "Muisha, I love you," he said. Several days later, when Muisha began repeating the word through dead eyes—"Uende, uende, uende"— his father murmured tenderly. A week went by like this. Slowly, Muisha's father's assurances faded to silence.

As Muisha gained the strength to sit up, one of the nurses in the ward brought him a toy car. With a blank look on his face, Muisha stared at the car in front of him. Assuming that Muisha needed a bit of encouragement, the nurse began driving the car around the bed. "Vroom vroom," she said with a smile. "Uende," Muisha replied flatly.

Several weeks later when I visited Muisha, I found him sitting in bed with a wet diaper. As I scanned the room for Baba Muisha, a woman in the neighboring bed offered that Muisha's father had been gone since the morning. Muisha had clearly been wet for some time, and he still did not have the strength to change himself. As I started to rummage through the bags on the floor for a clean strip of cloth, his father walked in. In response to his father's arrival, Muisha started talking, saying words that I did not understand. I listened for a minute, then asked his father for clarification. "Perhaps he is speaking Kinyarwanda?" I asked. His father emitted a sardonic laugh and replied, "No, that's not Kinyarwanda. His head is already ruined [*ichwa yake kilishaaribika*]." As he turned back to Muisha, his face grew stern, his movements mechanical.

Seventy-six days after Muisha was admitted, his father was served discharge papers with instructions to take his son to the mental health hospital in Goma. I ran into father and son in the hallway, papers in hand, on their way to begin packing. After reading through the paperwork, I asked how Muisha was doing. Baba Muisha happily reported that Muisha was now eating on his own and walking, but added that the doctors in Kishabe had said they couldn't do anything for his head [*kichwa yake*]. "I don't understand why they can't help. He used to be such a talkative, happy child," Baba Muisha said, "and now he just speaks gibberish." When Baba Muisha left to gather their affairs, I sought out one of the physicians at Kishabe whom I knew well. I didn't know the answers to Baba Muisha's questions about Muisha's anger and his transformed speech, and I didn't know whether Muisha would truly benefit from the mental health hospital. It was early in my time in Kishabe, and I had not yet seen many cases of severe malnutrition. Was it the malnutrition that had made him lose his mind? I wondered.

Dr. Aimé shook his head and sighed. "We don't know what happened to him," he replied in resignation. Perhaps Muisha had had meningitis, Dr. Aimé speculated. Perhaps it was the malnutrition that "ruined his head." Regardless, there was nothing further to be done for this child in Kishabe. The feeding tube had been out for some time; Muisha was now eating and able to get around on his own. Still, his frequent and sudden angry outbursts rendered him a danger to himself and others. "That's why we want him to get more help," Dr. Aimé said. "But I know he'll never make it." The mental health hospital in Goma, the only one in the province, was prohibitively expensive. As a miner, Baba Muisha was cash poor at baseline. Now, having been unemployed for several months as he cared for Muisha, he would not have the means to pay the daily bed fee. From the steps of the hospital, Dr. Aimé and I watched Baba Muisha load Muisha and their affairs onto a motorcycle. As they turned south, away from the mental hospital and toward their home, Dr. Aimé clucked, "That kid is going to end up tied up somewhere [a practice used to safely manage mental illness where institutionalization and medication are not possible]. He's an angry, mentally ill person [*fou*] now. As he gets stronger, he'll hurt someone or himself."

While there is data that indicates that acute malnutrition in early childhood can have significant effects on cognitive ability later in life—lower test scores, less precise fine motor skills—the medical literature doesn't mention madness as a possible side effect of malnutrition.[10] Importantly, mothers in the Kishabe malnutrition ward insisted that, actually, the causation went in the other direction. According to these women, Muisha was not malnourished; rather, he had *bwaki*, a condition that begins when children volitionally stop eating. One woman, who had lost her first two children to *bwaki*, explained that her third child, who was at the time hospitalized in the Kishabe ward, "started refusing food [*kukataa chakula*], not because she didn't like it, not because it was different, but for no reason at all [*hakuna hata sababu*]."

In the biomedical understanding of acute malnutrition, malnutrition precedes, and indeed causes, appetite loss. But this mother—together with Muisha's father and so many other parents in the ward—maintained that the doctors had the order of these two events reversed. First, children with *bwaki* stopped eating; then they became malnourished. In response to my questions about why children developed *bwaki*, parents insisted that it didn't do any good to search for a reason why the children stopped eating— nothing had changed in the children's diet; nothing had changed in their taste buds; there was no violence in the home. Rather, some children simply decided to stop eating. This decision marked the beginning of their *bwaki*.

If we apply this definition of *bwaki* to Muisha—and his father certainly described Muisha's illness as *bwaki*—then Muisha actually fell ill long before the doctors in Kishabe thought he did. For it wasn't when Muisha became acutely malnourished that he became ill, but rather when he stopped eating weeks or months before he came to the hospital. The question then arises as to why Muisha stopped eating in the first place. Muisha's father, like the other parents in the malnutrition ward, was clear that nothing in the household changed before Muisha stopped eating. Even though the family was poor, there had been food in the house, even beans—protein, Muisha's father insisted. But none of that mattered. "Alianza kukataa tu." He just started refusing.

I have tried to imagine what was going through his head the day that Muisha stopped eating. Had his little nine-year-old self looked around, at his thin mother, father, and siblings, and decided that chronic, low-level hunger was no life for him? Had he heard his mother or his older siblings tell a war story—of running, of plunder—and not been able to stomach another bite? Or, given that he and his family lived in a camp for displaced people where theft and rape were relatively common, perhaps he had witnessed violence, and the bodily knowledge that he might someday become a victim extinguished his appetite?[11]

In the end, I think there are many possibilities for what lay behind Muisha's refusal of food. His and his family's life circumstances were devastating: as Banyarwanda whose familial origins lay in Rwanda, their right to reside in Congo remained in question.[12] While their families had farmed land in the Congolese hills for decades, Baba Muisha and his wife had left the hills a year earlier to escape the violence that had been meted out on their neighbors. Now Muisha's mother stayed with the children in a camp for the internally displaced, while Baba Muisha went to the forest for weeks at a time to mine. Baba Muisha was clear that he and his family led *maisha buchungu*—a bitter life—and yet he did not see any different way forward. His family, like many of those living in the hills, had moved to eastern Congo prior to Congolese independence. Despite their long tenure in the country, Congolese law was ambiguous about their legal tenure in the country—and this legal ambiguousness led to cyclical violence.[13] As long as the violence continued in the hills, Baba Muisha was clear that his family would not be returning home. With a shrug of resignation, he added, "Na tungeenda wapi ingine?" And where else would we go? "Congo ni kwetu." Congo is home. By the age of nine, Muisha had lived enough bitter life in the place that his father called home to know that he no longer wanted to stick around.

****

One would think that, given the war and the hunger, the running and the violence, that people would leave en masse.

State failure in eastern Congo, and the predatory government that has arisen in its wake, has its roots in the example set by Mobutu Sese Seko, president and then dictator of the country between 1965 and 1997.[14] When Mobutu first wrested control of the country five years after independence, he did so to applause. At first, he ousted Belgian corporations, claiming that profit from Congolese (Zairean) minerals should go the Congolese (Zairean) people.[15] Several years later, he rolled out a new national health system, which provided primary health care for all—for free.[16] However, within a decade of Mobutu taking office, the nation began to come apart at the seams. The divisions fostered in the colonial era left scars that persisted despite public corporations and health care for all. As these divisions began to threaten his grip on power, Mobutu began emptying state coffers to ensure allegiance (and his own comfort). For another decade, Mobutu maintained power by pitting various challengers of his authority against themselves—a practice William Reno has termed "warlord politics"; however, with the falling copper prices in the 1970s and then the structural adjustment policies in the 1980s, Mobutu's largesse overwhelmed the state coffers.[17] In the early 1990s, when there was no longer money to pay the salary of the army, Mobutu granted the military implicit permission to extract their salary directly from the population.[18] By the mid-1990s, violent plunder had become commonplace and hunger was widespread. In 1995, anthropologist René Devisch quoted a resident of the capital saying dryly, "In the days of the Belgian, we could eat three times a day. During the First Republic [1960–65] one ate but two meals. With the second [1965–97] we can afford only one. Where will progress end?"[19]

Some people do leave Congo. The Migration Policy Institute quantifies them as a proportion: Congo's "net migration rate" is listed as "–0.1/1000 population (2018 est.)."[20] This represents a greater out-migration than Nigeria sees; but less flight than South Sudan. Many who leave end up just next door, in Rwanda or Uganda, where formal employment is more plentiful. Others go farther. Despite the DRC's geographic location on the continent, just south of center, Congolese make up 10 percent of the migrants who seek to cross the Mediterranean.[21] They often make many stops on the continent: first, there is Brazzaville, just north of DRC—perhaps it is safer there, they muse. Then Cameroon, where they have family. Then Libya, where a prospect of work presents itself. On the job site in Libya, a husband learns from a Moroccan colleague about the opportunity to cross the sea. And so, when his contract comes to an end, he decides "to risk it" and pay for a one-way passage in a less-than-seaworthy vessel to a better life. Some make it to the other side; if there are storms, or too many people on the boat, others join their ancestors at the bottom of the sea.[22]

But leaving also happens internally, such as when entire villages run from war. Perhaps heavy artillery nearby made them leave. Perhaps it was the news of people hacked to death last night the town over. There are pictures that circulate—abdomens cut open, bodies dismembered—although unless you know the person who took one, one never knows if they represent atrocities committed last night, the town over, or whether they were taken before, somewhere else. The inability to pin these images down to a specific time and place renders them even more unsettling. And so, entire villages pack their essential belongings—mattresses, pots, enough charcoal and food to make it for several days—and join the others on the road.[23]

The character of the flight depends on the character of the violence. Large-scale war leads to roads packed with moving people and their livestock, slow sorrowful crowds moving in waves over landscapes; whereas individual face-to-face dismembering creates trickles, single-file lines of people who have decided that the violence has gotten too close this time; it's just too much to bear now. In some places, the internally displaced are welcomed into homes, where they stay, seven or eight new mouths sleeping on a mattress in the living room, for days, months, or years. And in other situations, new homes are made: UNHCR tarps stretched over found wood, each hut nearly touching the next. Perhaps this kind of human touch feels safe for a while, after being so near to the blade of a machete. But how does it feel after years of the same free lentils and cornmeal, just enough to meet your caloric requirement for the day? At some point, does the camp, which is tangled up in profit-making ventures of UNHCR, US foreign policy, and the inhabitants themselves, ever feel like home?[24] Or are the 5.01 million internally displaced in Congo always in a state of flight?

And then what of those whose minds leave even as their bodies stay? There are various versions of this mind-body split. There are those who live too close to the gold mines and to the gold extraction that happens nearby. With time, the mercury used in extraction accumulates in their bodies, causing tremor, insomnia, and memory problems.[25] There are those who, running from war, do not have time to dry their cassava properly, who, as a consequence, ingest toxic levels of cyanide and develop the dizziness and confusion that are characteristic of konzo.[26] There are also the raped, who dissociate when their husbands come home, their minds in flight to somewhere else. Where do they go when he mounts them, I wonder but never ask. How are they related to the truly mad who wander the streets in handcuffs, restrained by their families in the name of protecting themselves and their communities? Or to the dreamers, who speak of a time when streets will be paved and clean water will run from the spigots across Congo? For those who remain physically present during devastating violence, where are the lines between madness and dissociation, dissociation and imagination?

Frantz Fanon, a French Martinican psychiatrist who took part in the Algerian war of independence, wrote extensively on the ways in which colonial regimes' denial of the subjectivity of the colonized contributed to the development of madness. He begins his treatise "Colonial War and Mental Disorders" by stating the root of the illness, the origin of the pathology. He writes, "Because it is a systematized negation of the other, a frenzied determination to deny the other any attribute of humanity, colonialism forces the colonized to constantly ask the question: 'Who am I in reality?'"[27] After establishing how deep this negation cuts, he goes on to describe its effects on the minds of the colonized: "When colonization remains unchallenged by armed resistance, when the sum of harmful stimulants exceeds a certain threshold, the colonized's defenses collapse, and many of them end up in psychiatric institutions. In the calm of this period of triumphant colonization, a constant and considerable stream of mental symptoms are direct sequels of this oppression."[28]

In his treatise on postcolonial power, which draws much from Fanon's work, Mbembe asserts that, because colonial race relations continue in the present, so too does the eternal suspension between life and death to which today's subaltern subjects remain confined. He writes, "In this zero world neither matter nor life ends as such. They do not return to nothingness. They merely pursue a movement of exiting toward something else, with the end being deferred each time and the very question of finitude left hanging. The zero world is a world in which becoming is difficult to figure because the time of which it is woven cannot be captured through the traditional categories of the present, past, and future."[29] Mbembe argues, the subaltern of today, like the colonized before him, is denied recognition, restricted to negation, to a permanent state of becoming—except if he refuses the zero world to which he has been confined.

Having devoted his life to caring for those with mental illness, Fanon believed in the possibility of rehabilitation, that those driven to madness under colonialism could recover. He also believed strongly in the power of refusal. As Mbembe points out, in his clinical practice as in his political treatises, Fanon imagined that radical decolonization, and thus recognition of true subjecthood for the colonized subject, was achieved through refusal.[30] Often, Fanon wrote about the two processes—healing for the subject driven mad under colonization, and ascension to subjecthood through refusal of colonial power—as if they were linked. This inseparability of healing and refusal in Fanon lays the groundwork for Mbembe's theory of necropolitics.

In Fanon's writing, the "no" of the colonized takes the form of violent resistance to colonial oppression—the colonial war. In the postcolony (or the settler colony), Mbembe asserts, refusal becomes necropolitical. Thus, the negated becomes subject at the moment when he refuses the zero world to which he has been confined through an embrace of death. In this chapter, I am interested in the many forms that refusal takes in Congo. Might we hear a rejection of life amid negation and hunger in Muisha's *bwaki*? Further, might Muisha's "no," his *uende*, which resulted in his referral to the psychiatric hospital, actually be his clearest moments?[31] What does this do to our understanding of healing if a nine-year-old child's death drive contains therapeutic potential? And does it change our analysis if the child's refusal is performed individually, as in Muisha's case, or takes the form of collective action, wherein an occupying military force is the subject of the "no"?

M23 in Rutshuru: Playing with Violence

M23 entered Rutshuru on July 25, 2012. Like most residents of the eastern Congolese town, Trésor, a man in his early twenties, knew the date by heart. It was at least the fifth time the town had been invaded by a foreign force in the last two decades.[32] When the fight for the town between the national army and M23 had first begun, many families had fled to Uganda, Goma, or the refugee camp on the outskirts of Goma. Others, like Trésor, had locked their doors and hunkered down at home. When M23 won the firefight and entered the town victorious, people feared for what might happen—but they also hoped. Maybe this time it would be different. After all, Sultani Makenga, the group's leader, was from Rutshuru, and in his speeches, he promised roads, courts, an end to corruption and to war—the kind of change for which people deeply yearned. As a tribute to the soldiers who some said had "liberated" the town from Congolese national troops, *peace* was painted on a monument in the center of town.[33]

The optimism, guarded as it was, was short lived. Within months of their arrival in Rutshuru, M23's cash stores ran out. To raise the funds necessary to support military recruitment, training, and armament, M23 begin collecting taxes on the main commercial thoroughfare that ran through Rutshuru. When they first launched collections, M23 justified their actions by insisting that taxation was a normal part of any government and claimed that the rates would be lower than those that bandits and the Congolese army had charged prior to their arrival.[34] And yet, when eighteen-seater buses began paying $300 to pass and lorries $700, much of the traffic traveling to Goma from the Kenyan ports began to be rerouted through Rwanda and Uganda. Within weeks, road traffic had diminished significantly, and many Rutshuru residents who had previously made their living on the lorries could no longer put food on the table. As for M23, the road taxes were not as lucrative as they hoped; they would have to find other means to raise funds. As they prepared for the attack on Goma, they began levying taxes on individual homes in Rutshuru in addition to the road taxes. Again, the occupying force announced their plans ahead of time, thus attempting to differentiate themselves from the arbitrary taxes the government soldiers were known to demand. However, even if they were more standardized, the taxes M23 elicited further eroded households' food stores, and the population grew more and more critical of the regime.

In November 2012, having recruited sufficient numbers and readied an armament, M23 left Rutshuru to invade Goma. For a few weeks, the population of Rutshuru experienced a brief reprieve from the taxes and exploitation. In the quietness that overtook the town, a curiosity grew. Few had believed that M23 could successfully capture Goma. Now, given their dramatic victory, people wondered whether the group would actually push to Kinshasa. If so, what would that mean for Rutshuru, M23's first base in Congo, Makenga's hometown? In Congo, the hometowns of politicians benefited significantly from them being in office. Was this a possibility for Rutshuru? "If Makenga marches to Kinshasa, will we get electricity?" a text from Rutshuru read. People listened eagerly to the radio for hints about what the future held.

Two weeks after the soldiers had left, they returned. People told of the entry of a long line of civilian cars and government vehicles that the troops had "repossessed" in Goma that preceded the foot soldiers. "Things were different when they came back," Trésor remembered. "They returned from Goma with anger." When their pillaged goods had been sold and the profits consumed, M23 soldiers began looting from individual houses in Rutshuru. Trésor explained, "They wouldn't take everything—just a few things, your TV if you had one, some money." Though not terribly violent, the unpredictability of this raiding made people in Rutshuru nervous. For the troops didn't just come once or twice—they kept coming back. In January, soldiers added another technique to their income-generating activities: they began kidnapping for ransom. A neighborhood leader in Rutshuru described the practice: "They would do research and figure out a family that had money. Then, they would kidnap him and take him to the forest. His family would have to sell property to get him back." The leader added, "But it wasn't just M23. M23 brought out the worst in the population, too. The population began using the soldiers to settle their internal disputes. They would tell the soldiers to kidnap a certain person with whom they had had an argument. The soldiers would keep the ransom for their efforts, and the person who had arranged the kidnapping would prove that they were more powerful than the person who was kidnapped."

In the spring of 2013, the security situation worsened in Rutshuru. A shop owner told of the heightened danger in town after repeated pillage. Where the soldiers had already taken so much, little of value remained in houses. If soldiers entered and did not find anything to take, they were known to beat men or rape women. Also, as ability to pay ransoms declined, fewer men came back from the forest. "The soldiers were frustrated [*découragés*]," the shop owner said. "While [their leaders] were getting $100 a day in per diems at the peace treaties in Kampala, the soldiers in town were starving."

More of Rutshuru's population left. Most of the shops in the town center shuttered. Music disappeared from the streets. The hospital became a refuge. During daylight hours, Rutshuru's population went to their fields or circulated around town for work. By 6 p.m., however, many began to seek refuge in the courtyard of the reference hospital in town. John, a friend of Trésor, spent most of his nights in the hospital. He explained, "Soldiers came to my house one night. There were so many of them, and we didn't know what they wanted. They didn't take anything. They just came in and left. Since then, I've slept at the hospital. My head is not good when I sleep at home. It's the not-knowing that ruins our courage."

While some hid in the hospital and others fled the town altogether, two groups of young men and women began daily affronts against M23. The first group was an armed group, with ties to PARECO, one of the splinter groups formed after a previous failed demobilization process. These youths carried guns, spoke of self-protection, and intermittently engaged in armed attacks and shoot-outs with M23.[35] Meanwhile, motivated by their indignation about the politics that kept their country at war, a second group took a different tactic. Instead of fighting M23 with firepower, they used the tactic of disruption to "show [M23] that Rutshuru is no longer for them." It is this second group that I find most interesting. Though M23 possessed significant firepower with no bars against using it, the unarmed youths brazenly stole the soldiers' livestock, lit their camp on fire at night, and created noise in the forest that confused M23's patrols to the point that they shot at themselves. Trésor explained,

> [M23] used to control us night and day, but now we control ourselves during the day. The soldiers can't do anything to us during the day. They've still got the night, but they're even losing control of that. The kids [*watoto*] hunt them in the forest. We used to be scared. We thought they would just kill people. But now, we can't live like this.

Our whole life has been like this, another armed group. We've had enough. We're not scared anymore. Now it is the soldiers who are scared. The soldiers are more scared of the kids than they are of [the Congolese army].[36]

The youths' resistance contained a playful element: in addition to acts meant to scare or confuse the soldiers, the youths waged *vita ya kinywa*, or war of the mouth. The youths insulted the soldiers, mocking them publicly. They brazenly disobeyed military rule, walking the town at night despite the curfew set by M23. And though they recognized that "[their] mouths were starting to start trouble," they spoke flippantly, even gaily, of taunting death. "They can't kill us," one youth said. "We are the autochthons [sons of the soil]." Their descriptions of their defiance of M23 were more often than not accompanied with chittering laughter.

As the youths' blatant challenges to M23's authority grew, so did tension in the town. When I returned again to Rutshuru in June 2012, the signs of an oppressive occupation were immediately apparent. Despite it being daylight, most storefronts were closed and padlocked, with little foot traffic, and the usual backdrop of music and spirited conversation was replaced by an almost eerie silence. Even behind closed doors, mothers and fathers in Rutshuru worried about talking directly about the challenge to authority that the youth groups posed. For as long as M23 still had some firepower, they still posed a threat to the population.

In early November 2013, the Congolese army won a decisive military victory against M23. M23 was first chased into the forest; then several hundred soldiers together with their leader, Makenga, were captured in Uganda. Analysts described it as the first military victory over Rwandan-based rebels in the Congolese history of the war, the end of an era of Rwandan intervention.[37] In Goma, there was jubilance. Colonel Mamadou Ndala, the army commander who had led the army to the momentous victory, was carried through the streets on people's shoulders. A movie circulated on people's phones that showed government soldiers killing M23 soldiers and then mocking their corpses. In response to the normal Swahili greeting, people responded triumphantly with a version of "We have chased them, chased them from the whole of Congo!"

In Rutshuru, the celebrations were even more enthusiastic. For weeks, rumba music echoed from every store and open-air bar in town, and people danced in the street in the middle of the day. Speeches were given; flags for the reigning political party were placed all around town. Ecstatic to be back in school after a year of vacation, children milled around town in their school uniforms well after school had let out for the day. Commerce returned: merchants restocked for the first time in many months, and agricultural goods were once again brought in the from the surrounding farms. People spoke openly about the atrocities during M23's rule: "Before, we had already died [(Fr) *On ne vivait plus*; (Sw) *Watu walikuwa walishakufa*]. Now, we're in Congo. Our country has come back to us." One man put it more strongly: "If I die today, I have seen heaven."

Since this time, Rutshuru has moved on; these days, the time spent under M23's occupation seem distant. And yet I am interested in its story for what it reveals about subject formation in a regime of death. For a brief time in 2013, a group of civilian youths in M23-occupied Rutshuru established themselves as political subjects in a region characterized by terror. While others hid or fled, when faced with the possibility of living in a long-term way under the rule of an occupying force, a group of youths waged a war of disruption. "Our whole lives have been like this. We've had enough," Trésor said. As they ignored curfews, confused patrols, and lit a military camp on fire, they demanded recognition from the soldiers. "We are the autochthons," the youth repeated. Their actions were, in many ways, small scale, individual. Their numbers were small, and, Trésor speculated, they lost more lives than they took. And yet their very presence—an unarmed group of youths brazenly challenging an army in daylight—opened the door for the beginning of something new. "Before we had died," people said. "Now, we're in Congo. Our country has come back to us." And for a while it was so.

Until now, I have used Mbembe's theory of necropolitics to describe the experience of living in a necropolitical regime, wherein political subjecthood is continuously denied, and the only clear path to agency is through self-sacrifice. For many who live in this nocturnal world, death is experienced as "a release from terror and bondage."[38] But this refusal of the present conditions of living which leads through death is only one aspect of Mbembe's theorization of necropolitics. There is another critical aspect of necropolitical sovereignty, which extends beyond dying to taking life with you as you go. In this third and final section, I begin to think about the relationship between killing, agency, and healing in eastern Congo. The knot is wound tight, and its unraveling an ethically complex task; and a query about what killing might generate (besides death) feels essential to understanding the continuation of violence in Congo today.

Killing to Become Subject?

In the fall of 2014, a pattern of repeated brutal massacres began in the Beni region of North Kivu, 220 miles north of Goma and 180 miles north of Rutshuru. For weeks, entire villages in the area were attacked, men, women, and children slaughtered at night with machetes. Then there would be several weeks without massacres. Sometimes months would elapse, enough time that people would return to their routines, to their fields. And then the massacres would start up again. Twenty people one night, a few nights later dozens more. People in the area attributed the attacks to the group Allied Democratic Forces, the ADF, a small group that had originated in Uganda and migrated to eastern Congo during the wars of the 1990s.[39] But the true perpetrators of the attacks, as well as their motives, have remained largely opaque: over the years, the Congolese army has been implicated as have smaller local militias.[40]

For several years, I read about the attacks from afar. I knew few people in the region, and I had no real business in the area. And still I found myself seeking out information about the killings, which continued sporadically. In the years I had spent studying eastern Congo, I had heard people tell of many kinds of violence—but these massacres felt different from other narratives that I had recorded or witnessed. For starters, they were shrouded in opacity: no one really knew who was responsible for them or what their motivations were. But also, in many ways, they seemed to be oddly devoid of the usual political, economic, and ideological underpinnings that normally motivated armed groups in the region. The people killed were poor, subsistence farmers and hunters; they would have nothing theft worthy. But it wasn't either about local politics or land conflicts: the killings were spread over an entire region, involving people of different ethnicities. And, despite the fact that much changed on the national political stage, the massacres continued. What drove them then, I wondered, and how did those affected make sense of them?

Five years after the attacks started, I traveled to the region for research. The year prior, an Ebola epidemic had emerged in a rural community not far from Beni, and I had been hired to examine the effects of this epidemic on the Congolese health system there. While the ADF—or whoever was behind the violence—was still active in the area, the massacres had become more sporadic, and it was now Ebola, a viral disease with a mortality rate as high as 90 percent, that was threatening life in and around Beni—or so the situation had been portrayed.[41] In preliminary interviews, it quickly became clear that this was not the case. In response to my questions about their experience with Ebola, people stated, "It's not Ebola that is killing us, but the ADF." When asked for their opinions about how Ebola had been handled thus far, people answered with a version of, "For years, we've been killed by ADF. We are being slaughtered [*tunachinjwa*]. And now, four years later, the international community decides to intervene, when there is Ebola. Do our deaths not matter unless they are contagious, unless we risk infecting whites when we die?" Anytime I brought up the risk Ebola posed to the region, people shifted the conversation to postulate about whether the upcoming military operations would send the ADF into hiding or make things worse.

In November 2019, there was a spate of killings. These were followed by a small reprieve. At the end of January 2020, the attacks began again. During a particularly violent two-week span, there were attacks every other day. Seven killed, fourteen, once thirty-one. Pictures of dismembered bodies circulated on WhatsApp groups. When presented with these images, I found myself trying to piece bodies back together—which head fit with which hands. At some point, I began deleting the images before they loaded. But talk of the violence was everywhere: families fleeing villages when the previous night's attack was too close, demonstrations in the center of town. "Il n'y a pas de Congo sans Beni," the signs read. There is no Congo without Beni.

During a particularly intense period, I sat with a European conflict researcher with a decade of experience in the region to talk about the violence that was taking place. At first, we talked about the history of the ADF—the splinterings and rearrangements of various armed groups in the region that led to the current group assumed to be responsible for the massacres. For half an hour, he traced specific battalions and military leaders through the region over the last two decades.[42] When he reached the present, he paused. While most armed groups in eastern Congo have a long history, the ADF's story was particularly complex. But even if the *who* seemed clearer now, I still could not make sense of why these soldiers operated as they did. I asked, "Of all the ways to kill, with guns everywhere, why do they hack people apart?"[43] In discussions with inhabitants of the regions, this was a question I rarely heard posed. And still, as someone who performs amputations in the operating room, I was curious as to why this group—or those who were mimicking it—killed through such a labor-intensive process. "Do you know that the amputation of a single limb can be physically demanding?" There are many layers, I explained—first the skin, then the muscle, then the bone, and then the vessels and the nerve. Afterward, I find blood and bone flecks on my shoes or on my scrub cap. "Why are the ADF killing with a machete?" I repeated. If ethnic conflict was not undergirding the vivisection-esque killings—and it did not seem that it was this simple—then why were the perpetrators subjecting themselves to the fatigue, to the gore that such massacres require?[44]

For several minutes, my friend seemed to be pondering my question. Then he answered, with a shrug, "I guess hacking is qualitatively different than shooting."

In his book on the Lord's Resistance Army in Uganda, Sam Dubal argues that the barbaric nature of the violence that the group perpetrates has resulted in their exclusion from the category of humanity.[45] In an effort to demonstrate how problematic such an exclusion is, Dubal first historicizes and contextualizes the LRA, who, like the ADF, operate in an area deeply scarred by decades of state violence and systematic neglect. Then he goes on to illustrate the ethics by which the LRA live in the bush, which, if taken seriously, challenge liberal ideas about modernity, kinship, and morality. According to Dubal, the LRA does not default to face-to-face killing because they lack guns or ammunition or because, as they have been presented in the media, they are depraved, savages, animals. In fact, Dubal argues, the reality is quite the opposite. In line with Acholi theories of justice, the LRA strategically employs brutal tactics to intimidate those who might try to stop them and to achieve recognition. One LRA member in Dubal's research explains thus: "It's nice to kill in this way, especially those who have intentions of killing you. You have to kill for it to be heard for some time, that it becomes historic. You can kill in any way that scares people who remained, even if it's chopping them into pieces, leaving only the skin of a person, or using a bayonet."[46]

When reading Dubal's work, I am brought back to the conversation I had with my conflict researcher friend about the ADF. Unlike my Congolese interlocutors, I had become preoccupied by the brutality of the violence. I had pictured the ADF washing bone fragments out of their hair, and I had wondered what made them kill in this particularly proximate way. I had thought that my experience as a surgeon, as someone who conducts amputations in my daily life, generated this question. In reality, however, it was my distance from a life of negation that rendered the ADF's violence particularly baffling to me. The Congolese who lived in and around Beni intimately understood the burning quest for recognition, the urgent desire to be seen and heard. Occasionally, they compared the ADF to the Congolese national army who often said explicitly, "We pick up arms to have a voice." And so the population did not wonder about the technicalities of how they were killed; they were not preoccupied with who was killing them or why. In many ways, these questions were all answerable. Instead, the questions that people returned to again and again were why Congolese continued to "die like insects [*kama vidudu*]," why their deaths were met with continued indifference by the Congolese government and the international community, why the international community had sent incredible resources into Congo to manage the Ebola epidemic when the disease would kill nowhere near as many people as violence would. For many in the Beni area, given the context, the turn toward killing seemed to make sense; the acceptance of continued Congolese dying, as if early and violent death of Black/African people were natural, did not.

In the past three decades, conflict researchers, journalists, and legal experts have written much about Congo. Interviews and statistics are quoted, rumors are analyzed, a plausible cast of actors and course of events is presented. Regardless of the subject matter, a common assumption runs through much of this work—that, if only the truth were told, if the curtain might be pulled back, that the violence might stop, justice could be served. Surely, among those living in eastern Congo, calls for justice and for peace are loud. And where so many have for so long been excluded from modernity, humanity, the common good, people are desperate to be seen, to be heard, to have a say in the direction of their life and in the timing of their death. Some trek along what Mbembe calls the "solar body," wherein recognition is conferred by the courts of law, through the democratic process.[47] But, for many, the antiblackness is too thick, and the "nocturnal" route— dying, taunting death, and killing—is the sole path available to being heard, to becoming subject. Those on this route—the ADF and their many counterparts—act without knowing what may come, without knowing whether they are ushering in more destruction or life otherwise.

Violence, like dying, in eastern Congo is devastating. It is also generative, a motivating force that has the capacity to bring into being a new kind of existence. By killing, even brutally so, less than an arm's length away, looking people in their eyes as they hack, armed actors achieve a recognition, a subjecthood that they are otherwise denied. As the killer becomes subject, he interrupts, if briefly, the regime that has otherwise confined him to nothingness.[48] Where subjecthood has been elusive for decades, a turn toward violence might open the door to a present otherwise.

Refusal, Recognition, Healing

There are many dangers to thinking of dying and violence as healing; drawing from the lessons of the Holocaust, Hannah Arendt articulates these.[49] At the same time, where violence has been, and continues to be, so deep and so chronic, all possible routes to healing must be considered. In this chapter, I have taken seriously Mbembe's statement that, in the necropolitical present, war has become both remedy and poison, and I have examined whether violence might force open the door to reimagining Black presents and futures. After telling stories of dying and killing in eastern Congo, I have asked whether violence might create entirely new possibilities of being, of being together, of being in common.[50] I stand with Congolese who decry local, national, and international inaction despite recurring, brutal massacres. And I am interested in the new worlds created when Congolese receive recognition as political actors, when their "no," "that's enough," is heard in harmony across the globe. Might refusal beget recognition and recognition beget an emphasis on tomorrow, on durable healing?

FIGURE 4.2. Peace monument near Rutshuru, 2013. I took this picture, of a monument in Rutshuru that reads *peace* in Kinyarwanda, during the M23 occupation. At the time, it seemed like a cruel joke—that there would be a monument to peace in an occupied territory. The occupation ended, as people knew it would; and then M23 returned to North Kivu. And still, this monument continues to declare—propose? command?—what could be. Photograph by author.

Bullets in Congo cost $15 a piece.[1] And soldiers and their families are one of Congo's most vulnerable populations.[2] Learning these two facts has dramatically changed my interpretation of the pictures of armed men grinning while wearing strings of bullets like necklaces. After they pose for the flak-jacketed journalists, I have heard them tell of returning to camp and trading bullets for food. Perhaps they grin because their acquisition of the bullet necklaces means that they will eat on that day. Or perhaps this victory has felt especially satisfying. The soldiers with whom I have spoken cannot pin down when exactly war buoys their spirits—but they are clear that the work of war has many good moments too, and they sometimes speak of joy.

In an essay called "Joy," Zadie Smith works to differentiate between pleasure and joy. After describing such pleasures as eating a good sandwich or anthropomorphizing a dog, she hypothesizes that children might be an example of the "human madness" we call joy. She offers, "Occasionally the child, too, is a pleasure, though mostly she is a joy, which means in fact she gives us not much pleasure at all, but rather that strange admixture of terror, pain, and delight that I have come to recognize as joy, and now must find some way to live with daily."[3]

There was, perhaps, a joy-filled phone theft on January 12, 2013. As he handed over his phone, the boy reportedly laughed at the men who pointed an AK-47 in his face. When the boy retold the story and I asked why he had laughed—wasn't he scared of these men who threatened his life?—he simply laughed again. Hearing his laughter, and imagining it as a response to the soldiers' gruff and threatening demand, brought all of those to whom he told the story to tears. He never could explain why he laughed, but it seemed he didn't need to: like Smith, those around him also understood the strange ways that terror, pain, and delight can combine to produce joy.

Congo has always been a dark spot in the (white) imaginary, a site for continued devastation, war. This is not a Congo that I recognize. Surely, there is a heaviness that clings to many stories in this book; and I have always been pushed by my Congolese interlocutors to wonder if another reading of the place might be possible, which sutures a devastating past with an otherwise. Even as the violence repeats in eastern Congo, there is a pleasure of discovering traces between past and future, a lust for nostalgic reminders of what was, and an excitement for wild imaginings of what could be.[4] How to archive these pleasures, these desires? If an archive can transmit sound, even the uncanny affect of repetitive violence, as Hunt has argued, can an archive also hold the feeling that reappropriating remains, recycling them, transforming them into something beautiful elicits in Congo?[5] Can an archive hold the delight that comes with knowing that another world is possible, or the joy that bubbles forth when a brilliant otherwise is spoken into existence?

"We Are Creating a World We Have Never Seen"

there is prayer in poem.
—Nayyirah Waheed, *Nejma*

won't you celebrate with me
what I have shaped into
a kind of life? I had no model.
born in Babylon
both nonwhite and woman
what did I see to be except myself?
i made it up
here on this bridge between starshine and clay,
my one hand holding tight
my other hand; come celebrate
with me that everyday
something has tried to kill me
and has failed.
—Lucille Clifton, *The Book of Light*

FIGURE 5.1. *Wakanda* by Justin Kasereka. This was one of many incredible Afrofuturist-oriented paintings displayed in Kasereka's exhibit at l'Alliance Française in Goma in fall 2019. Interspersed with drawings like these, of characters who could have starred in a Marvel movie, were drawings of Lumumba and Mobutu, Congolese leaders and radical thinkers who embodied a future orientation in a different way. Photograph by author.

It's 5:30 on Friday evening. The large converted attic above l'Alliance Française is abuzz with energy. The crowd is young, vibrant, trendsetting with their creative haircuts and bold outfits. A collection of local artist Justin Kasereka's pieces was hung up last week. People are now circulating through intricate black-and-white sketches of previous liberation leaders and stunning, bright portraits of fierce warriors engaged in futuristic fights. "It's Wakanda," a young woman perusing the art says aloud, referencing the fictional home of the superhero Black Panther. Since the Marvel film came out several years ago, there has been a running conversation in Congo about how the Panther's creators must have based the utopian country on Congo. Surely Congo's coltan is Wakanda's vibranium, and Congo's peasants, Wakanda's Border Tribe. Tonight, this Afrofuturist vision seems especially compelling.

We have assembled for a poetry slam, which happens monthly now in Goma. Over the course of two hours, young men and women will get up in front of the crowd and recite, rap, or sing the pieces that they have worked on for the past month. The jokes will be rewarded with raucous laughter. Silence or tears will accompany the more somber pieces. Regardless of what emotions capture the room during the performances, enthusiastic applause always follows. Even when the slammers speak in the first person, this crowd makes it clear that the artist is but the medium for their message, that the experiences that are spoken are shared, uniting, and vital.

There has always been a thriving art community in Goma, even when the war felt most proximate. Talented dancers, comedians, and musicians who now have international followings have had their start at Yole Center in Goma. The Amani Festival, Swahili for *peace*, which has been held yearly in Goma since 2014, attracts artists and spectators from across the region. Tonight's stars, poetry *slammeurs*, are a relatively new addition to the scene. I first heard about their emergence from a friend of a friend who made a short documentary film about the club. After being introduced to one of the club's founders, I began corresponding with several of the club's most active members. One of the women, who played a key role in the documentary, sends me a new slam every few months. She has a soft voice and cutting lyrics and talks about slamming as a way that she gives voice to her pain and her dreams. Tonight, she gets onstage and begins, "My name is Rita Zaburi, and this slam is called 'I Am'":

Je suis une page remplie de métaphores
Même sous silence mon slam crie haut et fort

Dans un Monde des sourds c'est lourd
Le poids que porte la femme marginalisée
Qui finit par la paralysée
Je suis une voix qui vient tamiser ses misères . . .

I am a page full of metaphors
Even in silence my slam shouts loud and strong
In a world of the deaf it is heavy
The weight that the marginalized woman carries
That ends up paralyzing her
I am a voice that comes to sift her miseries . . .

Rita continues like this for several minutes. She blasts school for import-
ing "ideas of white colonizers" and decries those who think of women as a
machine of production. She is direct, she spits fire, and she receives a standing ovation. After the slam session, I get in line to congratulate Rita on a
job well done. We continue our correspondence, and several months later,
I receive a fundraising WhatsApp that announces her plan, together with
other *slammeurs*, to travel to an international slam competition. The message reads, "We are Goma Slam Session. For three years we have been doing
societal therapy [*une thérapie sociétale*] through words. For three years our
word has become the word of a whole people."

Throughout this book, I have explored different ways that Congolese remake the worlds that recurrent violence has ripped apart, returning to their
wounds and forging new paths out of the rubble. In this chapter, I follow
these paths through dreamworlds and future imaginings. Even as the global
regime of antiblackness has been so crushing, Congolese articulate wild
visions of lives beyond war, hunger, and marginalization. Much has been
written about the future worlding that Congolese *sapeurs* and musicians
accomplish.[1] But visions of what could be occupy other registers too—and
necessarily must. As Audre Lorde asserts, amid the prohibitions imposed by
dense antiblackness, poetic epistemology opens to ways of seeing, speaking,
being, creating otherwise. Lorde writes,

> When we view living, in the European mode, only as a problem to be
> solved, we then rely solely upon our ideas to make us free, for these
> were what the white fathers told us were precious.
>
> But as we become more in touch with our own ancient, black,
> non-European view of living as a situation to be experienced and in-
> teracted with, we learn more and more to cherish our feelings, and to

respect those hidden sources of our power from where true knowledge and therefore lasting action comes. . . .

For women, then, poetry is not a luxury. It is a vital necessity of our existence. It forms the quality of the light within which we predicate our hopes and dreams toward survival and change, first made into language, then into idea, then into more tangible action.[2]

For Lorde, it is not just that the poetic register has the capacity to contain certain forms of (Black) knowledge—feelings, hopes, dreams, fears; it is also that because the poetic gives home to the earliest subjunctive utterances, wild imaginations of what could be, it also serves as a medium for transformation— "where true knowledge and therefore lasting action comes." For those living in the wake, where talk of violence and death dominates, the poetic register embraces visions of life otherwise. It accepts the what-ifs, the perhaps-it-could-be-like-this, the not-yet-not-ever-linear ideas. And it encourages speech as a performative act, wherein what were once distant, indeterminate thoughts are spoken into existence. In the words of Black poet and visionary fiction writer adrienne maree brown, "we are creating a world we have never seen."[3] For Rita, this is healing. As it gives voice to the collective subjunctive, slam does "vital societal therapy," "become[s] the word of a whole people."

Where the previous chapters have examined repair work aimed at healing past wrongs and asserting the necessity of presents otherwise, this chapter queries the performative power of speech acts in the creation of a new world.[4] I begin by telling the story of the Congolese space program. Poetic in the broadest sense, this is a story of play and imagination that fundamentally challenges our notions of the present-futurity of Black worlds.[5] I then move to query the intersection of performance and prophecy as it relates to Congolese self-determination. Congolese freedom fighter Patrice Lumumba is part of this story; so, too, are the youths who summon him into being. Finally, I move inward, to the dreamworlds of interpersonal intimacy.[6] I examine a vision that does not die despite every indication that it should; then, with recourse to queer writings on love, I question what this kind of attachment does to our understandings of the possible and impossible in Congo. In the conclusion, I return to the healing power of articulations of Black/Congolese survival. As I move through this exploration of the poetic register in Congo, I frame the narratives with excerpts from the manifesto of a prominent social justice group, LUCHA, or Lutte pour le changement (Struggle for Change).[7] For it was LUCHA that first taught me about creating worlds that have never been seen.

LUCHA is a political movement that was formed in 2012 when a group of vocal Congolese youth came together to organize protests against state violence in Congo. LUCHA's initial efforts focused on calling attention to areas of state neglect—roads, water, education. However, over the years, it has developed a reputation for denouncing all forms of state violence, oppression, and neglect, whether perpetrated by the Congolese state or other entities that have power in Congo. While high-level government officials have called it "tomorrow's terrorists," LUCHA is militantly nonviolent. Neither a political party nor a civil society organization, LUCHA issues policy statements, distributes tracts, organizes marches, and holds peaceful sit-ins. With these tactics, it has waged successful advocacy campaigns against the targeted killing of opposition leaders, persistent massacres, fraudulent humanitarian projects, ineffective military action, and criminal corporate deals that characterize political life in Congo. Between 2015 and 2017, LUCHA activists played key roles in the protests denouncing the growing autocratic tendencies of the Kabila regime. Eventually, their advocacy led to national elections in December 2018, two years after they were constitutionally mandated.[8]

In 2012, as I was finishing a year of fieldwork in Kishabe, one of my friends began speaking LUCHA into existence. Within a few years, LUCHA was a household name across the country. As LUCHA has gained popular backing, the national government has sought to thwart its efforts. In 2015, prominent LUCHA activists were beaten and jailed by the national government. Since then, there have been other arrests of LUCHA members and at least one death.[9] Under threats of violence, my friend, the LUCHA cofounder, left the country. And still the group continues to envision a different Congo— and to demand the necessary changes to make this possibility a reality. I once expressed my doubts about the potential for a different Congo to another friend in LUCHA leadership. He replied, "Even if neither me nor my children will see Congolese freedom, the next generation might. For nonviolence to work, the population must rise—and that will take time." He paused briefly before concluding confidently, "But we are the solution." S., this chapter is for you. May your words become a chorus, and may they be sung and sung until it is so.

Two Manifestos

The Congolese state is peculiar. Its components, territory, institution, and population, which would guarantee its functions and internal and international prestige, infect each other.

A territory that extends over two million three hundred and forty thousand square kilometers, but whose borders are disrupted by regional and international economic interests. The natural resources are scattered over the soil and subsoil, but are systematically plundered by multinationals and private companies in connivance with selfish Congolese politicians and thieves. Existing public and parastatal companies limit themselves to the extraction of nonrenewable materials, and export a large part of them through organized fraud. The exaggerated bureaucracy combined with various forms of corruption complicates and blocks the creativity of young entrepreneurs, deters potential serious investors and promotes tax evasion and fraud, causing the state to lose huge sums of money to the few "state agents." Thus, more and more employees of management in state enterprises or ministries are richer than the institutions they run. Agriculture and livestock farming, which could be the [country's] economic pillars, are sectors that suffer from widespread insecurity, poor infrastructure and lack of adequate support. . . .

We are the children of war, but we dream and fight for peace.

—LUCHA, *Manifeste du Congo Nouveau* (Manifesto of the New Congo)

Since the 1970s, the Congolese government has been interested and invested in getting to space. With the goal of launching telecommunication satellites, then-president Mobutu signed a twenty-five-year lease on a plot of land the size of Indiana that was supposed serve as "the private Cape Canaveral of Africa." One rocket was launched before the president, under pressure from the Soviet Union, cut ties with its West German astronautics partner. Then the Zairean state collapsed, and the country became the battleground for two regional wars, effectively putting any Congolese space travel on hold for decades.

In 2005, when Jean-Patrice Keka gathered several of the country's best engineers in the western capital and started the Congolese space program anew, the east of the country was still embroiled in active conflict. Thus the program got very little attention until the launch of Troposphere IV two years later. Troposphere IV, which flew nine miles into the atmosphere and reached Mach 2.7, was hailed as a success. While it had not technically made it to space, defined as fifty miles above the Earth's surface, it had demonstrated that the launch of a rocket made from milk tins and other discarded objects was possible. Additionally, Troposphere IV paved the way for Troposphere V, a two-stage rocket designed to reach twenty-two miles into the atmosphere and to carry the first Congolese being, a rat, into space. On March 28, 2008, Troposphere V was launched to great fanfare; however, it crashed soon after launch, and the rat on board was named the first life lost in the quest for Congolese space travel.[10]

When Troposphere V plunged to the ground, the Congolese space program seemed doomed, having lost much of the momentum and funds that

it had acquired since 2005; however, on May 31, 2018, the space program re-
leased a video on YouTube that attested to the continuation of the space program, dubbed "une aventure extraordinaire," an extraordinary adventure.[11]
The video opens with the successful launch of Troposphere IV and the celebrations that followed. Then the screen cuts to Keka introducing "ce projet
fou," this crazy project, that is the Congolese space program. Footage from
the failed Troposphere V launch is shown before the space program's team
members begin to make a case for the necessity of continuing the project.
Nestor Wembo, chief engineer, speaks about the fact that all space programs
necessarily have many failures. He asserts, "Beaucoup de gens ne voient que
ce qui ne marche pas." Many people only see that which does not work. Another voice continues, "Vous pouvez penser que la République democratique
du Congo a besoin de bien d'autres choses que un programme spatial." You
could think that Congo needs many other things than a space program.
Then a female physician involved in the space program fills the screen and
argues, "Mais nous avons aussi besoin de nous projeter dans l'avenir. Mon-
trer au gens de notre pays qu'il est possible de rêver à de grandes choses."
But we also need to project ourselves into the future. Show the people of our
country that it is possible to dream of big things. The expressed goal for
the video is fundraising for the space project; and yet the possibility that it
proposes—that a rocket constructed of repurposed electric boards and discarded plastic might launch a satellite into orbit that will send pictures back
to the control center in Congo, subsequently expanding notions of possibility for the Congolese population—is radical.

As of this writing, four years have passed since the release of the video,
and Troposphere VI has yet to launch. Given back-to-back Ebola epidemics, and the concurrent measles epidemic and COVID-19 pandemic, it is
possible that attention, and funds, have been diverted elsewhere. And yet
the fact that there ever existed, if briefly, a Congolese space program is itself
a fact worth contemplating. I am deeply interested in this fact—that, as war
continued, as homes were destroyed, bodies were mutilated, lives were cut
short on one side of the country, a rocket was launched into the atmosphere
from the other.

Surely, one possible reaction to this act is dismissal. As the voice in the
video asserts, "Vous pouvez penser que la République democratique du
Congo a besoin de bien d'autres choses que un programme spatial." You
could think that Congo needs many other things than a space program.
What superfluousness, what egotism, what waste. And yet I wonder if there
might be a different reading: if instead, the existence of a space program in

a country with extremely limited resources to devote to wildly creative projects might be read otherwise.

Prior to Mobutu's gestures toward space, the Zambian government made their own. In an article examining the Zambian space program, historian Namwali Serpell describes the training that the Zambian Afronauts undertook: rolling down hills in fifty-gallon drums, swinging on rope swings.[12] She discusses the way that the leader of the program, Edward Mukuka Nkoloso, was ridiculed in Western media. She reprints a headline from the time that read, "Zambia warns Russia, US: We'll beat you to the moon." She then discusses the approach *San Francisco Chronicle* columnist Arthur Hoppe took in his 1964 series on the topic. Framing the Zambian space program as a satire of the Americans' multibillion-dollar space race against the Russians, Hoppe interprets its claims about upcoming space travel as playful, jockeying. Serpell then points to a 1964 op-ed written by Nkoloso in which he seems to use the space program to parody British colonialism. She quotes,

> "We have been studying the planet through telescopes at our headquarters and are now certain Mars is populated by primitive natives," he wrote. "Our rocket crew is ready. Specially trained spacegirl Matha Mwamba, two cats (also specially trained) and a missionary will be launched in our first rocket. But I have warned the missionary he must not force Christianity on the people if they do not want it." Nkoloso accuses American and Russian operators of trying to steal his space secrets: "Detention without trial for all spies is what we need."[13]

Given such a clear gesture to the absurd, Serpell asks, why have so few others imagined that the Zambian space program might have been created in jest?[14]

I make reference to Serpell's work on the Zambian space program not (necessarily) to argue that the Congolese space program has also been created as a parody. This may or may not be the case. But what is clear from reading Serpell's analysis of the Zambian space program is that there is much to gain from truly listening to—and learning from—those who advance visions that appear radically different than those we are currently living. Jean-Patrice Keka's claim that a rocket made of Nido cans will successfully travel fifty miles from earth is wild. And yet, I ask, what might we learn if we became curious about such a claim?

It is an audacious and emboldened notion that Congolese might be protagonists in the creation of a collective future. It is radical to think Blackness as infinite, fungible, fluid, pluripotential, spectacular, and ever evolving. And yet this is what the creation of the Congolese space program encourages. Steeped in Afrofuturist tradition, Keka and his colleagues assert that other futures are possible in Congo, something other than survival, something other than pain.[15] What might it change if we followed those who imagined Blackness otherwise and remained open to whatever new paths might emerge?

"The Future of Congo is Splendid"

The great richness of Congo, which gives it its height, is its population. A courageous people. A population happy with its diversity, speaking more than 400 languages and thousands of dialects, each with a culture rich in history and life. A people that has survived with dignity the crimes of the slave trade, colonization, dictatorship, and still struggles today against a disfigured democracy. A resilient people that, after each ordeal, straightens its spine and moves forward without having to look like its oppressors. A people that hopes. But, in order to survive the institutions that crush it, reinvents itself every day.

—LUCHA, *Manifeste du Congo Nouveau*

On June 30, 1960, Congo became an independent nation, and Patrice Lumumba, a vocal leader in the independence movement, was named the first prime minister. A self-proclaimed anti-imperialist, Lumumba quickly found himself at odds with the West as he worked to create a self-governed country, independent from Western influence. In speeches, he voiced commitment to Congolese unity, national control over Congolese mineral wealth, and Pan-African solidarity. But given its vested economic and political interests in the region, the West was fearful of Lumumba's rigorous cultivation of independence.

For years, Belgian colonists had manipulated class and ethnic divisions to retain power. After independence, motivated by Cold War politics and the fear that Congo might become a communist nation, Western powers continued to exploit these tensions so as to ensure their continued presence in the region. Within a month of Congo's independence celebrations, the national army mutinied, and the largest southern province had announced its secession. While Lumumba was still very wary of foreign influence, he also felt backed into a corner. Eventually, he declared a national state of emergency and asked the UN for military intervention. He felt strongly that "la main qui donne est la main qui dirige" (the hand that gives is the hand that directs) and yet, given the army's mutiny, he saw no other way to reunite the country.[16]

It has been reported that Lumumba's decision to invite UN troops to Congo in the weeks following the country's independence was what put him at odds with Joseph Kasa-Vubu, the Belgium-appointed president. Perhaps there were other clashes, too. After all, Kasa-Vubu believed in a more gradual phase-out of the colonial regime, and Lumumba was working to start anew. And yet it was international interference, rather than political ideology, that caused their ultimate rift. In early September 1960, Kasa-Vubu, under pressure from the United States and Belgium to rid the country of a so-called communist threat, dismissed Lumumba from power. Several days later, the Congolese army arrested and imprisoned him. From prison, Lumumba wrote a letter to his family, which is quoted frequently in present-day Congo around independence celebrations. It reads: "To my sons, whom I am leaving and whom, perhaps, I shall not see again, I want to say that the future of the Congo is splendid and that I expect from them, as from every Congolese, the fulfilment of the sacred task of restoring our independence and our sovereignty."[17]

On January 17, 1961, Lumumba was assassinated by a Congolese firing squad with Belgian and CIA assistance. Initially, his body was buried, only to be exhumed several days later by Belgian police commissioners Gerard Soete and Frans Verschure. With the intention of preventing a "martyr's" grave, these officers dismembered Lumumba's body and dissolved the remaining pieces in sulfuric acid.[18] Almost forty years later, in a macabre and almost celebratory reminiscence of this act, Soete claimed to have kept for himself two of Lumumba's teeth.[19] Despite decades of calls for their return, Lumumba's two teeth were finally repatriated to Congolese soil in 2022; however, many Congolese believe more remains remain at large.

For Congolese, the fact that Lumumba's remains remained at large for so many years—and might still—is symbolic of the fact that Congolese generally lack sovereignty over their own soil. Sixty years have passed since independence, and still it is the international community—in the form of UN troops, mining corporations, humanitarian organizations, and neighboring countries that continue to instigate conflict in the region—not the Congolese government or the Congolese people that dictates much of what happens on Congolese soil.[20]

Importantly, however, for some Congolese, the fact that Lumumba's body remained(/remains) outside Congo holds another meaning too. Some speculate that if Congolese soil is not the ultimate resting place for the country's greatest freedom fighter, then Lumumba must still be present in some way. For Lumumba was so fierce, and so committed to the country, that his ghost will haunt until his full remains are returned. Besides, with the country in such shambles, he surely still has work to do. People speculate: perhaps it is

Lumumba's spirit that helped free the country from Mobutu, the crony of Western imperialism; or perhaps it was Lumumba who led the Congolese army to victory against M23 in 2012.

****

In Goma, a young man walks down the street with a slicked-over side part, formally called the Lumumba, and a pair of black-and-wire-rimmed Ray-Bans like those that Lumumba shared with Malcolm X. I ask the youth why he is, today, paying homage to the Congolese freedom fighter. It is not Independence Day; neither is it the anniversary of Lumumba's birth nor that of his death. The young man replies with a smile and a shrug, says he just wants to *kupendeza*—to look good.

I am left standing on the street wondering whether I have just seen a version of Patrice Lumumba. In coifing oneself as a Lumumba, does one summon his spirit to descend?

Achille Mbembe has written about postcolonial subjects' mimicry of the domineering autocrat; however, instead of engaging mimicry to make light of the crushing weight of power, these youth in Goma seem to have the goal of channeling, becoming a medium for Lumumba.[21] Lumumba was a radical thinker, a visionary. The Congo of his dreams has never come to be. And yet, this youth, and so many others, continue to wear his haircut, his glasses. I wonder if, by making oneself into Lumumba's image, one embodies the possibility of which Lumumba spoke. When one wears the Lumumba and then looks into the mirror, does one see not oneself, but the man who insisted that the future of Congo is splendid? Perhaps it is in becoming Lumumba that one fulfills "the sacred task of restoring [Congo's] independence and [Congo's] sovereignty."

In an article titled "Prophecy in the Present Tense," Alexis Pauline Gumbs queries the discursive relationship between (Black) dreaming and (Black) freedom. Martin Luther King Jr. proclaimed, "I have a dream," but there were many dreamers prior to this, and many since. Harriet Tubman was one such dreamer. It seems that Tubman began dreaming after a head injury that she sustained at the hands of her enslaver. One day, before she began working to free the enslaved, she was reported to have woken up triumphantly after a dream and "to have repeated all day with gratitude and wonder a prophecy in the present tense: 'My people are free!'"[22] A year later, she led the Combahee River Raid, the first US military victory organized and led by a woman, which freed eight hundred enslaved people. For Gumbs, Tubman's story demonstrates the transformative potential of dreaming, of envisioning a different future.[23]

Harriet Tubman said, "My people are free," before making it so. Lumumba asserted, "The future of the Congo is splendid," before his assassination. Sixty years later, Lumumba's body remains at large, and his likenesses are everyday sightings on the streets of Goma. Perhaps these Congolese youths summon him; perhaps they embody his spirit. Whatever the exact mechanism, they evoke memories of the man who dreamed of a free and splendid future for Congo as they amble about town in his image. If there is, indeed, a discursive relationship between (Black) dreaming and (Black) freedom, as Gumbs argues, re-membering this freedom fighter and his dreams seems to have transformative potential.

"The solution will come from the people"

The solution will come from the people.

Certainly, the problem of Congo is complex and often seems absurd for its multiple mutations. But there is an effective way out: the commitment of the people. A people that imposes a new political, economic, cultural system. A people that imposes revolution, the final struggle.

This revolution will come through the rejection of this daily life that we currently have. The choice to fight for something other than survival. The mobilization of the people for the establishment of another, more legitimate and more accountable system. . . . We are the only ones who can liberate our country, liberating ourselves.

—LUCHA, *Manifeste du Congo Nouveau*

We had finished eating, and I asked to see a picture of her husband. For all of the conversations Debora and I had had about him over nearly a decade of friendship, I had no idea what this man, who had left so long ago, looked like. Debora smiled, reached under the heavy tablecloth that covered the coffee table, and pulled out a photo album. As I flipped through the photos, Debora narrated.

First, there was an album of weddings, graduations, and New Year's celebrations. Ones that she attended, ones that she was a part of; the events that marked time in her and her family's lives. "Is that him?" I asked as I tried to find her husband in every picture. Debora shook her head again and again. "No, that's my brother," she said. "No, that was a neighbor." "No, that was after he was gone."

When one photo album was finished, Debora pulled out a large stack of loose pictures and handed them to me. As I flipped, the colorful matte prints gradually gave way to older, shinier photographs. There were several pictures of her siblings from their childhood. Their giddiness made Debora smile. We lingered for a while as Debora explained a game she and her siblings played in one of the pictures. Then I flipped again. Debora drew in a sharp breath and pulled the photo from my hand. "That's him!" she said excitedly. Now, with satisfaction: "That's my husband." The picture she held was a faded image of a younger man holding hands with a young boy. Debora held the picture for a moment before returning it to my hand. "That's Anthony [her firstborn son]. He must have been two or three." I flipped the page. "And that's another of him," Debora said. A short man in military fatigues was sitting at a round table surrounded by several other men. Holding a beer in the air as if to make a toast, he looked directly at the camera.

"He was handsome," I said before correcting myself: "he is handsome."

I met Debora in Goma in 2010. At the time, she was thirty-three, a single mother to two teenage boys. She lived in a compound with her mother and several other family members and worked as domestic help in a guesthouse that catered to expatriates. She laughed heartily and made the best cassava leaves and tomato sauce in town. And she harbored an ambivalent love for a man who had left her years ago, a man that she sometimes referred to as her husband in the present tense and sometimes referred to as having passed long ago.

Debora can still remember the day they met: she had been a teenager, sent to the lake by her family with a jug to bring water home for the family's cooking; he had been sitting on a rock on the lakeshore watching the foot traffic come and go. He had whistled at her; she had walked over to where he sat; he had said that she was beautiful and that he would like to see her again. The next day, he had stopped by her family's house and asked permission to talk to her. That day they had spoken giddily behind her family's house. But things were not good at home. After Debora's father had died, her mother had begun selling beer at the house. Like the rest of her siblings, Debora served men beer when she got home from school. At first, it had been all right, but as her body began developing, she had started to attract the wrong kind of attention. "Men's wives had started coming by the house saying that I was sleeping with their husbands. I needed out," Debora reminisced. Several weeks after she and Moïse started speaking, Debora made up her mind. One day after he visited, Debora accompanied him out of the family's compound, and then she kept going. "And that was it," Debora says. "Once you leave your father's house, you can't go back, not even to get your things." So she stayed, and soon she was pregnant. Debora was seventeen.

Debora and Moïse never got married. He was a soldier and didn't have the money. "But we loved each other," Debora says. He left Goma soon after

Debora got pregnant. Wherever he went, there were always other women. When she was seven months pregnant, another woman dropped an infant off at the house—the woman claimed that Moïse had gotten her pregnant and demanded that he take financial responsibility for the child. Debora's family got involved; they took responsibility for the child so as to clear Moïse's name. However, several months later, when Debora's firstborn was several months old, Moïse called to tell her that he had taken a second wife. And still, despite his repeated infidelity, Debora's affection for her husband was unwavering. When he was sick, she brought him food; when he was thrown in jail far from where she was living, Debora got on a bus with her infant child and moved closer to him.

In 1996, large-scale fighting began, and much of the population was displaced.[24] Debora and her family left their home in Goma and stayed with extended family in the hills for a week. Several hundred miles away, her husband was captured by the invading force. So as to save his life, he defected from Mobutu's army to the ranks of the invading army. Then, when his battalion marched west to take the capital, he remained behind to guard over the territory they had gained in the east. For a year, Debora, Moïse, and their firstborn child lived together in South Kivu. Life was easy: the soldiers were being paid well, and there wasn't any war.

However, within a year, the leader of the invading troops, who had overthrown Mobutu and become president, had been assassinated, and another armed group entered the east of the country.[25] Fearful of being captured by this round of invading troops, Moïse ran again. Pregnant and with a toddler on her back, Debora stayed behind in South Kivu. Eventually, when it became clear that her husband was not coming back for her, she got on a bus and returned to her mother's house in Goma. With no job and no access to land to farm, she needed help to feed her child.

In the months directly following the start of the Second Congo War, Moïse called Debora often on the phone. First he was running from war in Congo; then he was in Zambia working as a mercenary. Then she received a letter from UNHCR, informing her that Moïse was in a refugee camp in Tanzania. But, with time, his phone stopping working. Six years passed in silence; Debora feared the worst. Then, in early 2006, a couple came by her family's house bearing news: Moïse was living in Mozambique. In the intervening years, he had married and had had several children with another woman, but he had befriended the couple and had given them his phone number to give to Debora when they got to Goma. Soon after the couple left her family's house, Debora dialed the number. For nine months, she and Moïse spoke nearly every day. Despite the distance and his other family, they planned a new future together. Then one day in October, his phone was disconnected. That was in October 2006. Debora had not heard from Moïse since.[26]

This is the story that Debora told me as we flipped through photos one evening after dinner. Prior to this evening, information about him had only come in wisps: once she talked about how her eldest son had written a new request to the refugee camp to see if they had any new information. "Bwana yangu," she had called this man who had long since disappeared. My husband. Despite the amount of time that had lapsed since she had seen or spoken with him, she usually referred to him in the present tense. Debora was confident, sometimes even expectant. "He is alive," she insisted. "Once the war ends, he will come back, and we will restart a life together."

And yet, even as she asserted the possibility of her husband's eventual return, she also held onto other eventualities. Occasionally, a flicker of frustration was discernible in her speech. Instead of calling him her husband, she referred to him as "baba ya watoto"—the father of the children. "He has two children in Congo," she steamed. "Why doesn't he care about those too?" On the day that we were looking at pictures, Debora spoke of the possibility that her husband might be dead. I had asked Debora what she would do if her husband called. She had replied simply, "Which husband?," half a question and half a statement. She continued, "I'm like a widow whose husband will not die."

In Debora's narrative, the spread of large-scale conflict in the 1996 war forced her and her husband apart, rendering their relationship, like Debora's life more generally, uncertain. Fighting, as he was, on the wrong side of the conflict, her husband had no choice but to flee. And, because war had persisted in eastern Congo over the past two decades, he had been forced to maintain the separation. And yet, even though she and her husband had not spoken for almost a decade, Debora held onto a future with her husband. Importantly, this future had three possible orientations: perhaps her husband would return to Congo, and the two lovers would once again be reunited; perhaps they would remain forever separated, with him staying with his new family in Mozambique and Debora continuing to raise their children on her own in Goma; and perhaps she would become a widow and would mourn his death. The prospects seemed impossibly orthogonal; however, Debora did not attempt resolution. She never allowed herself to fully believe or completely discard any one of the possibilities. Instead, she embraced all three concurrently, ambivalently.

For Debora, as for many in eastern Congo, living amid recurrent violence created ambivalence. The depth of her loss made her wish sometimes that she could forget this man whom she loved with her whole being. On these days, she spoke of him as the children's father and of herself as a widow. Her husband was dead, she insisted. However, on other days, she reminisced about Moïse, how good a husband he had been. Regardless of the hurt he had caused when they were together or the time that had elapsed since they had last spoken, she found herself attached to the husband that she had lost in the early years of fighting. For, as she fought every day to feed and clothe her children, as she strove despite all odds to keep them safe from the violence that threatened their existence, the idea that Moïse might still be alive, might one day come back to her, kept her going. "Our love is so strong," she insisted.

In a series of articles dedicated to thinking about how affect might remake politics, Lauren Berlant outlines what she calls "a properly political concept of love."[27] Because love has the power to "open spaces for really dealing with the discomfort of the radical contingency that a genuine democracy—like any attachment—would demand," Berlant proposes that love could (re)build worlds.[28] Love pushes people to dream of otherwise. It motivates change; it creates new kinds of belonging. It is "one of the few situations where we desire to have patience for what isn't working, and affective binding that allows us to iron things out, or to be elastic, or to try a new incoherence."[29] Surely, love can be greedy and narcissistic and unethical; but, Berlant asserts, this is precisely the point—that people are willing to risk it all for love. What if love, then, as opposed to money or ethics or a sense of the good, were the irrational force that underlay our institutions, Berlant asks? What if love, rather than nation-states, was the glue that held us together, that which motivated attachment?

In my conversations with Debora, I have never gotten the sense that she thought of her love for her husband as a political act, as a force that countered the neglect and violence of the Congolese state with affective solidarity. And yet I am struck by the ways in which her radically ambivalent love, like Berlant's vision, creates belonging amid flight, fantasies of futures otherwise where war and loss otherwise dominate. While Debora's mobility is limited by war, poverty, and citizenship, her love spans multiple temporalities and geographies. Although war renders her life so uncertain, her love for her husband remains long-suffering. And still, even as it gestures toward the possibility of home in war, of permanence in a regime of consumption, Debora's love also threatens further pain: Debora asserts that she is "a widow whose husband will not die." Though it often brings her great sadness, she refuses to either forget Moïse, mourn his death, or anticipate his return. Instead, in love, she allows for the emergence, and holding together, of radically conflicting futures. In a place dominated by "warlord politics," I am curious about thinking Debora's love on a larger scale.[30] What might governance look like in Congo if Debora's greedy and sentimental love were to substitute for the currently dominant forms of attachment? What might the state become if it had "patience for what isn't working, and affective binding that allow[ed it] to iron things out, or to be elastic, or to try a new incoherence"?[31] What would be the form of an economic system built on Black aliveness—inclusive of Black desire, subjunctivity, and ambivalence—instead of Black death?[32] What might come if Black aspiration, Black yearning, were allowed to create planetary change?

An Audatious Notion

In this chapter, I have sought to collate some of the present and future worlding that is taking place in eastern Congo today. For people of African descent, it is an audacious and emboldened notion to envisage a collective future. For generations, amid trauma and oppression, the very idea of a Black future has been, at the very least, an oxymoronic phrase. But a new discourse is emerging in Congo, an epistemology of Black survival, which questions and affirms how Congolese will survive in the future, not if they will.[33] In LUCHA's manifesto, as in Rita's slam and the youth who became Lumumba, we hear Congolese insisting that other futures are possible. Following Alexis Pauline Gumbs, I have called these prophecies in the present tense. In these narratives, thriving is not relegated to the always-distant future—will Africa someday ascend to, arrive at, Western modernity, to democracy, peace, rationality, order? Rather, the future, a future defined by Black aliveness, is very near, and in Lumumba's words, it is brilliant.[34]

FIGURE 5.2. Children playing on a tank, 2013. For months after M23 took Goma, a burned-out tank sat in a field just north of Goma. Initially, the tank seemed to remind people of the death and destruction that accompanied the war—previously jovial conversations grew silent when the tank came into view. With the passage of time, however, the tank, like the war more generally, faded into the background. As it lost its association with the trauma of the war, children began to use the tank as a play structure. Photograph by author.

After finishing a long stretch of research in Beni, Kahindo and I were driving home. Several planes had gone down recently, and the roads through Virunga Park were too dangerous to take the direct route back to Goma, so we had decided to drive sixteen hours from Congo, through Uganda and Rwanda, and then back into Congo in order to get home. We had spent the first several hours catching up—on the project, on our personal lives—before the conversation turned, inevitably, to Congolese politics. An important army general had just been murdered, and we exchanged various theories we had heard about who had killed him and why. Eventually, the conversation tapered, and we both looked ahead toward the Congolese mountaintops in the distance. In the silence that separated us, Kahindo asked, "Do you ever think, where is Congo going? Perhaps, ten years from now, there will be a new government installed, one strong enough to ignore the West. Imagine, a government that put the needs of Congolese people first. So much would have to change. Can you even imagine what this would be like?"

Discussions like these about what might come in Congo were commonplace. When the conversation about Congolese politics had run its course and there was nothing else concrete to say, people proposed all kinds of possibilities for the country—maybe there would be another regional war, maybe a new leader would bring peace and paved roads, maybe the current president would finally have his fill and stop the graft, maybe there was a way to reform land tenure so that everyone could feed their families. Speculating was a pastime, and everyone was welcome to join.

***

There is a genre of writing called speculative nonfiction. It harnesses the strange, uncanny, and fantastical aspects of our lives—our daydreams, our imaginations—to develop fuller stories. So as to remain true to nonfiction, moments of speculation are highlighted as such. *Perhaps* cues the reader that the author is making a transition between factual and speculative. *It could have been* is another commonly used transition.[1]

I learned about speculative nonfiction when I began writing this book. In my dissertation, I had used three tenses—what was, what is, and what would be in eastern Congo. However, when returning to my field notes, I began to see so many *maybes* (*labda*), so much about what could be. Speculation abounded. It should be included in the book, I reasoned. But how to fit speculation in ethnography? There were several road maps: Diane Nelson's, Michael Taussig's work.[2] And still, I continued to question how I might represent the Congo that I knew while also maintaining the integrity of scholarly work; how I might balance archiving utopian speculations and their darker counterparts in a country that has always been a black hole for our imaginary. Surely, archiving is always only partial—and the ethnographic archive, which contains only that which the ethnographer records, even more so; but writing an ethnographic archive that integrated speculation felt especially fraught with questions of authorship—how to portray the worlds of shared knowledge that undergirded imaginings about what could be?[3]

***

Beginning with studies on the long-term psychological effects of the Holocaust, a field of research has arisen around the heredity of trauma. Some of it subscribes to a certain biological determinism, searching for the genetic codes that make people more susceptible to PTSD. And some is significantly more nuanced, looking at the neurobiology of the traumatic event. Prior to this research on epigenetics, the inheritance of trauma was attributed to environmental factors. So if depression, anxiety, and some psychotic states are more common among survivors of trauma as well as their offspring—whether the latter have directly experienced trauma or not—this is because hurt people hurt people. And yet the effects of the parents' traumatic experience on the child are only partially mitigated by secure attachment to a loving family.

Research on the epigenetics of trauma suggests that something deeper happens when mammals—humans and rodents alike—witness extreme violence or deprivation. The early waves of epigenetic research demonstrated the phenomenon of intergenerational inheritance, wherein a trauma that occurs exclusively to the parent can be felt by a child who has never experienced trauma.[4] Papers attested to children of Holocaust survivors who had terrible nightmares in which they are chased, persecuted, tortured, or annihilated, despite the fact that their parents had never spoken to their children about the experiences they endured in the camps. This was a remarkable discovery, but what was its mechanism? Some scientists proposed that trauma is etched into our DNA via methylation. Others argued that modifications to histones, or perhaps noncoding RNA, explain the fact that our children can recount their parents' trauma without having ever heard of the experience in question. Importantly, a second wave of papers pointed out, the transmission of trauma does not seem to be limited to the first generation. Rather, offspring two and three generations removed from the traumatic event have also been observed to inhabit posttraumatic states.[5] When reading these papers, I imagine trauma rippling out in waves of transgenerational inheritance.

In eastern Congo, even if some parents were able to protect their children from physical violence, they often could not shield them from the hunger, the running, and the too-early death that war created. Neither could they hide from their children the physical violence that they had directly endured. One mother who told me of being raped in front of her young daughter remarked, "After what they have seen, how many times they have hidden under their bed, they need to know the rest of the story. They need to know the whole history of Congo, how the Rwandans came in 1994, how war has ravaged our country." Even when parents tried to shield their children from the effects of war, pain was transmitted. For, as Sharika Thiranagama argues in the Sri Lankan context, loss can also be sensed, "through living with the desires, secrets, and silences of a previous generation's experience of those events."[6] Even when children did not know the details of the destruction that their parents had experienced, they knew generally that war had ruined bodies, identities, families, and land. And this awareness, of a history of traumatic events that had so deeply transformed the country and its inhabitants, shaped them.

But when did this knowing begin? asked a group of researchers in July 2010. Could a mother's historical trauma be detected in neonates shortly after birth, and did this have physical ramifications? With the goal of elucidating the mechanism of intergenerational inheritance, the researchers designed a study that compared the blood of women in labor in eastern Congo with the cord blood of their newly delivered infant—and looked for associations between mothers' self-reports of trauma, mothers' and babies' genetic code, and babies' birth weights.[7] Given how common traumatic experience was in eastern Congo, the study design seemed promising. And, indeed, the researchers found a statistically significant correlation between mothers' testimonies of "war stress" and methylation of their newborns' DNA at a particular genetic focus, which they call NR3C1. Because the NR3C1 locus is implicated in babies' response to stressors, the authors suggest that methylation at this locus "may constrain plasticity in expression at stress-related genes in later life and thus restrict the range of stress adaptation responses possible in the affected individuals." Perhaps, the authors propose, NR3C1 is involved in the epigenetic transmission of trauma.

Given that we don't yet know what methylation of the NR3C1 focus actually means, given that the study began and ended at birth rather than following the babies through to adulthood, I wonder whether another interpretation of this data is possible. Rather than coding for trauma, as the authors propose, might methylation of the NR3C1 receptor code for aliveness instead?[8] Is it possible that, instead of inheriting their mothers' traumatic experience, these infants inherited something else? Surely, war most often annihilates. The study methods do not talk about the women and infants who died during the study. But for those who are born healthy despite being sung bullet lullabies in the womb, perhaps methylation produces something besides higher rates of depression or psychosis? Is it possible that in addition to the nightmares, the children and grandchildren and great-grandchildren of those who run from war also inherit dreams, wild notions of a world otherwise?

Cohabitation

This is what you must remember: the ending of one story is just the beginning of another. This has happened before after all. People die, old orders pass, new societies have begun. When we say "the world has ended," it's usually a lie because the planet is still alive.
—N. K. Jemisin, *The Fifth Season*

Consider this text an experiment, an index, an oracle, an archive.
—Alexis Pauline Gumbs, м *Archive*

In September 2019, I returned to eastern Congo. It had been three years since I had last visited, and my grueling clinical training had meant that my communication with friends and informants had been limited. As I returned to the living rooms of old friends, my Swahili and French came out in fits and starts. After the initial exchange of news—deaths, births, marriages—I asked people what their lives were like now. Much had changed in the intervening years: the war that engulfed my field site years earlier had ceased; the world's

FIGURE C.1. Masisi hills, 2012. Paths that lead elsewhere. Photograph by author.

largest camp for internally displaced people located outside Goma had been closed; there had been national elections (if stolen); some roads had been paved. And still, my friends insisted, "Vita, njala ingali." War and hunger are still here. In 2019, UNHCR reported record high numbers of internal displacement, and the World Food Program distributed the largest amount of food aid in Congo in its history.[1] Now, in addition to the violence and the hunger, a deadly virus, and the international response it generated, threatened further disruption.

The tenth Ebola epidemic in Congo was declared in North Kivu on August 1, 2018. While the west of the country had seen nine previous epidemics, this was the first time Ebola had affected eastern Congo; it was also the first time Ebola had been managed in a conflict zone. Fearing "another West Africa," wherein the disease escaped the African continent, the international community prepared a massive epidemic response. In less than two years, more than half a billion dollars of international aid flowed into the country. Additionally, a newly approved, highly protective vaccine was distributed, and effective novel therapeutic agents utilized. And still, despite the enormous level of logistical, scientific, and financial support, Ebola continued to spread, and to kill in record numbers.[2] In fact, the situation was worse: not only was the large public health apparatus that assembled to fight Ebola not able to contain the disease, the massive cash inflows associated with the humanitarian Response (hereafter, the Response) also destabilized existing conflict networks, thus worsening violence in the area. While official counts differ, some two hundred to three hundred episodes of violence took place over a two-year period that could be directly tied to the Ebola epidemic and/or the national and international Response that it generated.[3]

In the fall of 2019, the European Union commissioned a study to investigate why the large public health response to the tenth epidemic had caused so much friction in communities in eastern Congo. As an anthropologist and a physician who had worked in the area for years, I was hired to lead one arm of this study. As a team of twelve researchers, all Congolese save me, we developed a mixed-methods study that sought to understand what roles the Congolese health system, the Response, and the community each played in managing the epidemic. During the period of data collection, my colleagues and I circulated around Ebola-affected areas. We administered household surveys, collected quantitative data from the registers of hospitals, tracked down people with Ebola who had fled the Ebola apparatus, spoke with politicians and local militias, and conducted ethnographic research in Ebola treatment centers. Through this process, I learned about Ebola; I also learned more about living together.

Since the discovery of Ebola in 1976, Congo's Ministry of Health has been engaged in the detection and management of Ebola epidemics. For many years, epidemic control followed the same logic: there was no treatment for this disease that often killed 90 percent of the people it infected; instead, isolation was the sole means of control. Then Ebola erupted in West Africa. As the disease took more than eleven thousand lives, and for the first time arrived on Western soil, Ebola captured the attention of international funders, researchers, and clinicians for the first time. A flurry of scientific and clinical developments were made. By the time the first tests in North Kivu returned positive, Ebola had become a preventable disease; months later, it became both preventable and treatable. While the news of a protective vaccine and effective treatment molecules should have given a reason to celebrate, it instead provoked significant fear. For a people already distrustful of the biomedical apparatus, the rapidly changing therapeutic environment that surrounded Ebola was less than comforting. "Is the Ebola Response here to help us, or to profit from us?" some people asked. When the answer to this question remained spectacularly unclear, people began running. As people infected with Ebola sought to evade the Response's surveillance teams, Ebola spread across the region. Case numbers rose, and the Response buckled down. Before long, armed men began accompanying surveillance teams and carrying those suspected of Ebola away to treatment centers. The Response's guns were met with other guns, and in the standoff that resulted, Ebola continued to spread.[4]

It was in this context that our team circulated to nearly four thousand households and deployed a qualitative survey that sought to better understand the Congolese population's viewpoint. We asked many questions about fear, about running, about dying from Ebola. Everyone gave the questions thought; some people expounded on them. In one of the most rural areas we traveled to, a woman gave voice to a common sentiment that we had begun to observe. "Ebola is not the problem," she said. "For years now in Congo, we have lived with Ebola [*on vivait avec*]. You white people [*mzungu*] are scared of Ebola—you're scared of it coming to you, of dying like we are used to dying [*kama tumeshazowea kufa*], in our own excrement. And so you come here with your Land Cruisers. But Congolese live with [*tunaishi na*] this disease of ours [*ugonjwa wetu*]. We have since Kikwit [one of the early outbreaks], and we will forever [*kwa milile*]."

I never saw the woman who spoke these words again—once she finished the survey, she faded back to household survey #2316, as we had committed she would. But after we recorded her words, we heard others echoing her words. At our weekly research meetings, our research team began discussing the idea of living with Ebola. The Response kept talking about "getting to zero [transmission]" and the scientific community had uttered the word "eradicate." But people in rural eastern Congo, those most threatened by the disease, spoke of living with. We wondered, what would it mean for the international community to think like our Congolese interlocutors, to transition from thinking of Ebola as an epidemic that could be eradicated to an endemic disease, which would always be present?[5] We began brainstorming how communities and health care facilities might manage Ebola differently if individual consent and community well-being were more valued than getting to zero. We made lists of the expertise, the personnel, and the materials that would be necessary for Congolese to live with such a fatal virus in a dignified way. In the end, these lists never made it into our final report— they were too speculative, and stakeholders wanted to know concrete things that could have been done differently.[6] And still, despite all that the project produced—the press releases, interviews, an academic paper, a blog series—I have not been able to shake the idea that we haven't yet written about the greatest lesson the epidemic had to teach. We haven't yet shared the idea of scrapping the epidemic Response—which led to so much division and violence and likely prolonged an epidemic that became endemic anyway—and living with the deadly disease. "This disease of ours," survey respondent #2316 had said.

In November 2019, shortly before we began our fieldwork on Ebola, prominent HIV researcher Eileen Moyer stood at the annual gathering of the American Anthropologist Association and gave a talk about living with. Moyer began by tracing the fear associated with HIV from the 1980s, when it was a death sentence, through the early 2000s, when antiretrovirals (ARVs) turned it into a chronic disease, to the present, when the introduction of pre-exposure prophylaxis (PrEP) allowed scientists and policy makers to predict the elimination of HIV. As HIV has shifted from a disease that can be tamed to a disease that can be completely avoided, Moyer asked, what of the still-infected? There was a time period before PrEP, when ARVs made it possible to love those with HIV, to live together. Will the new focus on eradication destroy the forms of cohabitation that have been developed and inadvertently ostracize those with a positive test?[7] If cohabitation is a not just a feel-good concept but a political act, a decision to live together despite the risks of doing so, what does it mean for humanity when eradication takes the place of living together more globally?

Early in my writing about Ebola, I returned to the words of survey respondent #2316, to my notes from Moyer's talk, and found myself doubting whether the globe could learn to cohabitate with HIV or with Ebola. With my research team, we had imagined a health system that could prioritize living with over eradication. But was this really desirable? I wondered. Ebola kills quickly, and HIV is a slow death; but both diseases attack one's most intimate circle—one's caregivers, one's lovers. And so the living with would be so proximate; there would be no real protection. Could anyone live like this? And then, I remembered the Congolese army that raided Kishabe and then came back two weeks later and asked for roofs over their heads; I remembered Trésor speaking of the knock-knock-open-up in Rutshuru, of walking the same streets, shopping in the same marketplace with an armed group that terrorized them at night; I remembered the phone thefts that were so quotidian and yet so frightening that they elicited absurd laughter—and I realized that long before Ebola came to eastern Congo, Congolese were cohabitating with death. Like Black folks across the world, living in the wake. And thus, the idea of cohabitating with Ebola is not a new one, but rather a continuation of the same commitment to survive, to breathe, to aspire in a world committed to Black death. Even after enduring centuries of violence, of neglect, of destruction, Congolese continue to insist that other worlds are possible. Their visions are not of worlds without disease, hunger, violence. Rather, they insist that by living with, by cohabitating, other presents, which take as their foundation Black life instead of Black death, might come into existence. For those of us interested in documenting the ends of some worlds, and the emergence of others, we would do well to listen to Congolese song. As the survival of our species becomes more and more tenuous, their voices are growing louder.

****

Much has been written about postcolonial violence, war in Africa, presents and futures on the continent. This literature forms the scaffolding for this book; and using Black critical theory to understand eastern Congo has, I believe, brought me somewhere new. Disciplinary conventions would have had me rely most heavily on regional specialists to understand Congo. Surely, Congo is shaped by regional forces; and Congo is also produced by and with the category of the human. Ideas of progress and modernity arise in relation to Congo, with Congo (and blackness more generally) as their foil. In order to dismantle the hierarchy of possibility that confines a book on Congo to African studies, analysis must be deflected upward from a country or region to the level of the human. Weheliye, Wynter, Sharpe, and others have used material from the North American context to establish that the human cannot be theorized without attention to global antiblackness. In this book, I have queried the Congolese context to understand the particular ways in which antiblackness delimits life and possibility there. By describing both the chronic violence that characterizes the region alongside the registers of healing that Congolese have developed to propel themselves beyond war, I have suggested that Congo might offer a glimpse of the human beyond antiblackness, where all lives have value and all futures are commensurable. This, I believe, marks a shift in the way we understand Congo: here, aporia is not an end, but rather a radical threshold at which the human is being redefined. Further, this redefinition of Congo suggests an "epistemic reorientation" in African studies more broadly, a turn away from writing difference, and a turn toward recording commensurable visions of the human.[8]

The impact of this research reaches far beyond scholarly contribution, however; my encounter with healing in eastern Congo has shifted my North Star. As I was instrumentalized in logging this archive—recording, holding, facilitating, witnessing, and transforming it into language[9]—my focus shifted away from global surgery. Instead of remaining focused on decimated health systems, I wrote stories of social and political action in the face of violence. Rather than logging surgical burden of disease, I described new registers of healing, which extended far beyond the physical body, toward the deep metaphysical wounds that antiblackness creates. Where I began research in Congo to impact morbidity and mortality, during the writing of this book, I turned down a fellowship that would have involved implementing a national surgical plan across the continent; for, I had begun to wonder if the kind of healing that I observed in Congo might actually contain more possibility for life otherwise than any imported health policy. Somewhere amid ethnographic contact, I began to see the possibilities for a collective future that my Congolese interlocutors envisioned. I am proud of this tack, in what it has meant for my professional and personal spheres. And I am forever grateful to my Congolese friends and interlocuters for teaching me the difference between health and healing. It has changed the way I doctor and the way that I live.

****

As I was in the final stages of writing this book, a wave of renewed violence encompassed eastern Congo. Reports of daily massacres dominated my news feed. A video appeared in my inbox. The video is grainy. It is taken as a group of people drive in Ituri, the province just north of North Kivu. From the passenger window, one can see men, women, and children lining both sides of a red dirt road. Everyone is carrying their life's possessions on their heads and backs—they are clearly in flight. A voice from behind the camera—the driver?—narrates sorrowfully, almost hauntingly, "Until when? Until when will we continue to suffer like this? [*Jusqu'à quand? Mpaka siku gani tutaendelea kuteseka hii.*] Look [*Uone*]. A good country, no peace [*Nchi nzuri, amani hamna*].... There are crops. I see cassava, corn, beans [*Kule ni mimea, ninaona mihogo, mihindi, marahage*]. And the people are leaving. They are abandoning their houses, their fields [*Et les gens sont en trein de fuire, ils sont en trein d'abandoner leurs maisons, leurs champs*].... Send us prayers [*Matupia mu maombi*]."

Many years after the official end of war was declared, war continues to be a crushing force in eastern Congo; and there is no end in sight. Since I first sent this book to the publisher, M23 has come back to occupy North Kivu; a state of siege has been invoked and a military government has displaced the civilian government in the eastern provinces; and Kivu Security Tracker has recorded a sharp uptick in violent incidents. As a Congolese friend said, "I was born in war, I grew up in war, and I live in war [*Nilizaliwa mu vita, nilikomaa mu vita, na minaishi mu vita*]." In spite of peace talks and treaties, regardless of transitions of power and new governments, with and without international aid, more wounds continue to accrue. And if war is the underside of liberal democracy, the sacrament of our time, as Mbembe has argued, the dying will not stop. Rather, living with war, with sickness and loss and death is one of the few constants in a regime governed by antiblackness.

And still, I am struck by the diversity of forms that life takes in war, in the wake. Certainly, there are those who are caught in the currents of antiblackness, and so many of these currents lead down, under, toward the zero world. And also, there are other paths being forged, other presents being demanded, other futures being spoken into existence. It is my hope that, by putting these possibilities otherwise into writing, both the devastating and liberatory ones, I will have created an archive of what could be.[10] After five centuries of rule, the racialized world of Man is on its way out; and it must be—so many beings have died under its rule, the planet destroyed. What the transition will look like, and what will come after, in my mind, remains an open question. Perhaps this archive of possibilities, recorded at a time when Black imaginings are far more radical than any of the stale climate conferences or attempts at public action currently taking place,[11] might open new conversations about the forms that living together might take. Of the new narratives emerging on the African continent, Mbembe writes, "To repair is to be alive. So that's the first sense of reparation—to be alive and to take care of something that matters because that thing is a very condition of my survival with others, my being with others, my moving on with others, my leaving something behind for others, something through which they might remember me."[12]

I ask, following my work in Congo, where eradication has in so many ways become the stated goal of the liberal world—the eradication of disease, of war, of emissions—what it would mean to focus instead on repair and healing, to learn from those who cohabitate, who live with because the very condition of their survival depends on it? This is not the unidimensional version of healing that biomedicine proposes, which I attempt to provide as a physician, cutting open bodies and removing an ailing organ, suturing up that which bleeds. Rather, it is a plural, multisited understanding of healing. It is a vision of healing that is emerging from the undercommons, the wild places "beyond the beyond" of liberal, democratic society, which is devoted to trying out other ways of living in a broken world.[13] It's a healing that incorporates scars instead of seeking to minimize them, that traces paths forward from devastation to what could be instead.

FIGURE C.2. Sunset at Lake Kivu, 2020. Photograph by author.

INTRODUCTION. WHERE THE SCARS ARE SO THICK

1 For more on Goma as border town, see Büscher and Vlassenroot, "Humanitarian Presence and Urban Development"; Vlassenroot and Büscher, "Borderlands, Identity and Urban Development."

2 On the traffic robots, see Al Jazeera, "DR Congo Recruits Robots as Traffic Police"; as well as the brilliant short story inspired by them, Okorafor and Kahiu, "Rusties." Thanks to Martha Saavedra for this latter recommendation.

3 See, for example, Csete and Kippenberg, "War within the War."

4 Onsrud et al., "Sexual Violence–Related Fistulas in the Democratic Republic of Congo." For a similar argument, see D'Errico et al., "'You Say Rape, I Say Hospitals.'"

5 Within DRC, a discussion also arose about armed groups' use of rape to gain international attention. See especially Autesserre, *Trouble with the Congo*; Autesserre, "Dangerous Tales."

6 See James, "Political Economy of 'Trauma' in Haiti"; James, "Ruptures, Rights, and Repair."

7 Utas, "West-African Warscapes."

8 Hunt, "Acoustic Register"; Baaz and Stern, "Complexity of Violence."

9 Here, I use quotation marks to denote the nebulousness of this category. While there is good data (cited above) that the majority of women with fistulas have fistulas as a result of obstetric complications, Mukwege nonetheless is recognized for his efforts with victims of sexual violence. "Denis Mukwege: Facts," Nobel Peace Prize 2018, accessed April 26, 2023, https://www.nobelprize.org/prizes/peace/2018/mukwege/facts/.

10 See World Food Program, "WFP Democratic Republic of Congo Country Brief"; Trefon, *Congo's Environmental Paradox*; Hunt, "Le Bébé en Brousse"; Hunt, *Colonial Lexicon*.

11 On precolonial Congolese history, see Mathys, "Bringing History Back In"; Vansina, *Paths in the Rainforests*; Hunt, *Colonial Lexicon*; Newbury, "Lake Kivu Regional Trade in the Nineteenth Century"; Chrétien, *Great Lakes of Africa*.

12 Schoenbrun, "Conjuring the Modern in Africa," 1407.

13 On middle figures in Congo, see Hunt, *Colonial Lexicon*; Hunt, *Nervous State*. On middle figures in colonialism more generally, see Fanon, *Black Skin, White Masks*.

14 Chapter 5 features a longer discussion on Lumumba's assassination with more extensive references. Nzongola-Ntalaja, *Patrice Lumumba*, provides a nice starting point. Lemarchand, *Political Awakening in the Belgian Congo*, provides a nice historiography of the "political awakening," in his words, that led to the Congolese demand for independence.

15 Between 1971 and 1997, the Democratic Republic of Congo was known as Zaire.

16 This tactic, which William Reno has termed "warlord politics," simultaneously ingratiated his opposition with him, while also pitting his enemies against each other. On governance in postcolonial Congo, see Reno, *Warlord Politics and African States*; Schatzberg, *Dialectics of Oppression in Zaire*; Nzongola-Ntalaja, *Congo from Leopold to Kabila*; MacGaffey, *Real Economy of Zaire*; Young, *Postcolonial State in Africa*; Bayart, *State in Africa*; Vogel, *Conflict Minerals, Inc.*

17 For an ethnographic exploration of this time, see Devisch, "Frenzy, Violence, and Ethical Renewal in Kinshasa."

18 Much has been written about the events surrounding the beginning of regional war in the 1990s. Prunier, *Africa's World War*; Reyntjens, *Great African War*; Stearns, *Dancing in the Glory of Monsters*; and Mamdani, *When Victims Become Killers*, are among the most useful. Mararo, "Land, Power, and Ethnic Conflict in Masisi," writes a very local history of this time. Lemarchand, "Reflections on the Recent Historiography of Eastern Congo," points out the difficulty of writing the history of this region since war began.

19 The chronic war in eastern Congo has drawn significant scholarly attention. Autesserre, *Trouble with the Congo*; Englebert and Tull, "Postconflict Reconstruction in Africa"; Raeymaekers, "Post-war Conflict and the Market for Protection"; Vlassenroot and Raeymaekers, *Conflict and Social Transformation in Eastern DR Congo*; Vogel and Raeymaekers, "Terr(it)or(ies) of Peace?"; Verweijen, "Ambiguity of Militarization"; and Stearns, *War That Doesn't Say Its Name*, are especially helpful in understanding the multitude of forces that perpetuate violence in the region.

20 Christina Sharpe asserts that the regime of antiblackness, which precludes some people from durable action, from satisfaction, from social life, is a global phenomenon, a "predictable and constitutive aspect" of the present moment (*In the Wake*, 7).

21 Mararo, "Land, Power, and Ethnic Conflict in Masisi"; Vlassenroot and Huggins, "Land, Migration and Conflict in Eastern DRC"; Chrétien, *Great Lakes of Africa*.

22 Mbembe argues that it is not just that Black life is disposable. Rather, because the enlightened towers of Western democracy—the solar body—rest on fixing disorder, bringing democracy elsewhere across the globe, war must continue in the nocturnal body. For the solar body to continue, which it must, there must always be someone to save. In Mbembe's words, "war . . . has become the sacrament of our times" (*Necropolitics*, 2). See also chapter 4 of this book.

23 On the enduring work that this trope continues to do, see Dunn, *Imagining the Congo*; Vogel et al., "Cliches Can Kill in Congo."

24 Wynter, "Unsettling the Coloniality of Being/Power/Truth/Freedom."

25 Weheliye, *Habeas Viscus*, 22.

26 To emphasize this point: I understand Wynter, Wehileye, Sharpe, Moten, and others to be writing a theory of Man (using examples from the North American context), just as Foucault writes a theory of Man (using examples from the European context). The fact that Foucault builds his theories of Man on European history does not limit the use of his work only to European contexts. Similarly, the fact that many Black critical theorists use material from North America to build their theories of antiblackness cannot limit the use of this work to only North American contexts. A smaller, but important corrective to one possible reading of this text: when I use *antiblackness* and race theory more generally to think about Congo, I am in no way conflating chattel slavery in Atlantic and North American histories of violence and slavery with the history of the slave trade in eastern Africa, which was mainly directed to Indian Ocean trade networks and the Middle East. These were two completely separate historical processes, which are connected only by the process that underlies them both—the devaluing of Black life everywhere, so that people could be owned, so that they could become, in the eyes of whites, (maimable, killable) property.

27 De Boeck, "Apocalyptic Interlude," 247.

28 Here I borrow language from prominent Black critical theorists including Harney and Moten, *Undercommons*; Spillers, "Mama's Baby, Papa's Maybe"; Sharpe, *In the Wake*.

29 See Attia, *RepaiR*.

30 *Art Daily*, "Exhibition Invites Visitors."

31 See Mbembe's critique of the future in writing on Africa, especially Mbembe, *On the Postcolony*; Mbembe, "Africa in Theory." Also see Guyer, "Prophecy and the Near Future."

32 Campt, "Black Feminist Futures and the Practice of Fugitivity." See especially minutes 29:15–30:30 of this talk.

33 Comaroff and Comaroff, *Theory from the South*, 2019.

34 To protect the identity of my interlocutors, "Kishabe" and all names used in this book for patients, staff, and local informants are pseudonyms.

35 This is certainly not a constant in Congo or elsewhere. Dewachi, "Blurred Lines," writes about the ways in which the sites of health care provision have become targets—and active participants—in contemporary warscapes. During the tenth Ebola epidemic in Congo, hundreds of assaults against health care sites and providers were recorded. For further analysis of the forces that gave rise to this phenomenon in DRC, see Congo Research Group, "Rebels, Doctors, and Merchants of Violence."

36 I described the visceral sensation of the inequality present in my fieldwork in a talk I gave at the European Conference on African Studies in Lisbon: Niehuus, "Going Rogue."

37   This has certainly been observed elsewhere. Of her ethnographic research in postwar Guatemala, Linda Green writes, "Fear joined me to the people and yet separated me from them as well" (*Fear as a Way of Life*, 20). In her first book, *The Pastoral Clinic*, Angela Garcia writes about incommensurability more generally in the ethnographic encounter.

38   Saidiya Hartman writes about the desire for stories to recuperate that which has been erased: "Loss gives rise to longing, and in these circumstances, it would not be far-fetched to consider stories as a form of compensation or even as reparations, perhaps the only kind we will ever receive" ("Venus in Two Acts," sx26).

39   Stewart, *Ordinary Affects*, 2.

40   Stewart, *Ordinary Affects*, 129.

41   In this idea, I owe a large intellectual debt to Alexis Pauline Gumbs. Gumbs describes her book *M Archive* as a "speculative documentary work" that seeks to "[depict] a species at the edge of its integrity, on the verge or in the practice of transforming into something beyond the luxuries and limitations of what some call 'the human'" (*M Archive*, xi).

42   The fact that ethnographic methodology was used to create this text means that my presence has affected the shape of the archive itself: surely, lives unfolded and possibilities opened and closed every day outside of my presence, and yet only the things that I observed, the activities that I participated in, the stories that I recorded appear in this text. This archive is, thus, partial, delimited by my experience of eastern Congo; and, if archives, in Geissler et al.'s words, have the capacity to "trigger new affective responses, provoke moments of recognition and refusal, and thus invite further conversation, opening new futures rather than turning another page on the past" (Geissler et al., *Traces of the Future*, 27), the partiality of this archive might limit the kinds of futures it opens.

43   See De Boeck, "Apocalyptic Interlude."

44   Mbembe, *Necropolitics*, 2.

CHAPTER 1. DIRT WORK

1   Trefon, *Congo's Environmental Paradox*, 21.

2   UNICEF DR Congo (@UNICEFDRCongo), Twitter, February 6, 2013.

3   Farming as the most common occupation is an older statistic from Trefon, *Reinventing Order in the Congo*. A household survey that we conducted in North Kivu as part of research for a different project demonstrated this number was closer to 50 percent (Congo Research Group, "Ebola in the DRC"). On the 2021 crisis, see World Food Program, "wfp Democratic Republic of Congo Country Brief." As Alex de Waal previously demonstrated in Sudan, instead of being the result of a drought or a flood, hunger is often politically created. In Congo, like Sudan, a predatory government comes together with a humanitarian sector that intervenes in crises without ensuring durable political reform to create a situation in which the millions experiencing hunger are surrounded by huge swaths of fertile land. Waal, *Famine Crimes*.

4 For more on Congo's vast mineral wealth, see Trefon, *Congo's Environmental Paradox*; Vogel and Raeymaekers, "Terr(it)or(ies) of Peace?"; Vlassenroot and Raeymaekers, *Conflict and Social Transformation in Eastern DR Congo*; Vogel, *Conflict Minerals, Inc.*

5 Yusoff, *Billion Black Anthropocenes or None*.

6 My claim in this and the preceding paragraph that antiblackness is the ground on which we stand is, as one an anonymous reviewer pointed out, "a grand, assertive sweep about knowledge, power, violence and race." They warn, "If taken literally, [it] could be read in a way that would make the discipline of anthropology, for example, complicit everywhere and at all times in antiblack thought and practices." This book is part of a much larger movement to make their admonition a reality—that is, to elucidate how antiblackness undergirds every aspect of modern thought, language, and processes. Throughout, I argue that antiblackness is a generalized force that influences every aspect of our being, our thinking. (This is not to collapse different historical contexts, regimes of power, and resistances, but rather to demonstrate how the modern world is built on antiblackness.) Surely, anthropology—even works like my own that seek to elucidate the effects of antiblackness—is also complicit in perpetuating an antiblack world.

7 For more on land transformation from precolonial Congo and Rwanda through colonial times, see Chrétien, *Great Lakes of Africa*; Vansina, *Antecedents to Modern Rwanda*; Mararo, "Land, Power, and Ethnic Conflict in Masisi."

8 On the "red rubber" regime, see Hochschild, *King Leopold's Ghost*, as well as Hunt's superb correction to it in "Acoustic Register." Throughout her opus, Nancy Rose Hunt notes points at which Congolese middle figures were complicit in imperial and colonial rule. Surely, some Congolese participated in and profited financially or socially during enslavement, Belgian imperialism, and Belgian colonialism in eastern Congo. She is very clear, however, that the losses far outweighed any gains during these periods for the Congolese population taken as a whole.

9 Stearns et al., "Banyamulenge."

10 Mathys, "Bringing History Back In." Other names for Banyarwanda that refer specifically to the area in which they settled after immigration include Banyamulenge, Banyabwisha, and Banyamasisi. On the changing legal tenure of Kinyarwanda speakers in Congo, see also Jackson, "Sons of Which Soil?"; Mararo, "Land, Power, and Ethnic Conflict in Masisi"; Mamdani, *When Victims Become Killers*.

11 Jackson, "Sons of Which Soil?"

12 Acker, "Where Did All the Land Go?"

13 Mathys, "Bringing History Back In."

14 Comaroff and Comaroff, *Theory from the South*.

15 Jackson, "Sons of Which Soil?," 99.

16 For more on how conflict over land continues to undergird current conflict in eastern DRC, see Mararo, "Land, Power, and Ethnic Conflict in Masisi"; Leeuwen et al., "From Resolving Land Disputes to Agrarian Justice"; Acker, "Where Did All the Land Go?"; Vlassenroot and Huggins, "Land, Migration and Conflict in

Eastern DRC"; Autesserre, "Local Violence, National Peace?"; Kisangani, *Civil Wars in the Democratic Republic of Congo*; Stearns, *War That Doesn't Say Its Name*.

17 Vlassenroot and Huggins, "Land, Migration and Conflict in Eastern DRC."

18 See Vogel, "Armed Group Maps," for mapping of armed groups in the region.

19 Büscher, "Urbanisation and the Political Geographies of Violent Struggle."

20 Smith, "Tantalus in the Digital Age," 29.

21 Mbembe and Roitman, "Figures of the Subject in Times of Crisis," 324.

22 Wynter, "Unsettling the Coloniality of Being/Power/Truth/Freedom." For a brilliant synthesis of the way that Wynter's and Spiller's work calls into question the bounds of the human, see Weheliye, *Habeas Viscus*.

23 Sexton, "Social Life of Social Death," 6.

24 Sexton, "Social Life of Social Death"; Hartman and Wilderson, "The Position of the Unthought"; Sharpe, *In the Wake*; Spillers, "Mama's Baby, Papa's Maybe."

25 Mbembe, *Necropolitics*, 159.

26 Kalema, "Scars, Marked Bodies, and Suffering."

27 Derrida, *Aporias*, 17. Derrida continues, "The aporia is not a paralyzing structure, something that simply blocks the way with a simple negative effect. The aporia is the experience of responsibility. It is only by *going through* a set of contradictory injunctions, impossible choices, that we make a choice . . . for the responsible decision to be envisaged or taken, we have to go through pain and aporia, a situation in which I do not know what to do" (quoted in Bernstein, "Derrida," 399).

28 For an exploration of this phenomenon across the border in Zambia, see Ferguson, *Expectations of Modernity*.

29 On coltan mining in eastern DRC, see Smith, "Tantalus in the Digital Age"; Smith, "'May It Never End'"; Vogel, *Conflict Minerals, Inc.*

30 Feierman, "Healing as Social Criticism," 77. It should be noted here that Feierman starts at a more communal understanding of healing in the precolonial area to then argue that the colonial era brought about the individualization of healing in many African societies.

31 Schoenbrun, "Conjuring the Modern in Africa."

32 For the role of spirit mediums in public healing in precolonial Congo, see also Janzen, "Ideologies and Institutions"; Janzen, *Quest for Therapy in Lower Zaire*; Hunt, "Health and Healing"; Hunt, *Colonial Lexicon*.

33 Understanding little of precolonial public health rituals, Belgians often characterized them as opaque and/or chaotic—and thus direct threats to the mission of creating obedient subjects. As a result, public healing suffered fierce attacks with the arrival of the Belgian colonists. For more on the encounter between Congolese healing and Belgian medicine, see Hunt, "Le Bébé en Brousse"; Hunt, *Colonial Lexicon*; Schoenbrun, "Conjuring the Modern in Africa"; Feierman, "Healing as Social Criticism"; Janzen, "Ideologies and Institutions."

34 Jourdan, "Mayi-Mayi"; Jourdan, "Being at War, Being Young."

35 Schoenbrun describes public healing as "a moral community of seekers with a public face . . . [who] realize[d] their individual aims through a collective action

that promise[d] moral continuity and material consequence in the face of 'a world gone awry'" ("Conjuring the Modern in Africa," 1436). I thank an anonymous reviewer for the idea to use public healing here. For a historiography of the idea of public healing, see also Hunt, "Health and Healing."

36 See Penniman, *Farming While Black*.

37 On the state of phenomenological alienation in Congo, see De Boeck, "Apocalyptic Interlude"; Devisch, "Frenzy, Violence, and Ethical Renewal"; Mbembe, "Variations on the Beautiful."

38 Like bricks in postsocialist Vietnam, Congolese soil is "vibrant matter endowed with affective agency and potency" (Schwenkel, "Post/Socialist Affect," 254).

39 On this subject, see Camille Dungy's anthology of poetry *Black Nature*.

40 See Leeuwen et al., "From Resolving Land Disputes to Agrarian Justice."

41 Taken together, these three measures constitute the platform for agrarian reform that Leeuwen et al. propose. For policy recommendations aimed at decreasing land conflict, see also Vlassenroot and Huggins, "Land, Migration and Conflict in Eastern DRC."

42 At a screening for the documentary *Virunga* (2014), the director-general of UNESCO called Virunga National Park a "natural lung" (UNESCO World Heritage Convention, "Virunga").

43 It is said that if the park were made into arable land, it would provide the people living around it $1 billion in income. Therefore, efforts are ongoing to make it more profitable for those who live around the park to stay out rather than enter it to farm. On conservation in Virunga, see Marijnen, "Public Authority and Conservation"; Marijnen and Verweijen, "Selling Green Militarization"; Marijnen and Verweijen, "Pluralising Political Forests."

44 This is a pseudonym for a local NGO working in development and women's empowerment.

45 Bboxx, "DRC Government Partnership."

46 In this, they join Black and indigenous scholars across the globe. For discussions about the importance of the ecological register to Black healing, see especially brown, *Emergent Strategy*; Penniman, *Farming While Black*; Gumbs, *Undrowned*. In an interview on her relationality with the other-than-human, Alexis Pauline Gumbs states, "The individual is not a unit of care; the individual is a unit of capitalism. But care is an interconnected, ecological possibility" (Sagar, "Possibilities of Listening with Alexis Pauline Gumbs").

47 Mbembe, "Africa in Theory," 217.

CHAPTER 2. A SEA OF INSECURITY

1 On methane in Lake Kivu, see Rosen, "Lake Kivu's Great Gas Gamble." On Lake Nyos and limnic eruptions more generally, see Global Volcanism Program, "Report on Oku Volcanic Field."

2 Much of this paragraph comes from discussions with volcanologists in Goma in 2010 and 2011 who were present during the 2002 eruption.

3   For more on the Rwandan genocide, see Mamdani, *When Victims Become Killers*. On the relationship between the genocide in Rwanda and the beginnings of large-scale war in the DRC, see Stearns, *Dancing in the Glory of Monsters*; Reyntjens, *Great African War*; Prunier, *Africa's World War*.

4   These statistics come from the controversial report produced by Vinck et al., "Living with Fear." Slegh et al. ("Gender Relations") conducted a more recent household study in and around Goma with similar results: 73 percent of residents of North Kivu had lost property in the war, 25 percent had been personally injured, and 9 percent of men and 22 percent of women had experienced sexual violence.

5   Vansina (*Paths in the Rainforests*) and Schoenbrun ("Conjuring the Modern in Africa") both provide semantic analyses that attest to precolonial staying. See also Chrétien, *Great Lakes of Africa*.

6   As discussed in the introduction (see especially notes 11 and 13), these were different enslavers than those of the Atlantic slave trade, which established chattel slavery in North America. Additionally, it should be noted here that, surely, some Congolese people also participated in enslavement—selling their enemies, or even their less valuable kinspeople to the Arab enslavers for compensation—as some Congolese people also participated in the terrible violence of Belgian imperialism and colonialism. (On the latter, see especially Hunt, *Nervous State*; Hunt, *Colonial Lexicon*.) This should not deflect accountability from the authors of these processes.

7   On the brutality during the Belgian imperial regime, see Hunt, "Acoustic Register"; Hochschild, *King Leopold's Ghost*.

8   On the conflict that emerged in the immediate postcolonial period, see Nzongola-Ntalaja, *Congo from Leopold to Kabila*; Stearns, *Dancing in the Glory of Monsters*.

9   On the two Congolese wars, see Stearns, *Dancing in the Glory of Monsters*; Reyntjens, *Great African War*; Prunier, *Africa's World War*.

10 On the CNDP rebellion, see Stearns et al., "From CNDP to M23."

11 Here, I draw from Moten's description of Black social life as fugitive. See Moten, "Case of Blackness"; Harney and Moten, *Undercommons*.

12 For a discussion of the relationship between M23 and previous armed rebellions in the region, see Stearns et al, "From CNDP to M23."

13 For a description of Rwanda's relationship with M23, see United Nations, "Midterm Report."

14 The fact that M23 was able to take Goma said more about the weakness of the Congolese army than it did about the strength of M23. For a cinematographic exploration of this period, see McCabe, *This Is Congo*.

15 While the Congolese state is often spoken about as a failed state, and the army's retreat from M23 served as proof for many in Congo of how weak the state was, this moment demonstrated just how misleading the terms weak or failed state can be. As political scientist Michael Schatzberg writes, "The state, when viewed from abroad, may well be weak according to certain evaluative criteria analysts choose. But from the vantage point of villages and towns, even a ragtag, underpaid, poorly disciplined, and utterly corrupt platoon of Zairian soldiers represents a truly awesome power" (*Dialectics of Oppression in Zaire*, 68).

16 On the violence perpetrated in Minova during the FARDC's retreat from M23 and the trial that followed, see Human Rights Watch, "Justice on Trial"; Lake, "After Minova."

17 On the use of violence by the Mobutuist state, see Schatzberg, *Dialectics of Oppression in Zaire*; Reno, *Warlord Politics and African States*.

18 Laudati, "Beyond Minerals"; Verweijen, "Ambiguity of Militarization." For a larger discussion about how metaphors of eating are and have been used in politics on the African continent, see Bayart, *State in Africa*. This use of armed forces (whether the national army or other forces) by political leaders in Congo has been discussed as "warlord politics" (Reno, *Warlord Politics and African States*) and "the criminalization of the state" (Bayart, Ellis, and Hibou, *Criminalization of the State in Africa*).

19 For more on the extreme vulnerability of the national army, see Baaz and Stern, "Making Sense of Violence"; Baaz and Stern, "Why Do Soldiers Rape?"; Baaz and Verweijen, "Volatility of a Half-Cooked Bouillabaisse"; Stearns, Verweijen, and Baaz, "National Army and Armed Groups in the Eastern Congo."

20 Here, Anne-Marie is referring to the fact that, as with all government salaries, those with positions at the bottom of the hierarchy often find their salaries "eaten" by their superiors. Since 2012, the government has made several changes in an attempt to minimize this process; however, the processes aren't perfect, and the population often still refers to foot soldiers as "not being paid" or having their salaries "eaten." For more on the use of metaphors of eating to describe graft, see Bayart, *State in Africa*.

21 Kamari Clarke writes nicely on the ways in which the desire for justice on behalf of the victims relies on a clear split between victim and perpetrator—and on the fact that seeing victim and perpetrator as dichotomous entities is more common in Western epistemology than on the African continent. See, for example, Clarke, "Affective Justice"; Clarke and Knottnerus, *Africa and the ICC*.

22 See especially Verweijen, "Military Business and the Business of the Military"; Roitman, *Fiscal Disobedience*; Debos, *Living by the Gun in Chad*; Lombard, *State of Rebellion*.

23 On the slippage between civilian and military in Congo, see Verweijen, "Ambiguity of Militarization." On the slippage between war and peace in other contexts, see Green, *Fear as a Way of Life*; Nordstrom, *Different Kind of War Story*; Nordstrom, *Shadows of War*; Thiranagama, *In My Mother's House*; Lombard, *State of Rebellion*; Lubkemann, *Culture in Chaos*.

24 Debos, *Living by the Gun in Chad*.

25 See Verweijen, "Military Business and the Business of the Military."

26 See especially Baaz and Verweijen, "Volatility of a Half-Cooked Bouillabaisse."

27 Over the past decade, the Rift Valley Institute has produced a series of reports describing the main armed groups as well as the conflict dynamics in the region more generally. (See Stearns et al., "Banyamulenge"; Stearns et al., "From CNDP to M23"; Stearns et al., "PARECO"; and Verweijen, "Violent City"; among others.) The Usalama Project and the reports that it has generated nicely trace the groups'

relationships with each other and with the national army through time. They can be found at https//riftvalley.net/projects/usalama-project.

28 In the early 2000s, the Enough Project devoted significant resources to raising awareness about the militarization of the mining sector in the DRC. As a result of their efforts (together with Amnesty International and others), the United States passed section 1502 of the Dodd-Frank law in 2010, which sought to make traceable the paths of tin, tantalum, and tungsten from mine to consumer product. On this law and its effect on mining practices in Congo, see Vogel and Raeymaekers, "Terr(it)or(ies) of Peace?"; Stoop, Verpoorten, and Windt, "More Legislation, More Violence?"

29 See, for example, Fahey, "Rethinking the Resource Curse." In addition, the report titled "'Everything That Moves Will Be Taxed'" by Jaillon et al. nicely demonstrates the ways in which roadblocks allow armed groups to collect taxes on all sectors of the Congolese economy.

30 Laudati, "Beyond Minerals," 42–43. For more on military-civilian economic networks, see also Verweijen, "Military Business and the Business of the Military"; Larmer, Laudati, and Clark, "Neither War nor Peace"; Vlassenroot and Raeymaekers, *Conflict and Social Transformation*.

31 Roitman, "L'entrepôt-Garnison"; Debos, *Living by the Gun in Chad*.

32 Jourdan, "Mayi-Mayi."

33 Verweijen, "Ambiguity of Militarization."

34 This is a common problem in war, and one that is significantly unsettling. Writing on the experience of war in Mozambique, Carolyn Nordstrom states, "I have written 'factx' instead of 'facts' to underscore the observation that, at least in the context of war, something is always wrong with the facts one is given. The facts of war emerge as 'essentially contested' figures and representations everyone agrees are important, and no one agrees on" (*Different Kind of War Story*, 43).

35 In *On the Postcolony*, Mbembe writes about the way in which doubling is so generative in the postcolony, as both those in power and their subjects profit from the ambiguity created in the space between the thing and its double.

36 For fabulous deep dives on secrecy during violence and its aftermath—secrecy that allows getting by, and other effects—see Ferme, *Underneath of Things*; Last, "Importance of Knowing about Not Knowing"; Last, "Healing the Social Wounds of War."

37 As Michael Taussig demonstrates so eloquently, slippages are so productive in regimes of terror. He writes, "This problem of interpretation is decisive for terror, not only making effective counter discourse so difficult but also making the terribleness of death squads, disappearances, and torture all the more effective in crippling of peoples' capacity to resist. The problem of interpretation turned out to be an essential component of what had to be interpreted, just as resistance was necessary for control. Deeply dependent on sense and interpretation, terror nourished itself by destroying sense" (*Shamanism, Colonialism, and the Wild Man*, 128). This is certainly true in Congo, where fear and anxiety depend on the inability to know, to differentiate.

38   Janet Roitman (*Fiscal Disobedience*) and Louisa Lombard (*State of Rebellion*) have written at length about the function of roads amid insecurity. Roads are among the most democratic spaces, where the poor travel by necessity, the rich sometimes by choice. They are also by definition a liminal space, a space between, where things can happen that don't elsewhere, and where a certain degree of anonymity holds. In Kishabe, the road was all of these things at once. Learning to read the roads and understand their complexity was crucial to staying safe.

39   Sharpe, *In the Wake*, 105, emphasis added.

40   Sharpe, *In the Wake*, 16.

41   Sharika Thiranagama writes, "I see war not as along a continuum with other forms of social life, but as a powerful and distinct force, period, and subjectivity, a making on a site of unmaking" (*In My Mother's House*, 10).

42   Harney and Moten, *Undercommons*, 98.

INTERLUDE 2. RUNNING

1   Garcia, *Pastoral Clinic*.

CHAPTER 3. THE BODY, THE FLESH, AND THE HOSPITAL

1   Bwimana, "Health Sector Network Governance." In a study that examined the factors contributing to poor health, D'Errico et al. report, "When asked what was the single most significant factor influencing poor health, the majority of female respondents (82%) stated that food insecurity, past experiences with food insecurity, and fear of future food insecurity determine health and illness" ("'You Say Rape, I Say Hospitals,'" 58).

2   Certainly, the body in Congo has had different meanings at different times. Of the body in precolonial equatorial Africa, historian Florence Bernault writes, "As multiple and fragmentable, immaterial and material, the body could not be described simply as a neutral biological entity guided by an individual mind. Connecting the realm of the ancestors and the realm of the living, sheltering individual skills and ambivalent forces that served as the core material for public authority, it was entirely submerged by power" ("Body, Power, and Sacrifice," 215).

3   See Scheper-Hughes and Lock, "Mindful Body." While Spillers is not an anthropologist, her work on the body and the flesh (e.g., Spillers, "Mama's Baby, Papa's Maybe") has had a significant influence on the field.

4   Surely, all dichotomies are at least messy, if not exaggerated, and the dichotomy that juxtaposes Western medicine, as focusing on individual pathology, and African systems of healing, which take as their object the social causes of physiological affliction, is no exception. As Megan Vaughan points out in "Healing and Curing," whether African or Western, all healing systems take the individual body as their point of intervention.

5   Feierman and Janzen, *Social Basis of Health and Healing in Africa*, 14.

6 For this point, I am indebted to an anonymous reviewer, who astutely suggested the reframing of this chapter (and the book more generally) through historical studies of African healing.

7 On the way that the colonial encounter shaped the field of tropical medicine in the metropole, see Mertens and Lachenal, "History of 'Belgian' Tropical Medicine."

8 The irony that Belgian imperialists intervened to stop the Arab slave trade while proceeding to take part in much larger-scale massacres has not been lost. On the troubled morality of Belgian imperialism, see Hunt, "Acoustic Register"; Hochschild, *King Leopold's Ghost*.

9 On the mutilation photographs displayed in magic lantern shows in the early 1900s, see Hunt, "Acoustic Register."

10 Hunt, *Colonial Lexicon*, 10.

11 Hunt, *Colonial Lexicon*; Lyons, "Public Health in Colonial Africa."

12 Hunt, "Le Bébé en Brousse"; Hunt, *Colonial Lexicon*.

13 A publication of the World Health Organization reads, "When the first who staff members arrived in the Congo, the situation might be summarized as follows: there were first class hospitals, modern laboratories and good auxiliary staff. But the country had no Congolese doctors. . . . It was up to the World Health Organization to advise the Congolese authorities on how the many international medical teams might be employed to the best advantage of the country" (WHO, "World Health in the Congo").

14 Bwimana, "Health Sector Network Governance."

15 On the health system under Mobutu's early rule, see Waldman, "Health in Fragile States"; Bwimana, "Health Sector Network Governance"; Bukonda et al., "Health Care Entrepreneurship."

16 In 1990, Mobutu allocated 2.1 percent of state spending to health and education, compared with 17.5 percent in 1972 (Reno, *Warlord Politics and African States*, 153).

17 As Crawford Young and Thomas Turner (*Rise and Decline of the Zairian State*) demonstrate, seizure of public goods by private individuals was common under Mobutu's rule. On the way that the decline of the Zairean state affected health care provision in Congo, see Bwimana, "Health Sector Network Governance"; Bertone, Lurton, and Mutombo, "Investigating the Remuneration of Health Workers"; Waldman, "Health in Fragile States"; Seay, "Effective Responses."

18 Thus written, this history of health care in eastern Congo ignores the politics of health care financing. Surely, there is less money in the national Congolese budget per capita than most other places in the world, which means that health care remains chronically underfunded. And, as Luke Messac (*No More to Spend*) so brilliantly demonstrates in Malawi, colonial and postcolonial governments have also systematically constructed scarcity as a means to justify the poor state of health care in the country. In eastern Congo, the construction of scarcity extends to the current era, where governmental and nongovernmental entities financing health care in Congo also rationalize their limited action.

19 Zero Congolese physicians existed at independence in 1960. As a result, co-lonial relations continued to characterize medicine in Congo/Zaire long after independence had been declared. From the histories that were told to me by longtime Kishabe residents, this also held true in Kishabe despite the fact that the hospital was built in 1963.

20 "CENAB" here is a pseudonym.

21 During a speech in 1979, Mobutu had blamed the country's economic and social decline on the population's greediness and corruption, which he termed *le mal Zaïrois*. The population immediately turned the phrase on its head and began to use it to describe the pervasiveness of the president's graft (Dunn, *Imagining the Congo*, 131). For more on *le mal Zaïrois*, see Schatzberg, *Dialectics of Oppression in Zaire*; Young, *Postcolonial State in Africa*; Young and Turner, *Rise and Decline of the Zairian State*.

22 Bwimana, "Health Sector Network Governance," 1479.

23 Nancy Rose Hunt has written about hitting during labor in the colonial period. See Hunt, *Colonial Lexicon*, 219.

24 Hunt, *Colonial Lexicon*, 205.

25 As one reader has pointed out, this type of fleshy work—and surgery more broadly—was part of a new conception of the individual body, which entered the continent with Christianity. In a paper that looks at the introduction of tooth pulling in southern Africa, historian Paul Landau ("Explaining Surgical Evangelism") highlights the difference in agency between surgery, which puts the afflicted under maximum influence by the healer, and traditional African pharmacopeia, which the afflicted could choose not to take.

26 Julie Livingston's *Improvising Medicine* has been an incredible primer for the wide diversity of ways that health workers can care for their patients amid great structural violence.

27 All women in need of reproductive health care in Kishabe passed through the maternity ward. As in other public facilities, the maternity ward in Kishabe did not have the means or the staff to conduct preventative care for women (e.g., cervical exams, mammograms) and only offered minimal family planning options (mostly the rhythm method).

28 These family members served as part of the "therapy management group" proposed by John Janzen in *The Quest for Therapy in Lower Zaire*.

29 On the obligation to count in this context—and the different things that counting elides and makes possible—see Oni-Orisan, "Obligation to Count."

30 Diane Nelson writes, "One counts, but it is insufficient. It is telling—context, milieu, identities—that makes one (death) count" (*Reckoning*, 291).

31 See Hunt, *Colonial Lexicon*, 212. Also, Hunt, "Le Bébé en Brousse."

32 De Boeck, "On Being Shege in Kinshasa," 173.

33 This is notably different from Scheper-Hughes's description of the role of children in impoverished homes in Brazil, where their fragile bodies served as constant reminders of mothers' inability to act durably in the present, to build different futures (*Death without Weeping*).

34   Mbembe, "Variations on the Beautiful."

35   Mbembe, "Variations on the Beautiful," 74–75.

36   Mbembe, "Variations on the Beautiful," 78.

37   Mbembe, "Variations on the Beautiful," 81.

38   See also Mbembe's reading of Fanon on care in Mbembe, *Necropolitics*.

39   Or so the memories go.

40   Spillers, "Mama's Baby, Papa's Maybe," 167.

41   "Racializing assemblages" is a term used by Weheliye in his synthesis of Spillers's work with that of Sylvia Wynter. See Weheliye, *Habeas Viscus*.

42   Coghlan et al., "Mortality." Also see Coghlan et al., "Update on Mortality."

43   Significant controversy has surrounded this finding. D'Errico et al. ("'You Say Rape, I Say Hospitals,'" 54) provide a good review of this debate. In brief, epidemiologists criticize Coghlan et al. for using as a denominator for the study the average mortality rate of sub-Saharan Africa. Since this denominator does not take into account the very high prewar mortality in the DRC, they believe that the mortality rate that Coghlan et al. found is exaggerated.

CHAPTER 4. WHEN LIFE DEMANDS RELEASE

1   Janzen and MacGaffey, *An Anthology of Kongo Religion*. See also the testimony of the Congolese soldier in this chapter's second epigraph; quoted in Baaz and Stern, "Making Sense of Violence," 77.

2   See Hunt, "Acoustic Register."

3   Quoted from a woman interviewed at a women's empowerment program in 2013.

4   While I have never lived in Rutshuru, I began taking trips to visit several women's empowerment programs in the area in 2010 and 2011. Through this work, I gained multiple contacts in the town with whom I kept in close contact throughout 2012 and 2013. When it was safe to do so, I visited the town during its occupation by M23 and afterward, spending time with my previous contacts as well as with the youths to whom they introduced me.

5   While I discuss the impact of revolutionary violence on my thinking here, many other theorists of violence have contributed to my understanding of it. I owe a special debt to many conversations with Ian Whitmarsh about violence. And to the following authors: Hunt, *Nervous State*; Nelson, *Reckoning*; Scheper-Hughes and Bourgois, *Violence in War and Peace*; Green, *Fear as a Way of Life*; Finnström, *Living with Bad Surroundings*; Hoffman, *War Machines*; Richards, *Fighting for the Rain Forest*; Roitman, *Fiscal Disobedience*; Lombard, *State of Rebellion*; Thiranagama, *In My Mother's House*; Lubkemann, *Culture in Chaos*; Debos, *Living by the Gun in Chad*; Nordstrom, *Shadows of War*; Dubal, *Against Humanity*.

6   See X and Breitman, *Malcolm X Speaks*. See also Newton and Blake, Revolutionary Suicide.

7   See Fanon, *Wretched of the Earth*.

8   Mbembe, *Necropolitics*, 89.

9   Mbembe, *Necropolitics*, 3.

10   For more on the long-term effects of mal/undernutrition, see Sudfeld et al., "Malnutrition and Its Determinants"; Martins et al., "Long-Lasting Effects of Undernutrition."

11   For a characterization of life in a camp for internally displaced/refugees in the region, see Norman and Niehuus, "18 Years Displaced." In an article on the social value of hunger in Kinshasa, Filip De Boeck argues that hunger in Congo is understood not as merely an individual pathology but as an effect and a source of social disintegration. He writes, "The idiom of 'hunger' acts as a pivotal point between the breakdown and maintenance of vital relations of interdependence" ("'When Hunger Goes around the Land,'" 275). In addition to indicating the fragility of social relations, hunger also provides a medium for repairing social order, according to De Boeck.

12   On the problem of Banyarwanda land rights, see Stearns et al, "Banyamulenge."

13   This is covered in more depth in chapter 1, but see also Jackson, "Sons of Which Soil?"; Jackson, "War in the Making"; Geschiere and Jackson, "Autochthony and the Crisis of Citizenship."

14   On governance during Mobutu's era, see Schatzberg, *Dialectics of Oppression in Zaire*; Young and Turner, *Rise and Decline of the Zairian State*; Young, *Postcolonial State in Africa*; Reno, *Warlord Politics and African States*.

15   Mobutu renamed Congo "Zaire" in 1971. Under the auspices of returning Congolese (Zairean) wealth to the Congolese (Zairean people), he carried out a campaign of Zaireanization/*authenticité*, which included legislation that allowed for the state seizure of private wealth, as well as that which stipulated appropriate dress and national language. For more on *authenticité*, see Schatzberg, *Dialectics of Oppression in Zaire*.

16   On the health system under Mobutu, see Bertone, Lurton, and Mutombo, "Investigating the Remuneration of Health Workers"; Waldman, "Health in Fragile States"; Congo Research Group, "Ebola in the DRC."

17   Reno, *Warlord Politics and African States*.

18   Schatzberg, *Dialectics of Oppression in Zaire*, 59. Three decades later, Mobutu's statement, "The population is cornfield of the military," remains oft quoted and, to some extent, still practiced. Writing on governance in eastern Congo in the 2010s, Ann Laudati notes, "Pillage is not simply a negative symptom of war but may serve as the main instrument for troop retention" ("Beyond Minerals," 44).

19   Devisch, "Frenzy, Violence, and Ethical Renewal," 608.

20   Migration Policy Institute, "Democratic Republic of the Congo."

21   Collyer, "In-Between Places."

22   The trajectories of Congolese migrants across the Mediterranean, as well as some of their motivations, are discussed in Collyer, "In-Between Places"; Schapendonk, "Turbulent Trajectories"; Kassar and Dourgnon, "Big Crossing."

23   The inability to know what happened to whom when, I believe, is part of the terror of the violence. See chapter 3 on this, and also Nelson, *Reckoning*.

24   On the political economy of the camp, see Redfield, "Doctors, Borders, and Life in Crisis"; Waal, *Famine Crimes*.

25 On the toxic effects of gold mining in eastern DRC on people and the environment, see Nkuba, Bervoets, and Geenen, "Invisible and Ignored?"; Yard et al.,
   "Mercury Exposure among Artisanal Gold Miners." For toxic effects of cobalt and
   manganese mining, see Banza Lubaba Nkulu et al., "Sustainability of Artisanal
   Mining."

26 For an explanation of konzo in Congo and more generally, see Banea et al., "Control of Konzo in DRC"; Cliff et al., "Konzo and Continuing Cyanide Intoxication,"
   respectively.

27 Fanon, *Wretched of the Earth*, 182.

28 Fanon, *Wretched of the Earth*, 182.

29 Mbembe, *Necropolitics*, 168–69.

30 Mbembe writes, "Let us dwell, then, on this founding moment that, in Fanon, has
   a name: radical decolonization. In his work, this decolonization is likened to a
   force of refusal and it stands directly opposed to the passion of habituation. This
   force of refusal constitutes the first moment of the political and of the subject. In
   fact, the subject of the political—or the Fanonian subject period—is born to the
   world and to itself through this inaugural gesture, namely the capacity to say no"
   (*Necropolitics*, 139).

31 Huey Newton writes, "Revolutionary suicide does not mean that I and my com-
   rades have a death wish; it means just the opposite. We have such a strong desire
   to live with hope and human dignity that existence without them is impossible.
   When reactionary forces crush us, we must move against these forces, even at
   the risk of death. We will have to be driven out with a stick" (Newton and Blake,
   Revolutionary Suicide, 3).

32 I use the word *foreign* here because Trésor did. During the First and Second
   Congo Wars, foreign militaries operated in Congo. Since then, international
   meddling/graft has continued in the East, although in less overt ways. On the
   links between CNDP, M23, and Rwanda, see United Nations, "Midterm Report";
   Stearns et al, "From CNDP to M23."

33 The fact that *peace* was written in Rwanda's national languages—English and
   Kinyarwanda—did not go unnoticed.

34 On the militarized levying of taxes at roadblocks in Congo, see Jaillon et al.,
   "'Everything That Moves Will Be Taxed.'"

35 The acronym PARECO stands for Coalition des patriotes résistants congolais, or
   Alliance of Resistant Congolese Patriots.
      Surely, the emergence of these groups of militarized youths cannot be di-
   vorced from the influence of the networks of political and economic elites that
   run from Rwanda through North Kivu to Kinshasa. On the regional dynamics
   that drive conflict in Congo, see especially Stearns, *Dancing in the Glory of Monsters*; Reyntjens, *Great African War*; Vogel, *Conflict Minerals, Inc.*

36 Although they went by various names—PARECO, Nyatura—the youth combatants in Rutshuru were part of a larger self-defense movement called Mai Mai
   (also known as Mayi Mayi or Maji Maji). In the early 1990s, Mai Mai, or "water-
   water," emerged as a group of self-designated "autochthonous" fighters who first

took up arms in the name of "indigeneity." The protection of territorial sovereignty was their raison d'être; their broader mission was the cultivation of a pure Congolese identity, free from foreign influence. To this end, combatants in the Mai Mai movement observed a strict ethical regime that included various sexual and dietary prohibitions. And because they viewed an authentic Congolese way of life as being protective, they cleansed their bodies with *dawa*—literally, medicine, which often took the form of sacred water—before battle. For more on local militias including the Mai Mai, see Hoffmann, "Ethics of Child-Soldiering in the Congo"; Jourdan, "Mayi-Mayi"; Stearns et al, "PARECO."

37 See Vogel, "No More M23."

38 Mbembe, *Necropolitics*, 91.

39 On the origins of the ADF, see Congo Research Group, "Mass Killings in Beni Territory."

40 Because of the murkiness surrounding who exactly is committing massacres in the region, most journalists now use the term "suspected ADF" when describing the group's activity in the region. For a more recent analysis of who constitutes the ADF and how they are related to the violence in Beni, see the website produced by Congo Research Group titled "Inside the ADF" at https://insidetheadf.org/.

41 On the exacerbation of conflict by the Ebola epidemic and the response to it, see Wells et al., "Exacerbation of Ebola Outbreaks"; Congo Research Group, "Rebels, Doctors, and Merchants of Violence."

42 While his personal research served as the source for much of the discussion, many of the details this researcher presented find support in the reports that the UN Group of Experts produces biannually.

43 On the price of bullets and guns in the region, see Verweijen, "Violent Cities."

44 On why ethnic conflict motivates particularly intimate forms of violence, see Arjun Appadurai, who writes, "Combining Malkki's material on ethnic violence in Burundi with Geschiere's study of witchcraft in Cameroon, against the backdrop of Douglas's path-breaking work on category confusion, power, and taboo, allows us to see that the killing, torture, and rape associated with ethnocidal violence is not simply a matter of eliminating the ethnic other. It involves the use of the body to establish the parameters of this otherness, taking the body apart, so to speak, to divine the enemy within" ("Dead Certainty," 913).

45 Dubal, *Against Humanity*.

46 Dubal, *Against Humanity*, 70.

47 Mbembe, *Necropolitics*, 22.

48 Importantly, in his writings, Fanon identifies two kinds of violence: that which is carried out against fellow subalterns, which he calls "fratricidal violence" and describes as purely destructive, and that which is carried out against colonial regimes, which he celebrates as future oriented and liberatory. Given that the violence perpetrated by the ADF (and, for that matter, the LRA) is perpetrated against poor, rural, Black people, an argument could be made that it falls into Fanon's first category—that is, it is purely destructive violence. While I do not

think this is an incorrect reading of Fanon, I do think that it underestimates the disruptive work that these killings do. For more on the capacity of this type of violence to interrupt the status quo, see Congo Research Group, "Rebels, Doctors, and Merchants of Violence"; Congo Research Group, "Ebola in the DRC."

49 See Arendt, *On Violence.*

50 For further discussion of this future-oriented violence, see Mbembe and Goldberg, "In Conversation."

INTERLUDE 4. JOY

1 Verweijen, "Violent Cities."

2 Stearns, Verweijen, and Baaz, "National Army and Armed Groups"; Baaz and Stern, "Making Sense of Violence"; Baaz and Verweijen, "Between Integration and Disintegration."

3 Smith, "Joy."

4 On the affect of traces and nostalgia on the continent, see Geissler et al., *Traces of the Future*; Piot, *Nostalgia for the Future.*

5 See Hunt, "Acoustic Register."

CHAPTER 5. "WE ARE CREATING A WORLD WE HAVE NEVER SEEN"

1 MacGaffey and Bazenguissa-Ganga, *Congo-Paris*; Mbembe, "African Modes of Self-Writing"; Mbembe, "Variations on the Beautiful."

2 Lorde, *Sister Outsider*, 37.

3 See brown, "Afrofuturism and #blackspring." Also the chapter titled "creating more possibilities" in brown, *Emergent Strategy.*

4 Perhaps an Africa otherwise, as Roitman has suggested ("Africa Otherwise").

5 Here, I follow Simon Quashie, who writes, "the poetic, which invites us to live in subjunctivity, which casts subjunctivity as an essential condition of being alive; the poetic, which as an ontology asks 'what if'" (*Black Aliveness*, 28).

6 I am indebted to Susan Buck-Morss's *Dreamworld and Catastrophe* for its articulation of a dreamworld as a poetic description of a collective mental state, and as an analytical concept.

7 The manifesto, titled *Manifeste du Congo Nouveau* (Manifesto of the New Congo), can be viewed under "Nos idées" at LUCHA's website; accessed December 6, 2022, http://www.luchacongo.org/.

8 For more on LUCHA, see its website (http://www.luchacongo.org/) as well as Bantariza, Hirschel-Burns, and Schuster, "Lucha Continua"; Berwouts, "'La Lucha.'"

9 See the Human Rights Watch coverage of the imprisonment of LUCHA members, as well as obituaries for Luc Nkulula, for example, Human Rights Watch, "Congolese Authorities Arrest, Later Release 49 Activists"; Human Rights Watch, "DR Congo"; *Economist*, "Luc Nkulula Died on June 10th."

10 For more on the Congolese space program, see Monod, "Le programme spatial congolais Troposphère"; Voyages Extraordinaires, "Fusée spatiale congolaise

Troposphère 6"; Kovalchik, "Brief History of the Congolese Space Program"; Le Baron, "How's the Congolese Space Program Doing?"

11 I am not sure of the original title or author of the video; at the time of writing it appears at YouTube twice, posted by Voyages Extraordinaire, under the title "Fusée spatiale congolaise Troposphère 6," https://www.youtube.com/watch ?app=desktop&v=i--Ar4TWKuU; and under the title "Congolese Space Rocket Troposphère 6," https://www.youtube.com/watch?v=uAcD2AsMMBc. I cite the video in this book by the first title.

12 Serpell, "Meet 'The Afronauts.'" See also Nuotama Bodomo's film titled *Afronauts*.

13 Serpell, "Meet 'The Afronauts.'"

14 Thanks to Martha Saavedra for passing along this article.

15 According to Mbembe, in the Afrofuturist tradition, "The earthly condition is thus replaced by the cosmic condition, the stage of reconciliation between the human, the animal, the vegetal, the organic, the mineral, and all the other forces of the living, be they solar, nocturnal, or astral" (*Necropolitics*, 164). While neither Keka nor Nkoloso speak specifically about a human-nonhuman reconciliation, the manner in which they both speak about the possibilities of space travel gestures toward Afrofuturism as defined by Mbembe.

16 This is a phrase heard commonly in Congo. In Raoul Peck's biographical film *Lumumba*, Lumumba speaks these words.

17 For more on Lumumba, see George Nzongola-Ntalaja's biographical book *Patrice Lumumba*; and Peck, *Lumumba*. The letter from which this quotation is taken was republished in full online: Lumumba, "Dernière lettre à sa femme Pauline."

18 On Lumumba's assassination, see Devlin, *Chief of Station, Congo*, written by the chief of station for the CIA in Congo when Lumumba was killed.

19 See Fiston and Strauss, "Can a Tooth Settle the Mystery"; AFP, "Daughter of DR Congo Hero."

20 On the role of the international community in Congolese politics, see Stearns, *Dancing in the Glory of Monsters*; Vlassenroot and Raeymaekers, *Conflict and Social Transformation*; Vogel, *Conflict Minerals, Inc.*

21 Mbembe, *On the Postcolony*.

22 Gumbs, "Prophecy in the Present Tense," 143.

23 On Gumbs's reading of Harriet Tubman's dreams, see Gumbs, "Prophecy in the Present Tense"; brown and Brown, "Breathing Chorus with Alexis Pauline Gumbs."

24 This was the start of the First Congo War.

25 This was the start of the Second Congo War.

26 Since Debora told me this story, the ending has changed somewhat. In April 2020, Moïse returned to Goma. While Debora has sent me pictures of her and Moïse and reports over WhatsApp that they are doing well, I have not had a true conversation with Debora about Moïse's return, nor about the current state of their relationship. Without any information about the circumstances of Moïse's

return or how Debora understands this event, I have chosen to tell their story as of the last time I saw Debora in person, in March 2020.

27 This particular phrase is the title of an article she wrote as part of a conversation with Lawrence Cohen and Michael Hardt in *Cultural Anthropology*: Berlant, "Properly Political Concept of Love." See also Berlant, "Love, a Queer Feeling"; Berlant, "Intimacy"; Berlant, *Desire/Love*.

28 Berlant, "Properly Political Concept of Love," 690.

29 Berlant, "Properly Political Concept of Love," 685.

30 Reno, *Warlord Politics and African States*.

31 Berlant, "Properly Political Concept of Love," 685.

32 On Black aliveness, see Quashie, *Black Aliveness*.

33 Kevin Quashie writes, "This is what a poem does it orients you into openness, into being capable of the openness that is rightfully yours" (*Black Aliveness*, 138).

34 In Black science fiction writer Alexis De Veaux's words, "The future is our next breath"; from "Writing New Worlds," a discussion with Alexis Pauline Gumbs and Walida Imarsha at the Allied Media Conference, 2020; accessed July 18, 2023, http://alexisdeveaux.com/writing-new-worlds/.

INTERLUDE 5. OTHERWISE

1 For more on speculative nonfiction, see Knopp, "'Perhapsing.'"

2 Nelson, *Reckoning*; Taussig, *Shamanism, Colonialism, and the Wild Man*; Taussig, *Nervous System*.

3 I am thankful to Reader 3 for proposing that this question haunts the book throughout.

4 For a review of early epigenetics research, see Kim et al., "Neuroepigenetics of Post-traumatic Stress Disorder."

5 For a review of the biological research around transgenerational inheritance of trauma, see Jawaid, Roszkowski, and Mansuy, "Transgenerational Epigenetics of Traumatic Stress"; Kellerman, "Epigenetic Transmission of Holocaust Trauma." For an ethnographic account of the way that hauntings are passed on, see Schwab, *Haunting Legacies*.

6 Thiranagama, *In My Mother's House*, 99.

7 See Mulligan et al., "Methylation Changes at *NR3C1* in Newborns."

8 I borrow this term from Quashie, *Black Aliveness*.

CONCLUSION. COHABITATION

1 World Food Program, "WFP Democratic Republic of Congo Country Brief."

2 By the time the epidemic was finally declared over, it had become the largest epidemic to affect Congo, and, lasting twenty-three months and claiming 2,287 lives, the second largest and longest globally to date.

3 Congo Research Group, "Rebels, Doctors, and Merchants of Violence."

4   For more on the militarization of the Ebola Response in eastern Congo, see Congo Research Group, "Rebels, Doctors, and Merchants of Violence"; Congo Research Group, "Ebola in the DRC"; Nguyen, "Epidemic of Suspicion"; Wells et al., "Exacerbation of Ebola Outbreaks." On a similar phenomenon in West Africa, see Benton, "Whose Security?"; Burci, "Ebola, the Security Council and the Securitization"; Heymann et al., "Global Health Security."

5   At the time, this was a radical proposition, perhaps akin to suggesting the possibility that COVID-19 might become endemic in April 2020.

6   Congo Research Group, "Ebola in the DRC."

7   After Moyer sat down, Vinh-Kim Nguyen stood and continued the query. He proposed that the problem of exclusion, of boundaries, was not one limited to the community, to lovers making decisions behind closed doors. Rather, he suggested that the scientists, epidemiologists, and public health experts working on HIV were deathly afraid of cohabitating with the virus. For the discourse around HIV to change, he suggested, for cohabitation to become an acceptable public health message, those generating the messages, producing the expertise, would have to become comfortable with living with their own death.

8   Mbembe asks, "How to study the world? A single global system? A horizontally integrative macro history, one that seeks for the connections between the various events that are happening in regions that have traditionally been considered separate?" ("Africa in Theory," 228).

9   I am in debt to Reviewer 3 for this idea and this language.

10   The idea of archiving the ideas of a society on the edge of transformation came from Alexis Pauline Gumbs. Gumbs's book *M Archive* is, in her words, a "speculative documentary work" that seeks to "[depict] a species at the edge of its integrity, on the verge or in the practice of transforming into something beyond the luxuries and limitations of what some call 'the human'" (*M Archive*, xi).

11   A slight rewording of Comaroff and Comaroff's argument in *Theory from the South*.

12   These excerpts are taken from Mbembe's 2018 interview with David Theo Goldberg: Mbembe and Goldberg, "In Conversation." Mbembe covered similar ground in his December 8, 2018, keynote lecture at the "Recognition, Reparation, and Reconciliation" conference at Stellenbosch University.

13   In Fred Moten and Stefano Harney's conception of it, the undercommons is home to Black folks and queer folks and all other subaltern folks, a space that challenges rationality, order. It is a space where what survival looks like in the wake is being worked out, where what makes sense and what could be are constantly being redefined (Harney and Moten, *Undercommons*).

Acker, Frank Van. "Where Did All the Land Go? Enclosure and Social Struggle in Kivu (D.R.Congo)." *Review of African Political Economy* 32, no. 103 (March 1, 2005): 79–98. https://doi.org/10.1080/03056240500120984.

AFP. "Daughter of DR Congo Hero Demands Belgium Return Father's 'Relics.'" *France 24*, July 21, 2020. https://www.france24.com/en/20200721-daughter-of-dr-congo-hero-demands-belgium-return-father-s-relics.

Al Jazeera. "DR Congo Recruits Robots as Traffic Police." March 20, 2014, sec. Science and Technology. https://www.aljazeera.com/news/2014/3/20/dr-congo-recruits-robots-as-traffic-police.

Appadurai, Arjun. "Dead Certainty: Ethnic Violence in the Era of Globalization." *Development and Change* 29, no. 4 (October 1, 1998): 905–25. https://doi.org/10.1111/1467-7660.00103.

Arendt, Hannah. *On Violence*. N.p.: Important Books, 2014.

Art Daily. "Exhibition Invites Visitors to Gradually Learn about the Main Concepts in Kader Attia's Work." Accessed January 25, 2021. https://artdaily.cc/news/105399/Exhibition-invites-visitors-to-gradually-learn-about-the-main-concepts-in-Kader-Attia-s-work#.

Attia, Kader. *RepaiR*. Paris: Blackjack-Éd, 2014.

Autesserre, Séverine. "Dangerous Tales: Dominant Narratives on the Congo and Their Unintended Consequences." *African Affairs* 111, no. 443 (April 2012): 202–22. https://doi.org/10.1093/afraf/adr080.

Autesserre, Séverine. "Local Violence, National Peace? Postwar 'Settlement' in the Eastern D.R. Congo (2003–2006)." *African Studies Review* 49, no. 3 (December 2006): 1–29. https://doi.org/10.1353/arw.2007.0007.

Autesserre, Séverine. *The Trouble with the Congo: Local Violence and the Failure of International Peacebuilding*. Cambridge: Cambridge University Press, 2010.

Baaz, Maria Eriksson, and Maria Stern. "The Complexity of Violence: A Critical Analysis of Sexual Violence in the Democratic Republic of Congo (DRC)." Sida: Nordiska Afrikainstitutet, 2010. http://urn.kb.se/resolve?urn=urn:nbn:se:nai:diva-1119.

Baaz, Maria Eriksson, and Maria Stern. "Making Sense of Violence: Voices of Soldiers in the Congo (DRC)." *Journal of Modern African Studies* 46, no. 1 (2008): 57–86.

Baaz, Maria Eriksson, and Maria Stern. "Why Do Soldiers Rape? Masculinity, Violence, and Sexuality in the Armed Forces in the Congo (DRC)." *International*

Studies Quarterly 53, no. 2 (June 2009): 495–518. https://doi.org/10.1111/j.1468-2478 .2009.00543.x.

Baaz, Maria Eriksson, and Judith Verweijen. "Between Integration and Disintegration: The Erratic Trajectory of the Congolese Army." Social Science Research Council: DR Congo Affinity Group, April 29, 2013. https://www.ssrc.org/publications /between_integration_and_disintegration_the_erratic_trajectory/.

Baaz, Maria Eriksson, and Judith Verweijen. "The Volatility of a Half-Cooked Bouilla-baisse: Rebel–Military Integration and Conflict Dynamics in the Eastern DRC." *African Affairs* 112, no. 449 (October 2013): 563–82. https://doi.org/10.1093/afraf/adt044.

Banea, J. P., G. Nahimana, C. Mandombi, J. Howard Bradbury, Ian C. Denton, and N. Kuwa. "Control of Konzo in DRC Using the Wetting Method on Cassava Flour." *Food and Chemical Toxicology* 50, no. 5 (May 2012): 1517–23. https://doi.org/10.1016 /j.fct.2012.02.001.

Bantariza, Ruby, Tim Hirschel-Burns, and Sophia Schuster. "Lucha Continua: The Youth Movement Striking Fear into Congo's Elite." *African Arguments* (blog), May 31, 2017. https://africanarguments.org/2017/05/lucha-continua-the-youth -movement-striking-fear-into-congos-elite/.

Banza Lubaba Nkulu, Célestin, Lidia Casas, Vincent Haufroid, Thierry De Putter, Nelly D. Saenen, Tony Kayembe-Kitenge, Paul Musa Obadia, et al. "Sustainability of Artisanal Mining of Cobalt in DR Congo." *Nature Sustainability* 1, no. 9 (September 2018): 495–504. https://doi.org/10.1038/s41893-018-0139-4.

Bayart, Jean-François. *The State in Africa: The Politics of the Belly*. New York: Longman, 1993.

Bayart, Jean-François, Stephen Ellis, and Béatrice Hibou. *The Criminalization of the State in Africa*. International African Institute, 1999.

Bboxx. "DRC Government Partnership." January 21, 2020. https://www.bboxx.com /news/bboxx-partners-drc-government/.

Benton, Adia. "Whose Security? Militarization and Securitization during West Africa's Ebola Outbreak." In *The Politics of Fear: Médecins sans Frontières and the West African Ebola Epidemic*, edited by Michiel Hofman and Sokhieng Au, 25–50. New York: Oxford University Press, 2017.

Berlant, Lauren. *Desire/Love*. New York: Punctum, 2012.

Berlant, Lauren. "Intimacy: A Special Issue." *Critical Inquiry* 24, no. 2 (January 1998): 281–88. https://doi.org/10.1086/448875.

Berlant, Lauren. "Love, a Queer Feeling." In *Homosexuality and Psychoanalysis*, edited by Tim Dean and Christopher Lane, 432–51. Chicago: University of Chicago Press, 2001.

Berlant, Lauren. "A Properly Political Concept of Love: Three Approaches in Ten Pages." *Cultural Anthropology* 26, no. 4 (2011): 683–91. https://doi.org/10.1111/j.1548 -1360.2011.01120.x.

Bernault, Florence. "Body, Power, and Sacrifice in Equatorial Africa." *Journal of African History* 47, no. 2 (July 2006): 207–39. https://doi.org/10.1017 /S0021853706001836.

Bernstein, Richard J. "Derrida: The Aporia of Forgiveness?" *Constellations* 13, no. 3 (2006): 394–406. https://doi.org/10.1111/j.1467-8675.2006.00400.x.

Bertone, Maria Paola, Grégoire Lurton, and Paulin Beya Mutombo. "Investigating the Remuneration of Health Workers in the DR Congo: Implications for the Health Workforce and the Health System in a Fragile Setting." *Health Policy and Planning* 31, no. 9 (2016): 1143–51. https://doi.org/10.1093/heapol/czv131.

Berwouts, Kris. "'La Lucha': Goma's Own Brand of Indignados." *African Arguments* (blog), January 13, 2014. https://africanarguments.org/2014/01/la-lucha-gomas-own -brand-of-indignados-by-kris-berwouts/.

Bodomo, Nuotama, dir. *Afronauts*. Vimeo, July 30, 2019. https://vimeo.com /350994709.

brown, adrienne maree. "Afrofuturism and #blackspring (New School, #aroturismtns)." *Adrienne Maree Brown* (blog), May 2, 2015. https://adriennemareebrown .net/2015/05/02/afrofuturism-and-blackspring-new-school-afroturismtns/.

brown, adrienne maree. *Emergent Strategy: Shaping Change, Changing Worlds*. Chico, CA: AK Press, 2017.

brown, adrienne maree, and Autumn Brown. "A Breathing Chorus with Alexis Pauline Gumbs." *How to Survive the End of the World* (podcast), December 19, 2017. https://www.endoftheworldshow.org/blog/2017/12/19/a-breathing-chorus-with -alexis-pauline-gumbs.

Buck-Morss, Susan. *Dreamworld and Catastrophe: The Passing of Mass Utopia in East and West*. Cambridge, MA: MIT Press, 2002.

Bukonda, Ngoyi K. Z., Masud Chand, Tumba G. Disashi, Crispin wa Mbuyi Lumbala, and Benoit Mbiye. "Health Care Entrepreneurship in the Democratic Republic of the Congo: An Exploratory Study." *Journal of African Business* 13, no. 2 (May 2012): 87–100. https://doi.org/10.1080/15228916.2012.693433.

Burci, Gian. "Ebola, the Security Council and the Securitization of Public Health." *Questions of International Law* 10 (2014): 27–39.

Büscher, Karen. "Urbanisation and the Political Geographies of Violent Struggle for Power and Control: Mining Boomtowns in Eastern Congo." *International Development Policy | Revue Internationale de Politique de Développement*, no. 10 (October 1, 2018): 302–24. https://doi.org/10.4000/poldev.2769.

Büscher, Karen, and Koen Vlassenroot. "Humanitarian Presence and Urban Development: New Opportunities and Contrasts in Goma, DRC." *Disasters* 34, no. s2 (2010): S256–73. https://doi.org/10.1111/j.1467-7717.2010.01157.x.

Bwimana, Aembe. "Health Sector Network Governance and State-Building in South Kivu, Democratic Republic of Congo." *Health Policy and Planning* 32, no. 10 (December 2017): 1476–83. https://doi.org/10.1093/heapol/czx095.

Campt, Tina. "Black Feminist Futures and the Practice of Fugitivity." Barnard Center for Research on Women, October 7, 2014. https://bcrw.barnard.edu/videos/tina -campt-black-feminist-futures-and-the-practice-of-fugitivity/.

Chrétien, Jean-Pierre. *The Great Lakes of Africa: Two Thousand Years of History*. Translated by Scott Straus. Brooklyn: Zone, 2006.

Clarke, Kamari Maxine. "Affective Justice: The Racialized Imaginaries of International Justice." *PoLAR: Political and Legal Anthropology Review* 42, no. 2 (November 2019): 244–67. https://doi.org/10.1111/plar.12307.

Clarke, Kamari Maxine, and Abel Knottnerus, eds. *Africa and the ICC: Perceptions of Justice*. Cambridge: Cambridge University Press, 2016.

Cliff, J., H. Muquingue, D. Nhassico, H. Nzwalo, and J. H. Bradbury. "Konzo and Continuing Cyanide Intoxication from Cassava in Mozambique." *Food and Chemical Toxicology* 49, no. 3 (March 2011): 631–35. https://doi.org/10.1016/j.fct.2010.06.056.

Clifton, Lucille. *The Book of Light*. Port Townsend, WA: Copper Canyon, 1993.

Coghlan, Benjamin, Richard J. Brennan, Pascal Ngoy, David Dofara, Brad Otto, Mark Clements, and Tony Stewart. "Mortality in the Democratic Republic of Congo: An Ongoing Crisis." New York: International Rescue Committee, 2007.

Coghlan, Benjamin, Pascal Ngoy, Flavien Mulumba, Colleen Hardy, Valerie Nkamgang Bemo, Tony Stewart, Jennifer Lewis, and Richard J. Brennan. "Update on Mortality in the Democratic Republic of Congo: Results from a Third Nationwide Survey." *Disaster Medicine and Public Health Preparedness* 3, no. 2 (June 2009): 88–96. https://doi.org/10.1097/DMP.0b013e3181a6e952.

Collyer, Michael. "In-Between Places: Trans-Saharan Transit Migrants in Morocco and the Fragmented Journey to Europe." *Antipode* 39, no. 4 (2007): 668–90. https://doi.org/10.1111/j.1467-8330.2007.00546.x.

Comaroff, Jean, and John L. Comaroff. *Theory from the South: Or, How Euro-America Is Evolving toward Africa*. New York: Routledge, 2012.

Congo Research Group. "Ebola in the DRC: The Perverse Effects of a Parallel Health System." NYU, September 2020. https://www.alnap.org/help-library/ebola-in-the-drc-the-perverse-effects-of-a-parallel-health-system.

Congo Research Group. "Inside the ADF: A Glimpse into the Operations of Democratic Republic of Congo's Secretive Jihadist Group." Center on International Cooperation, New York University. November 2018. https://insidetheadf.org/.

Congo Research Group. "Mass Killings in Beni Territory: Political Violence, Cover Ups, and Cooptation." Center on International Cooperation at New York University, September 2017.

Congo Research Group. "Rebels, Doctors, and Merchants of Violence: How the Fight against Ebola Became Part of the Conflict in Eastern DRC." New York: New York University, 2021.

Csete, Joanne, and Juliane Kippenberg. "The War within the War: Sexual Violence against Women and Girls in Eastern Congo." Human Rights Watch, 2002.

De Boeck, Filip. "The Apocalyptic Interlude: Revealing Death in Kinshasa." *African Studies Review* 48, no. 2 (2005): 11–32.

De Boeck, Filip. "On Being Shege in Kinshasa: Children, the Occult, and the Street." In *Reinventing Order in the Congo: How People Respond to State Failure in Kinshasa*, edited by Theodore Trefon. London: Zed, 2013.

De Boeck, Filip. "'When Hunger Goes around the Land': Hunger and Food among the Aluund of Zaire." *Man* 29, no. 2 (1994): 257–82. https://doi.org/10.2307/2804474.

Debos, Marielle. *Living by the Gun in Chad: Combatants, Impunity and State Formation*. London: Zed, 2016.

D'Errico, Nicole C., Tshibangu Kalala, Louise Bashige Nzigire, Felicien Maisha, and Luc Malemo Kalisya. "'You Say Rape, I Say Hospitals. But Whose Voice Is Louder?' Health, Aid and Decision-Making in the Democratic Republic of Congo." *Review of African Political Economy* 40, no. 135 (March 2013): 51–66. https://doi.org/10.1080/03056244.2012.761962.

Derrida, Jacques. *Aporias*. Meridian: Crossing Aesthetics. Stanford, CA: Stanford University Press, 1993.

Devisch, René. "Frenzy, Violence, and Ethical Renewal in Kinshasa." *Public Culture* 7, no. 3 (1995): 593–629. https://doi.org/10.1215/08992363-7-3-593.

Devlin, Larry. *Chief of Station, Congo: Fighting the Cold War in a Hot Zone*. New York: PublicAffairs, 2008.

Dewachi, Omar. "Blurred Lines." *Medicine Anthropology Theory* 2, no. 2 (2015). https://doi.org/10.17157/mat.2.2.185.

Dubal, Sam. *Against Humanity: Lessons from the Lord's Resistance Army*. Oakland: University of California Press, 2018.

Dungy, Camille T. *Black Nature: Four Centuries of African American Nature Poetry*. Athens: University of Georgia Press, 2009.

Dunn, K. *Imagining the Congo: The International Relations of Identity*. New York: Palgrave Macmillan US, 2003. https://doi.org/10.1057/9781403979261.

Economist. "Luc Nkulula Died on June 10th." August 9, 2018. https://www.economist.com/obituary/2018/08/09/luc-nkulula-died-on-june-10th.

Einsiedel, Orlando von, dir. *Virunga*. Violet Films/Grain Media, 2014.

Englebert, Pierre, and Denis M. Tull. "Postconflict Reconstruction in Africa: Flawed Ideas about Failed States." *International Security* 32, no. 4 (Spring 2008): 106–39. https://doi.org/10.1162/isec.2008.32.4.106.

Fahey, Dan. "Rethinking the Resource Curse: Natural Resources and Polywar in the Ituri District, Democratic Republic of the Congo." PhD diss., UC Berkeley, 2011. https://escholarship.org/uc/item/320469nv.

Fanon, Frantz. *Black Skin, White Masks*. Translated by Richard Philcox. New York: Grove, 2008.

Fanon, Frantz. *The Wretched of the Earth*. New York: Grove, 1963. https://groveatlantic.com/book/the-wretched-of-the-earth/.

Feierman, Steven. "Healing as Social Criticism in the Time of Colonial Conquest." *African Studies* 54, no. 1 (January 1, 1995): 73–88. https://doi.org/10.1080/00020189508707816.

Feierman, Steven, and John M. Janzen, eds. *The Social Basis of Health and Healing in Africa*. Berkeley: University of California Press, 1992. https://www.ucpress.edu/book/9780520066816/the-social-basis-of-health-and-healing-in-africa.

Ferguson, James. *Expectations of Modernity*. Berkeley: University of California Press, 1999. https://www.ucpress.edu/book/9780520217027/expectations-of-modernity.

Ferme, Mariane Conchita. *The Underneath of Things: Violence, History, and the Everyday in Sierra Leone*. Berkeley: University of California Press, 2001.

Finnström, Sverker. *Living with Bad Surroundings: War, History, and Everyday Moments in Northern Uganda*. Durham, NC: Duke University Press, 2008.

Fiston, Mahamba, and Marine Strauss. "Can a Tooth Settle the Mystery over Congo's Independence Hero?" Reuters, September 11, 2020. https://www.reuters.com/article/us-congo-belgium-lumumba-idUSKBN26220N.

Garcia, Angela. *The Pastoral Clinic*. Berkeley: University of California Press, 2010. https://www.ucpress.edu/book/9780520262089/the-pastoral-clinic.

Geissler, Paul W., Guillaume Lachenal, John Manton, Noémi Tousignant, Evgenia Arbugaeva, Mariele Neudecker, and John Derek Manton, eds. *Traces of the Future: An Archaeology of Medical Science in Africa*. Bristol, UK: Intellect, 2016.

Geschiere, Peter, and Stephen Jackson. "Autochthony and the Crisis of Citizenship: Democratization, Decentralization, and the Politics of Belonging." *African Studies Review* 49, no. 2 (2006): 1–8. https://doi.org/10.1353/arw.2006.0104.

Global Volcanism Program. "Report on Oku Volcanic Field (Cameroon)." Edited by Lindsay McClelland. *Scientific Event Alert Network Bulletin* 11, no. 8 (1986). https://doi.org/10.5479/si.GVP.SEAN198608-224030.

Green, Linda. *Fear as a Way of Life: Mayan Widows in Rural Guatemala*. New York: Columbia University Press, 2013.

Gumbs, Alexis Pauline. м *Archive: After the End of the World*. Durham, NC: Duke University Press, 2018.

Gumbs, Alexis Pauline. "Prophecy in the Present Tense: Harriet Tubman, the Combahee Pilgrimage, and Dreams Coming True." *Meridians* 12, no. 2 (2014): 142–52. https://doi.org/10.2979/meridians.12.2.142.

Gumbs, Alexis Pauline. *Undrowned: Black Feminist Lessons from Marine Mammals*. Chico, CA: AK Press, 2020.

Guyer, Jane I. "Prophecy and the Near Future: Thoughts on Macroeconomic, Evangelical, and Punctuated Time." *American Ethnologist* 34, no. 3 (2007): 409–21. https://doi.org/10.1525/ae.2007.34.3.409.

Harney, Stefano, and Fred Moten. *The Undercommons: Fugitive Planning and Black Study*. New York: Minor Compositions, 2013.

Hartman, Saidiya. "Venus in Two Acts." *Small Axe* 12, no. 2 (2008): 1–14.

Hartman, Saidiya V., and Frank B. Wilderson. "The Position of the Unthought." *Qui Parle* 13, no. 2 (2003): 183–201.

Heymann, David L., Lincoln Chen, Keizo Takemi, David P. Fidler, Jordan W. Tappero, Mathew J. Thomas, Thomas A. Kenyon, et al. "Global Health Security: The Wider Lessons from the West African Ebola Virus Disease Epidemic." *The Lancet* 385, no. 9980 (May 2015): 1884–1901. https://doi.org/10.1016/S0140-6736(15)60858-3.

Hochschild, Adam. *King Leopold's Ghost: A Story of Greed, Terror, and Heroism in Colonial Africa*. Boston: Houghton Mifflin Harcourt, 1999.

Hoffman, Danny. *The War Machines: Young Men and Violence in Sierra Leone and Liberia*. Durham, NC: Duke University Press, 2011.

Hoffmann, Kasper. "The Ethics of Child-Soldiering in the Congo." *Young* 18, no. 3 (August 2010): 339–58. https://doi.org/10.1177/110330881001800306.

Human Rights Watch. "Congolese Authorities Arrest, Later Release 49 Activists Holding Anti-Kabila Protests." *Democratic Republic of Congo in Crisis* (blog), October 5, 2017. https://www.hrw.org/blog-feed/democratic-republic-congo-crisis#.

Human Rights Watch. "DR Congo: Free Youth Activists." *Human Rights Watch* (blog), July 19, 2021. https://www.hrw.org/news/2021/07/19/dr-congo-free-youth-activists.

Human Rights Watch. "Justice on Trial." New York: Human Rights Watch, October 1, 2015. https://www.hrw.org/report/2015/10/01/justice-trial/lessons-minova-rape-case -democratic-republic-congo.

Hunt, Nancy Rose. "An Acoustic Register, Tenacious Images, and Congolese Scenes of Rape and Repetition." *Cultural Anthropology* 23, no. 2 (2008): 220–53. https://doi .org/10.1111/j.1548-1360.2008.00008.x.

Hunt, Nancy Rose. *A Colonial Lexicon: Of Birth Ritual, Medicalization, and Mobility in the Congo.* Durham, NC: Duke University Press, 1999.

Hunt, Nancy Rose. "Health and Healing." In *The Oxford Handbook of Modern African History*, edited by John Parker and Richard Reid. Oxford: Oxford University Press, 2013. https://doi.org/10.1093/oxfordhb/9780199572472.013.0020.

Hunt, Nancy Rose. "'Le Bébé en Brousse': European Women, African Birth Spacing and Colonial Intervention in Breast Feeding in the Belgian Congo." *International Journal of African Historical Studies* 21, no. 3 (1988): 401–32. https://doi.org/10.2307/219448.

Hunt, Nancy Rose. *A Nervous State: Violence, Remedies, and Reverie in Colonial Congo.* Durham, NC: Duke University Press, 2015.

Jackson, Stephen. "Sons of Which Soil? The Language and Politics of Autochthony in Eastern D.R. Congo." *African Studies Review* 49, no. 2 (2006): 95–124. https://doi .org/10.1353/arw.2006.0107.

Jackson, Stephen. "War in the Making: Bordering on Violence in the Kivu Provinces, DR Congo, 1997–2002." PhD diss., Princeton University, 2003.

Jaillon, Alexandre, Janvier Murairi, Peer Schouten, and Saidi Kubuya. "'Everything That Moves Will Be Taxed': The Political Economy of Roadblocks in North and South Kivu." IPIS, December 6, 2017.

James, Erica Caple. "The Political Economy of 'Trauma' in Haiti in the Democratic Era of Insecurity." *Culture, Medicine and Psychiatry* 28, no. 2 (2004): 127–49. https://doi .org/10.1023/B:MEDI.0000034407.39471.d4.

James, Erica Caple. "Ruptures, Rights, and Repair: The Political Economy of Trauma in Haiti." *Social Science and Medicine* 70, no. 1 (January 2010): 106–13. https://doi .org/10.1016/j.socscimed.2009.09.040.

Janzen, John M. "Ideologies and Institutions in Precolonial Western Equatorial African Therapeutics." In *The Social Basis of Health and Healing in Africa*, edited by Steven Feierman and John M. Janzen, 195–211. Comparative Studies of Health Systems and Medical Care. Berkeley: University of California Press, 1992.

Janzen, John M. *The Quest for Therapy in Lower Zaire.* Berkeley: University of California Press, 1982. https://www.ucpress.edu/book/9780520046337/the-quest-for -therapy-in-lower-zaire.

Janzen, John M., and Wyatt MacGaffey. *An Anthology of Kongo Religion: Primary Texts from Lower Zaïre.* Lawrence: University of Kansas, 1974.

Jawaid, Ali, Martin Roszkowski, and Isabelle M. Mansuy. "Transgenerational Epigenetics of Traumatic Stress." *Progress in Molecular Biology and Translational Science* no. 158 (2018): 273–98. https://doi.org/10.1016/bs.pmbts.2018.03.003.

Jemisin, N. K. *The Fifth Season: Every Age Must Come to an End*. Broken Earth Trilogy. New York: Orbit, 2018.

Jourdan, Luca. "Being at War, Being Young: Violence and Youth in North Kivu." In *Conflict and Social Transformation in Eastern DR Congo*, edited by Koen Vlassenroot and Timothy Raeymaekers, 157–76. Ghent: Academia, 2004.

Jourdan, Luca. "Mayi-Mayi: Young Rebels in Kivu, DRC." *Africa Development* 36, no. 3–4 (2011): 89–112.

Kalema, Emery "Scars, Marked Bodies, and Suffering: The Mulele 'Rebellion' in Postcolonial Congo." *Journal of African History* 59, no. 2 (2018). https://doi.org/10.1017/S0021853718000348.

Kassar, H., and P. Dourgnon. "The Big Crossing: Illegal Boat Migrants in the Mediterranean." *European Journal of Public Health* 24, suppl 1 (August 1, 2014): 11–15. https://doi.org/10.1093/eurpub/cku099.

Kellerman, N. P. "Epigenetic Transmission of Holocaust Trauma: Can Nightmares Be Inherited?" *Israel Journal of Psychiatry and Related Sciences* 50, no. 1 (January 1, 2013): 33–39.

Kim, Grace S., Alicia K. Smith, Caroline M. Nievergelt, and Monica Uddin. "Neuroepigenetics of Post-traumatic Stress Disorder." *Progress in Molecular Biology and Translational Science* 158 (2018): 227–53. https://doi.org/10.1016/bs.pmbts.2018.04.001.

Kisangani, Emizet Fran. *Civil Wars in the Democratic Republic of Congo: 1960–2010*. Boulder, CO: Lynne Rienner, 2012.

Knopp, Lisa. "'Perhapsing': The Use of Speculation in Creative Nonfiction." *Brevity*, January 8, 2009. https://brevitymag.com/craft-essays/perhapsing-the-use-of-speculation-in-creative-nonfiction/.

Kovalchik, Kara. "A Brief History of the Congolese Space Program." Mental Floss, March 13, 2011. https://www.mentalfloss.com/article/27244/brief-history-congolese-space-program.

Lake, Milli. "After Minova: Can War Crimes Trials Overcome Violence in the DRC?" *African Arguments* (blog), May 8, 2014. http://africanarguments.org/2014/05/08/after-minova-can-war-crimes-trials-overcome-violence-in-the-drc-by-millie-lake/.

Landau, Paul S. "Explaining Surgical Evangelism in Colonial Southern Africa: Teeth, Pain and Faith." *Journal of African History* 37, no. 2 (1996): 261–81.

Larmer, Miles, Ann Laudati, and John F. Clark. "Neither War nor Peace in the Democratic Republic of Congo (DRC): Profiting and Coping amid Violence and Disorder." *Review of African Political Economy* 40, no. 135 (2013): 1–12. https://doi.org/10.1080/03056244.2013.762165.

Last, Murray. "Healing the Social Wounds of War." *Medicine, Conflict and Survival* 16, no. 4 (October 2000): 370–82. https://doi.org/10.1080/13623690008409537.

Last, Murray. "The Importance of Knowing about Not Knowing." *Social Science and Medicine. Part B: Medical Anthropology* 15, no. 3 (July 1981): 387–92. https://doi.org/10.1016/0160-7987(81)90064-8.

Laudati, Ann. "Beyond Minerals: Broadening 'Economies of Violence' in Eastern Democratic Republic of Congo." *Review of African Political Economy* 40, no. 135 (2013): 32–50. https://doi.org/10.1080/03056244.2012.760446.

Le Baron, Julie. "How's the Congolese Space Program Doing?" *Vice*, March 14, 2014. https://www.vice.com/en/article/8gddy3/hows-the-congolese-space-program-doing -0000261-v21n3.

Leeuwen, Mathijs van, Gillian Mathys, Lotje de Vries, and Gemma van der Haar. "From Resolving Land Disputes to Agrarian Justice: Dealing with the Structural Crisis of Plantation Agriculture in Eastern DR Congo." *Journal of Peasant Studies* 49, no. 2 (2022): 309–34. https://doi.org/10.1080/03066150.2020.1824179.

Lemarchand, René. *Political Awakening in the Belgian Congo*. Berkeley: University of California Press, 1964. https://www.degruyter.com/isbn/9780520338630.

Lemarchand, René. "Reflections on the Recent Historiography of Eastern Congo." *Journal of African History* 54, no. 3 (November 2013): 417–37. https://doi.org/10.1017 /S002185371300073X.

Livingston, Julie. *Improvising Medicine: An African Oncology Ward in an Emerging Cancer Epidemic*. Durham, NC: Duke University Press, 2012.

Lombard, Louisa. *State of Rebellion: Violence and Intervention in the Central African Republic*. London: Zed, 2016.

Lorde, Audre. *Sister Outsider: Essays and Speeches*. Berkeley, CA: Crossing Press, 2007.

Lubkemann, Stephen. *Culture in Chaos*. Chicago: University of Chicago Press, 2007. https://press.uchicago.edu/ucp/books/book/chicago/C/bo5568065.html.

LUCHA (Lutte pour le changement). *Manifeste du Congo Nouveau*. Accessed July 17, 2023. http://www.luchacongo.org.

Lumumba, Patrice. "Dernière lettre à sa femme Pauline." *Quartiers Libres*, January 17, 2014. https://quartierslibres.wordpress.com/2014/01/17/patrice-lumumba-derniere -lettre-a-sa-femme-pauline/

Lyons, Maryinez. "Public Health in Colonial Africa: The Belgian Congo." In *The History of Public Health and the Modern State*, edited by Dorothy Porter. Amsterdam: Rodopi, 1994.

MacGaffey, Janet. *The Real Economy of Zaire: The Contribution of Smuggling and Other Unofficial Activities to National Wealth*. Philadelphia: University of Pennsylvania Press, 1991.

MacGaffey, Janet, and Rémy Bazenguissa-Ganga. *Congo-Paris: Transnational Traders on the Margins of the Law*. Bloomington: Indiana University Press, 2000.

Mamdani, Mahmood. *When Victims Become Killers: Colonialism, Nativism, and the Genocide in Rwanda*. Princeton, NJ: Princeton University Press, 2001.

Mararo, Bucyalimwe. "Land, Power, and Ethnic Conflict in Masisi (Congo-Kinshasa), 1940s–1994." *International Journal of African Historical Studies* 30, no. 3 (1997): 503–38. https://doi.org/10.2307/220574.

Marijnen, Esther. "Public Authority and Conservation in Areas of Armed Conflict: Virunga National Park as a 'State within a State' in Eastern Congo." *Development and Change* 49, no. 3 (2018): 790–814. https://doi.org/10.1111/dech.12380.

Marijnen, Esther, and Judith Verweijen. "Pluralising Political Forests: Unpacking 'the State' by Tracing Virunga's Charcoal Chain." *Antipode* 52, no. 4 (2020): 996–1017. https://doi.org/10.1111/anti.12492.

Marijnen, Esther, and Judith Verweijen. "Selling Green Militarization: The Discursive (Re)Production of Militarized Conservation in the Virunga National Park, Democratic Republic of the Congo." *Geoforum* 75 (October 2016): 274–85. https://doi.org/10.1016/j.geoforum.2016.08.003.

Martins, Vinicius J. B., Telma M. M. Toledo Florêncio, Luciane P. Grillo, Maria do Carmo P. Franco, Paula A. Martins, Ana Paula G. Clemente, Carla D. L. Santos, Maria de Fatima A. Vieira, and Ana Lydia Sawaya. "Long-Lasting Effects of Undernutrition." *International Journal of Environmental Research and Public Health* 8, no. 6 (June 2011): 1817–46. https://doi.org/10.3390/ijerph8061817.

Mathys, Gillian. "Bringing History Back In: Past, Present, and Conflict in Rwanda and the Eastern Democratic Republic of Congo." *Journal of African History* 58, no. 3 (November 2017): 465–87. https://doi.org/10.1017/S0021853717000391.

Mbembe, Achille. "Africa in Theory." In *African Futures: Essays on Crisis, Emergence, and Possibility*, edited by Brian Goldstone and Juan Obarrio, 211–30. Chicago: University of Chicago Press, 2017.

Mbembe, Achille. "African Modes of Self-Writing." Translated by Steven Rendall. *Public Culture* 14, no. 1 (2002): 239–73.

Mbembe, Achille. *Necropolitics*. Durham, NC: Duke University Press, 2019.

Mbembe, Achille. *On the Postcolony*. Berkeley: University of California Press, 2001. https://www.ucpress.edu/book/9780520204355/on-the-postcolony.

Mbembe, Achille. "Variations on the Beautiful in the Congolese World of Sounds." *Politique africaine* 100, no. 4 (2005): 69–91.

Mbembe, Achille, and David Goldberg. "In Conversation: Achille Mbembe and David Theo Goldberg on 'Critique of Black Reason.'" *Theory, Culture and Society*, March 7, 2018. https://www.theoryculturesociety.org/blog/interviews-achille-mbembe-david-theo-goldberg-critique-black-reason.

Mbembe, Achille, and Janet Roitman. "Figures of the Subject in Times of Crisis." *Public Culture* 7, no. 2 (1995): 323–52.

McCabe, Dan, dir. *This Is Congo*. Vision Entertainment, 2017.

Mertens, Myriam, and Guillaume Lachenal. "The History of 'Belgian' Tropical Medicine from a Cross-Border Perspective." *Revue belge de philologie et d'histoire* 90, no. 4 (2012): 1249–71. https://doi.org/10.3406/rbph.2012.8285.

Messac, Luke. *No More to Spend: Neglect and the Construction of Scarcity in Malawi's History of Health Care*. Oxford: Oxford University Press, 2020.

Migration Policy Institute. "Democratic Republic of the Congo." February 22, 2018. https://www.migrationpolicy.org/country-resource/congo-democratic-republic.

Monod, Olivier. "Le programme spatial congolais Troposphère existe-t-il vraiment?" *Libération*, May 23, 2019. https://www.liberation.fr/checknews/2019/05/23/le-programme-spatial-congolais-troposphere-existe-t-il-vraiment_1727376/.

Moten, Fred. "The Case of Blackness." *Criticism* 50, no. 2 (2008): 177–218.

Mulligan, Connie, Nicole D'Errico, Jared Stees, and David Hughes. "Methylation Changes at $NR3C1$ in Newborns Associate with Maternal Prenatal Stress Exposure and Newborn Birth Weight." *Epigenetics* 7, no. 8 (August 18, 2012): 853–57. https://doi.org/10.4161/epi.21180.

Nelson, Diane M. *Reckoning: The Ends of War in Guatemala*. Durham, NC: Duke University Press, 2009.

Newbury, David S. "Lake Kivu Regional Trade in the Nineteenth Century." *Journal des Africanistes* 50, no. 2 (1980): 7–30. https://doi.org/10.3406/jafr.1980.2001.

Newton, Huey P., and J. Herman Blake. *Revolutionary Suicide*. Penguin Classics Deluxe Edition. New York: Penguin, 2009.

Nguyen, Vinh-Kim. "An Epidemic of Suspicion—Ebola and Violence in the DRC." *New England Journal of Medicine* 380, no. 14 (2019): 1298–99. https://doi.org/10.1056/NEJMp1902682.

Niehuus, Rachel. "Going Rogue, or the Ethnography of War as Ethical Practice." Presented at the European Conference on African Studies, Lisbon, June 2013.

Nkuba, Bossissi, Lieven Bervoets, and Sara Geenen. "Invisible and Ignored? Local Perspectives on Mercury in Congolese Gold Mining." *Journal of Cleaner Production* 221 (June 2019): 795–804. https://doi.org/10.1016/j.jclepro.2019.01.174.

Nordstrom, Carolyn. *A Different Kind of War Story*. Philadelphia: University of Pennsylvania Press, 1997.

Nordstrom, Carolyn. *Shadows of War: Violence, Power, and International Profiteering in the Twenty-First Century*. Berkeley: University of California Press, 2004.

Norman, Julie, and Rachel Niehuus. "18 Years Displaced: An Anthropological Study of Protection Concerns Facing Congolese Refugees in Nyarugusu Refugee Camp, Tanzania." New York: International Rescue Committee, January 2015.

Nzongola-Ntalaja, Georges. *The Congo from Leopold to Kabila: A People's History*. London: Zed, 2013.

Nzongola-Ntalaja, Georges. *Patrice Lumumba*. Athens: Ohio University Press, 2014.

Okorafor, Wanuri, and Wanuri Kahiu. "Rusties." *Clarkesworld*, October 2016. https://clarkesworldmagazine.com/okorafor-kahiu_10_16/.

Oni-Orisan, Adeola. "The Obligation to Count: The Politics of Monitoring Maternal Mortality in Nigeria." In *Metrics: What Counts in Global Health*, edited by Vincanne Adams, 82–104. Durham, NC: Duke University Press, 2016.

Onsrud, Mathias, Solbjørg Sjøveian, Roger Luhiriri, and Dennis Mukwege. "Sexual Violence-Related Fistulas in the Democratic Republic of Congo." *International Journal of Gynaecology and Obstetrics* 103, no. 3 (December 2008): 265–69. https://doi.org/10.1016/j.ijgo.2008.07.018.

Peck, Raoul, dir. *Lumumba*. Biography, 2000.

Penniman, Leah. *Farming While Black: Soul Fire Farm's Practical Guide to Liberation on the Land*. White River Junction, VT: Chelsea Green, 2018.

Piot, Charles. *Nostalgia for the Future: West Africa after the Cold War*. Chicago: University of Chicago Press, 2010.

Prunier, Gerard. *Africa's World War: Congo, the Rwandan Genocide, and the Making of a Continental Catastrophe*. New York: Oxford University Press, 2008.

Quashie, Kevin Everod. *Black Aliveness, or a Poetics of Being*. Durham, NC: Duke University Press, 2021.

Raeymaekers, Timothy. "Post-war Conflict and the Market for Protection: The Challenges to Congo's Hybrid Peace." *International Peacekeeping* 20, no. 5 (November 1, 2013): 600–617. https://doi.org/10.1080/13533312.2013.854591.

Rankine, Claudia. *Citizen: An American Lyric*. Minneapolis: Graywolf, 2014.

Redfield, Peter. "Doctors, Borders, and Life in Crisis." *Cultural Anthropology* 20, no. 3 (2005): 328–61. https://doi.org/10.1525/can.2005.20.3.328.

Reno, William. *Warlord Politics and African States*. Boulder, CO: Lynne Rienner, 1999.

Reyntjens, Filip. *The Great African War: Congo and Regional Geopolitics, 1996–2006*. New York: Cambridge University Press, 2009.

Richards, Paul. *Fighting for the Rain Forest: War, Youth and Resources in Sierra Leone*. African Issues. Portsmouth, NH: Heinemann, 1996.

Roitman, Janet. "Africa Otherwise." In *African Futures: Essays on Crisis, Emergence, and Possibility*, edited by Brian Goldstone and Juan Obarrio, 23–38. Chicago: University of Chicago Press, 2017.

Roitman, Janet. *Fiscal Disobedience: An Anthropology of Economic Regulation in Central Africa*. Princeton, NJ: Princeton University Press, 2005.

Roitman, Janet. "L'entrepôt-Garnison." *Cahiers d'Études Africaines* 38, no. 150/152 (1998): 297–329.

Rosen, Jonathan. "Lake Kivu's Great Gas Gamble." *MIT Technology Review*, April 16, 2015. https://www.technologyreview.com/2015/04/16/248915/lake-kivus-great-gas -gamble/.

Sagar, Umang Antariksh. "Possibilities of Listening with Alexis Pauline Gumbs" (transcript). *Possibilities Podcast*, season 1, episode 1, June 11, 2020. https://www .possibilitiespodcast.com/possibilities-of-listening-w-alexis.

Schapendonk, Joris. "Turbulent Trajectories: African Migrants on Their Way to the European Union." *Societies* 2, no. 2 (2012): 27–41. https://doi.org/10.3390/soc2020027.

Schatzberg, Michael G. *The Dialectics of Oppression in Zaire*. Bloomington: Indiana University Press, 1988.

Scheper-Hughes, Nancy. *Death without Weeping*. Berkeley: University of California Press, 1993. https://www.ucpress.edu/book/9780520075375/death-without-weeping.

Scheper-Hughes, Nancy, and Philippe I. Bourgois. *Violence in War and Peace: An Anthology*. Malden, MA: Blackwell, 2004.

Scheper-Hughes, Nancy, and Margaret M. Lock. "The Mindful Body: A Prolegomenon to Future Work in Medical Anthropology." *Medical Anthropology Quarterly* 1, no. 1 (1987): 6–41.

Schoenbrun, David L. "Conjuring the Modern in Africa: Durability and Rupture in Histories of Public Healing between the Great Lakes of East Africa." *American Historical Review* 111, no. 5 (December 1, 2006): 1403–39. https://doi.org/10.1086/ahr .111.5.1403.

Schwab, Gabriele. *Haunting Legacies: Violent Histories and Transgenerational Trauma*. New York: Columbia University Press, 2010.

Schwenkel, Christina. "Post/Socialist Affect: Ruination and Reconstruction of the Nation in Urban Vietnam." *Cultural Anthropology* 28, no. 2 (2013): 252–77. https://doi .org/10.1111/cuan.12003.

Seay, Laura. "Effective Responses: Protestants, Catholics and the Provision of Health Care in the Post-war Kivus." *Review of African Political Economy* 40, no. 135 (2013): 83–97. https://doi.org/10.1080/03056244.2012.761601.

Serpell, Namwali. "Meet 'The Afronauts': An Introduction to Zambia's Forgotten 1960s Space Program." *Open Culture* (blog), March 4, 2020. https://www.openculture.com/2020/03/meet-the-afronauts.html.

Sexton, Jared. "The Social Life of Social Death: On Afro-Pessimism and Black Optimism." *InTensions*, no. 5 (fall/winter 2011).

Sharpe, Christina. *In the Wake: On Blackness and Being*. Durham, NC: Duke University Press, 2016.

Slegh, Henny, Gary Barker, Benoit Ruratotoye, and Tim Shand. "Gender Relations, Sexual Violence and the Effects of Conflict on Women and Men in North Kivu, Eastern Democratic Republic of Congo: Preliminary Results of the International Men and Gender Equality Study (IMAGES)." Capetown: Sonke Gender Justice Network, 2012.

Smith, James H. "'May It Never End': Price Wars, Networks, and Temporality in the '3 Ts' Mining Trade of the Eastern DR Congo." *HAU: Journal of Ethnographic Theory* 5, no. 1 (2015): 1–34. https://doi.org/10.14318/hau5.1.002.

Smith, James H. "Tantalus in the Digital Age: Coltan Ore, Temporal Dispossession, and 'Movement' in the Eastern Democratic Republic of the Congo." *American Ethnologist* 38, no. 1 (February 2011): 17–35. https://doi.org/10.1111/j.1548-1425.2010.01289.x.

Smith, Zadie. "Joy." *New York Review*, January 10, 2013. https://www.nybooks.com/articles/2013/01/10/joy/.

Spillers, Hortense J. "Mama's Baby, Papa's Maybe: An American Grammar Book." *Diacritics* 17, no. 2 (1987): 65–81. https://doi.org/10.2307/464747.

Stearns, Jason. *Dancing in the Glory of Monsters: The Collapse of the Congo and the Great War of Africa*. New York: PublicAffairs, 2011.

Stearns, Jason K. *The War That Doesn't Say Its Name: The Unending Conflict in the Congo*. Princeton, NJ: Princeton University Press, 2021.

Stearns, Jason, et al. "Banyamulenge: Insurgency and Exclusion in the Mountains of South Kivu." Report. London: Rift Valley Institute, 2013.

Stearns, Jason, et al. "From CNDP to M23: The Evolution of an Armed Movement in Eastern Congo." Report. London: Rift Valley Institute, 2012.

Stearns, Jason, et al. "PARECO: Land, Local Strongmen, and the Roots of Militia Politics in North Kivu." Report. London: Rift Valley Institute, 2013.

Stearns, Jason, Judith Verweijen, and Maria Eriksson Baaz. "The National Army and Armed Groups in the Eastern Congo." Usalama Project. London: Rift Valley Institute, 2013. https://riftvalley.net/publication/national-army-and-armed-groups-eastern-congo.

Stewart, Kathleen. *Ordinary Affects*. Durham, NC: Duke University Press, 2007.

Stoop, Nik, Marijke Verpoorten, and Peter van der Windt. "More Legislation, More Violence? The Impact of Dodd-Frank in the DRC." *PLOS ONE* 13, no. 8 (August 9, 2018): e0201783. https://doi.org/10.1371/journal.pone.0201783.

Sudfeld, Christopher R., Dana Charles McCoy, Günther Fink, Alfa Muhihi, David C. Bellinger, Honorati Masanja, Emily R. Smith, et al. "Malnutrition and Its Determinants Are Associated with Suboptimal Cognitive, Communication, and Motor

Development in Tanzanian Children." *Journal of Nutrition* 145, no. 12 (December 2015): 2705–14. https://doi.org/10.3945/jn.115.215996.

Taussig, Michael. *The Nervous System.* New York: Routledge, 2012.

Taussig, Michael. *Shamanism, Colonialism, and the Wild Man: A Study in Terror and Healing.* Chicago: University of Chicago Press, 1991.

Thiranagama, Sharika. *In My Mother's House: Civil War in Sri Lanka.* Philadelphia: University of Pennsylvania Press, 2011.

Trefon, Theodore. *Congo's Environmental Paradox: Potential and Predation in a Land of Plenty.* London: Zed, 2016.

Trefon, Theodore. *Reinventing Order in the Congo: How People Respond to State Failure in Kinshasa.* London: Zed, 2004.

Tsing, Anna Lowenhaupt. *The Mushroom at the End of the World.* Princeton, NJ: Princeton University Press, 2017. https://press.princeton.edu/books/paperback /9780691178325/the-mushroom-at-the-end-of-the-world.

UNESCO World Heritage Convention. "Virunga: A Challenge for Conservation and Sustainable Development." April 23, 2015. https://whc.unesco.org/en/news/1265/.

United Nations. "Midterm Report of the Group of Experts Submitted in Accordance with Paragraph 16 of Security Council Resolution 2045." Geneva, 2012.

Utas, Mats. "West-African Warscapes: Victimcy, Girlfriending, Soldiering: Tactic Agency in a Young Woman's Social Navigation of the Liberian War Zone." *Anthropological Quarterly* 78, no. 2 (2005): 403–30.

Vansina, Jan. *Antecedents to Modern Rwanda: The Nyiginya Kingdom.* Madison: University of Wisconsin Press, 2004.

Vansina, Jan. *Paths in the Rainforests: Toward a History of Political Tradition in Equatorial Africa.* Madison: University of Wisconsin Press, 1990.

Vaughan, Megan. "Healing and Curing: Issues in the Social History and Anthropology of Medicine in Africa." *Social History of Medicine* 7, no. 2 (August 1994): 283–95. https://doi.org/10.1093/shm/7.2.283.

Verweijen, Judith. "The Ambiguity of Militarization: The Complex Interaction between the Congolese Armed Forces and Civilians in the Kivu Provinces, Eastern DR Congo." PhD diss., Utrecht University, 2015.

Verweijen, Judith. "Military Business and the Business of the Military in the Kivus." *Review of African Political Economy* 40, no. 135 (2013): 67–82. https://doi.org/10.1080 /03056244.2012.761602.

Verweijen, Judith. "Violent Cities, Violent Society: Analyzing Urban Violence in the Eastern Congo." Usalama Project. London: Rift Valley Institute, 2019. https:// riftvalley.net/publication/violent-cities-violent-society-analyzing-urban-violence -eastern-congo.

Vinck, Patrick, Phuong Pham, Suliman Baldo, and Rachel Shigekane. "Living with Fear: A Population-Based Survey on Attitudes about Peace, Justice, and Social Reconstruction in Eastern Democratic Republic of the Congo." Berkeley, CA: Human Rights Center, August 19, 2008.

Vlassenroot, Koen, and Karen Büscher. "Borderlands, Identity and Urban Development: The Case of Goma (Democratic Republic of the Congo)." *Urban Studies* 50, no. 15 (November 2013): 3168–84. https://doi.org/10.1177/0042098013487772.

Vlassenroot, Koen, and C. Huggins. "Land, Migration and Conflict in Eastern DRC." In *From the Ground Up: Land Rights, Conflict and Peace in Sub-Saharan Africa*, 115–94. Ghent: Institute for Security Studies (ISS), 2005. http://hdl.handle.net/1854 /LU-321408.

Vlassenroot, Koen, and Timothy Raeymaekers, eds. *Conflict and Social Transformation in Eastern DR Congo*. Ghent: Academia, 2004.

Vogel, Christoph. "Armed Group Maps." Suluhu, 2017. https://suluhu.org/congo /mapping/.

Vogel, Christoph. *Conflict Minerals, Inc.: War, Profit and White Saviourism in Eastern Congo*. London: Hurst, 2022.

Vogel, Christoph. "No More M23. The End of an Era? And What's Next?" *Christoph Vogel* (blog), November 5, 2013. http://christophvogel.net/2013/11/05/no-more-m23 -the-end-of-an-era-and-whats-next/.

Vogel, Christoph, Gillian Mathys, Judith Verweijen, Adia Benton, Rachel Sweet, and Esther Marijnen. "Cliches Can Kill in Congo." *Foreign Policy*, April 30, 2019. https:// foreignpolicy.com/2019/04/30/cliches-can-kill-in-congo-grand-nord-north-kivu -tropes-conflict-ebola-response/.

Vogel, Christoph, and Timothy Raeymaekers. "Terr(it)or(ies) of Peace? The Congolese Mining Frontier and the Fight against 'Conflict Minerals.'" *Antipode* 48, no. 4 (2016): 1102–21. https://doi.org/10.1111/anti.12236.

Voyages Extraordinaires. "Fusée spatiale congolaise Troposphère 6." YouTube, May 31, 2018. https://www.youtube.com/watch?app=desktop&v=i--Ar4TWKuU.

Waal, Alexander de. *Famine Crimes: Politics and the Disaster Relief Industry in Africa*. London: African Rights and the International African Institute, 1997.

Waheed, Nayyirah. *Nejma*. N.p.: CreateSpace, 2014.

Waldman, Ron. "Health in Fragile States, Country Case Study: Democratic Republic of the Congo." Arlington, VA: BASICS for USAID, 2006.

Weheliye, Alexander G. *Habeas Viscus: Racializing Assemblages, Biopolitics, and Black Feminist Theories of the Human*. Durham, NC: Duke University Press, 2014.

Wells, Chad R., Abhishek Pandey, Martial L. Ndeffo Mbah, Bernard-A. Gaüzère, Denis Malvy, Burton H. Singer, and Alison P. Galvani. "The Exacerbation of Ebola Outbreaks by Conflict in the Democratic Republic of the Congo." *Proceedings of the National Academy of Sciences* 116, no. 48 (2019): 24366–72. https://doi.org/10.1073 /pnas.1913980116.

WHO. "World Health in the Congo." World Health Organization, 1960. https:// apps.who.int/iris/bitstream/handle/10665/274647/WH-1960-Nov-Dec-eng.pdf ?sequence=1.

World Food Program. "WFP Democratic Republic of Congo Country Brief." April 2020. https://docs.wfp.org/api/documents/WFP-0000115192/download/?_ga =2.215498644.2016967829.1611514115-1209679793.1611514115.

Wynter, Sylvia. "Unsettling the Coloniality of Being/Power/Truth/Freedom: Towards the Human, After Man, Its Overrepresentation—an Argument." *CR: The New Centennial Review* 3, no. 3 (2003): 257–337. https://doi.org/10.1353/ncr.2004.0015.

X, Malcolm, and George Breitman. *Malcolm X Speaks: Selected Speeches and Statements*. New York: Grove Weidenfeld, 1990.

Yard, Ellen E., Jane Horton, Joshua G. Schier, Kathleen Caldwell, Carlos Sanchez, Lauren Lewis, and Carmen Gastañaga. "Mercury Exposure among Artisanal Gold Miners in Madre de Dios, Peru: A Cross-Sectional Study." *Journal of Medical Toxicology* 8, no. 4 (December 2012): 441–48. https://doi.org/10.1007/s13181-012-0252-0.

Young, Crawford. *The Postcolonial State in Africa: Fifty Years of Independence, 1960–2010.* Madison: University of Wisconsin Pres, 2012.

Young, Crawford, and Thomas Turner. *The Rise and Decline of the Zairian State.* Madison: University of Wisconsin Press, 1985.

Yusoff, Kathryn. *A Billion Black Anthropocenes or None.* Minneapolis: University of Minnesota Press, 2018.

Page locators in italics refer to figures.

epigenetic research, 144–46
European Union, 149
evangelization, 76–77
évolués Congolese, 7, 9
exit, 33, 37–38, 88

Fanon, Frantz, 19, 101, 107–8, 173n48; decolonization, radical, 108, 172n30
farming, 24, 91, 160n3; selling on credit, 57; by women, 31, 34–37
fear, 70–71, 159n37; associated with HIV, 151
Feierman, Steven, 38, 75, 162n30
fertility of Congo land, 24
"fifty-niners," 26–27
"Figures of the Subject in Times of Crisis" (Mbembe and Roitman), 32–33
First Congo War, 8
fistulas, vesicovaginal, 2–5, 157n9
flesh, 73, 75, 92–93. *See also* body
food insecurity, 15–16, 24, 167n1; staples needed for war, 95–97. *See also* malnutrition
Foucault, Michel, 159n26
future, 19, 123–41; alternative present, 39–40, *141*; archive of, 13, 17–18, 20; dreaming, 134–35; and intergenerational inheritance, 144–46; and intimate relationships, 135–40; lost in past, 24; LUCHA, 127–29, 132, 135; and movement, 34; poetic register, 19, 125–27, 174n5, 176n33; proximate, 13; space program, 127, 129–32, 175n15. *See also* Afrofuturism; possibilities; presents otherwise
future real conditional, 13

Garcia, Angela, 71
Goma (capital of North Kivu, eastern Congo), 1–5; art community, 125–26; M23 invasion of, 52–53; roads, 21–23, *22*; war in, 5; Yole Center, 125. *See also* hospital
Green, Linda, 159n37
Gumbs, Alexis Pauline, 1, 140, 147, 160n41, 163n45, 177n10

Harney, Stefano, 67
Hartman, Saidiya, 33, 160n38
healing, 162n30, 167n4; and affect, 67; belief in, 5; body's role in, 75; death, relationship with, 101, 113, 118; defined, 4; devastation and drive toward, 100–101; dirt work as

register of, 38; duality of African, 100–101, 117; harming register of, 100–101; hospital's promise of, 90–92, 93; "I am healed" as traditional response to sympathies, 84, 89; killing motivated by desire for, 101, 114–17, 118; *kupona*, 5; multisited understanding of, 13, 155; *nkisi* (medical charms and power objects), 100; and non-Occidental repair, 11; in precolonial central Africa, 38; public, 18, 38–39, 43, 162–63n35; and refusal, 108; rituals, 38–39, 162nn32, 33; social, 38, 75–76; by spirit mediums, 38, 162n32; of wound, four stages of, 12. *See also* body; repair
health, collective, 38
history, narrative structure of, 27
HIV, 151–52, 177n7
Holocaust, 118, 144–45
Hoppe, Arthur, 131
hospital, 19, *44*, 73–93, *74*; boutiques operated nearby, 89–92; "catastrophic cases," 83–84; cleanliness attempted, 78–79; deaths of neonates, 83–87; dirt in setting of, 78–79; educational role of, 81–82; employment offered by, 77–78, 90–91; funds used to treat soldiers, 55; as neutral in war, 14–15, 111, 159n35; pain in setting of, 79–81; promise of care, 89–92; as site of healing and harm, 76–82; socialization of suffering by, 89, 92, 93; staffing, 82–83; as target, 159n35. *See also* body
Huggins, Chris, 28
humanitarian aid: destabilization of existing conflict networks, 149; "legitimate recipients" of, 3; negative impacts of, 4; and Rwandan genocide, 49
humanitarian-industrial complex, 1–2, 107
humanity: Black, impossibility of, 33; massacres resulting from denial of, 116; self-questioning of, 32–33. *See also* subjectivity
Hunde people, 27
hunger, 35, 37, 171n11; and rape, 99; of soldiers, 52. *See also* malnutrition
Hunt, Nancy Rose, 76, 81, 100, 122, 161n8
Hutu militias, 8

images, online, 61, 106, 115
indigeneity, hierarchy of, 27

Médecins sans Frontières (MSF), 78, 90–91, 92
medicalization, 76
mental illness, 102–3, 107–8
methane, 48–49
methylation, 145–46
middle figures, 7, 161n8
Middle Passage, 33–34, 39
migration into Congo, 106, 161n10; four waves of, 26–27. *See also* refugee camps
Migration Policy Institute, 106
military enlistment by youth, 28
mineral extraction, 24, 35–36, 50; toxic effects of, 107
minerals in subsoil: trading, 35, 37
mining sector, 36, 166n28; pronatalist polices, 76
Ministry of Health (Congo), 150
"Mobutuist habitus," 59
Mobutu Sese Seko, 7–9, 27, 54, 88; and health care system, 77, 91, 103, 168n16; "le mal Zaïrois," 169n21; and space program, 129; and state failure, 103–4
modernity, enslavement written into, 10
Moten, Fred, 47, 67
Mount Nyiragongo, 1–2, 48
movement, 28, 32–34, 37; and wounding, 34
Moyer, Eileen, 151, 152
mtunzo (care), 91–92
Mugunga Refugee Camp, *98*
Mukwege, Denis, 3, 157n9
music, Congolese, 88–89

narrative structure of history, 27
Ndala, Mamadou, 112
necropolitics, 101, 108–9, 113, 118
Newton, Huey, 172n31
ngoma drumming ritual, 38, 39
Nguyen, Vinh-Kim, 177n7
nkisi (medical charms and power objects), 100
Nkoloso, Edward Mukuka, 131, 175n15
nongovernmental organizations (NGOs), 41; demilitarization efforts by, 59; funds used to treat soldiers, 55; hospital support by, 78
nonhuman world, 25
non-Occidental repair, 11
nonviolence, 128
Nordstrom, Carolyn, 166n34
North American context, 152

nostalgia, for more modern past, 23–24
NR3C1 locus, 145–46

Occidental repair, 11
On Injury and Repair (Attia), 11–12
otherwise, 122; commensurable, 72; and poetic epistemology, 126–27; trajectory of, 13. *See also* space program, Congolese
Oxford Handbook of Modern African History, The, 100

pain: and survival, 81–82
Palestinian suicide bombers, 101–2
PARECO (Coalition des patriotes résistant congolais) (Alliance of Resistant Congolese Patriots), 111
peace treaties, 8, 52, 56
pillage, 31, 37, 45, *46*, 55–56, 58, 63–65, *94*, 106, 171n8; in Rutshuru, 110–11
pleasure, 121–22
poetic register, 19, 125–27, 174n5, 176n33
"political awakening," 158n14
possibilities, 15, 20, 71–72; within atrocities, 117; and cohabitation, 152; Lumumba, spirit of, 132–35; of *mtunzo*, 91–92; in speculative nonfiction, 143–44. *See also* future; LUCHA (Lutte pour le changement) (Struggle for Change)
postcolonial era, 14, 18, 108, 152
postcolonial power, 108
poverty, 24; of soldiers, 54–55, *68*
pre-exposure prophylaxis (PrEP), 151
presents otherwise, 13, 17, 72, 122, 126–27, *141*; and body, 19, 75, 92–93; and dirt work, 37, 39–40, 51; and love, 139. *See also* future
pronatalist policies under colonial rule, 4, 76, 87
"Prophecy in the Present Tense" (Gumbs), 134
public health: under Belgian imperialism, 76; after independence, 38, 77; and Ebola epidemics, 149–51; precolonial African, 38

queer writings, 127

racialization, 10, 92
Rankine, Claudia, 73
rape, 99, 100–101
rape-as-a-weapon-of-war narrative, 2–4